"An easy-to-read, well-organized compilation of stories that demonstrates their power across a broad spectrum of business needs. Anyone choosing these techniques as part of their toolkit will appreciate the insights shared by the storytellers."

— **Ellen Bovarnick**, vice president, Business Process Excellence, The Coca-Cola Company

"Lori Silverman offers fresh ideas for introducing stories into organizations and inspiring better leadership through them. This is a well-researched and lively reference for leaders at every level."

— **John Alexander**, president, Center for Creative Leadership

"This book takes the concept of organizational stories from a pleasant idea to a practical means to advance strategy, product development, and ultimately shareholder value."

— **Anita Brick**, director, University of Chicago Graduate School of Business

"I love the book. Lori Silverman and her contributors have assembled a valuable compendium of information on how and why stories enable transformation and include how to do this in your own organization. My hope is that this book will create a new generation of leaders who will stop numbing people with spreadsheets and pie charts, and start inspiring them with stories that illuminate organizational mission, values, and goals."

— **Frank D. Byrne**, M.D., president of St. Mary's Hospital Medical Center, a part of the SSM Health Care system

"Storytelling, often thought to be a dying craft, is making a sensational comeback in modern-day organizational life. Leaders in all walks will benefit from Silverman's real-world accounts of storytelling successes in high-performing organizations."

— **Daniel M. Sprague**, CEO, The Council of State Governments

"Silverman reminds us that the best tools for connecting to and inspiring our teams are the oldest ones—stories. A customer service story, a story illustrating our history, or a story exhibiting commitment to share goals can inspire more deeply than a directive from on high. Put flesh on the bone. Tell a story."

— **Arne M. Sorenson**, chief financial officer, Marriott International

"When just about every fact on the planet is but one mouse click away, stories take on new importance in every business enterprise. From leadership to team building to branding to knowledge management, narrative has become a powerful—and essential—tool. This collection of essays offers an array of savvy advice on how to unleash the power of stories in your organization."
    — **Daniel H. Pink**, author of *A Whole New Mind*

"Achieving results through others is a key competency for everyone in a leadership role. Lori's book illustrates how the use of stories will help your organization achieve positive outcomes. A must-read for anyone in an organization facing significant change."
    — **Vicki L. Chvala**, executive vice president, American Family Insurance

"Organizations have a real issue: The fact that they are both community and hierarchy, and that the two are often at cross-purposes with one another. Stories are a vehicle for expressing this kind of understanding and connection that from time to time make a great difference."
    — **Art Kleiner**, editor in chief, *strategy + business*

"This book is excellent at introducing how stories can be used to communicate management principles and strategic ideas. It's the first to summarize the use of story in various business applications with *real* examples and results. I seriously will use the concepts presented in this book in my own company."
    — **David Coffman**, president, Coffman Engineers, Inc.

"A captivating and inspirational read that reveals the power of stories to influence change in organizations! Lori Silverman does a masterful job of weaving a tapestry of stories from publicly traded companies and small businesses to governmental agencies and nonprofits that exemplify best practices in customer service, project management, teamwork, leadership, organizational change, and more."
    — **Kirby Rosplock**, vice president, Research & Development, Asset Management Advisors

"If your success as an executive depends upon your ability to engage your people, your leadership, and other vital stakeholders, you have to read this book. Using this proven technique will enhance the organization's success as well as your communications, and also transcend your activities and ultimate effectiveness. This book is a resource you'll refer to time and time again."

— **William J. Carbone**, CEO, American Association of Physician Specialists & American Board of Physician Specialties

"*Wake Me Up When the Data Is Over* is an invaluable set of insights about how business stories are being used in practical ways in a wide variety of organizational contexts…essential reading for anyone interested in learning how to use story—the most ancient of technologies—for very modern purposes."

— **Stephen Denning**, author of *The Leader's Guide to Storytelling* (2005)

"Wow! This is a really great read—unique and pertinent to day-to-day leadership. It provides a very fresh perspective on a very old subject."

— **Carson F. Dye**, partner, Witt/Kieffer

"What a wonderful book. Instead of theory and ideas, this book teaches by telling us stories that focus on the everyday life of an organization and the things that make a difference. The book introduces a new form of business education that is vivid, inspirational, and helpful."

— **Dennis T. Jaffe**, Ph.D., professor of organizational systems, Saybrook Graduate School

"As a person who has worked in the nonprofit world and 'fought hunger' for the past 17 years, I can totally attest to the strategies outlined in *Wake Me Up*. Charts cannot convey the loss of hope or dignity that comes with poverty, nor will statistics inspire citizens to see their role in finding solutions. Stories help people see the bigger world, and they can often give people the courage and understanding they need to step forward and become engaged. I never leave home without a story in my pocket."

— **Robert Egger**, president of DC Central Kitchen and author of *Begging for Change*

"The book is fabulous. The case studies are eye-opening to new and pragmatic ideas that can be implemented at all levels of an organization."

— **Cheryl Grandolfo**, manager, Strategic Alliances, Lending Solutions, Inc.; board member, American Marketing Association–Chicago Chapter

"Companies that use fact-based selling techniques struggle to differentiate themselves from their competition. This insightful and groundbreaking book teaches storytelling techniques that can transform any such organization from simply being competitive to being unforgettable."

> — **Vik Bangia**, managing director, Strategic Services,
> Corporate Real Estate Services, United Properties

"Every organization has its stories. Anyone wanting to understand an organization's culture need only listen to the stories people tell. This book is a must-read in that it describes ways to use storytelling and story-hearing to affect an organization's culture to create desired results."

> — **Judy Schector**, director, Developing Leadership in Reducing
> Substance Abuse, Portland State University

"Storytelling and corporate lore play an important role in communicating strategies, intentions, operating styles, and especially values. The organizational and topical breadth of the stories gathered together in this volume will inspire you to tell the most meaningful story of all—yours."

> — **Alph Bingham**, CEO, InnoCentive, Inc.

"Storytelling sounds so simple. And it was, once upon a time. This book is a reminder that storytelling allows deeper understanding of and commitment to a situation or a person, and it's a reference to jump-start the thinking required to tell your story."

> — **Susan Hughes**, senior vice president, Edelman

"This book will reshape your view of storytelling and give you lots of practical ways to use stories in your organization to capture the hearts and minds of people."

> — **Scott Hayes**, manager of organization development and
> training, Peoples Energy Corporation

"Business leaders in all arenas will be inspired by *Wake Me Up* to explore and harness the power of their individual and collective experiences to affect change and influence success."

> — **Pamela S. Gilley**, COO, American Legion Auxiliary
> National Headquarters

Wake Me Up When
the Data Is Over

Lori L. Silverman

Wake Me Up When the Data Is Over

How Organizations Use Stories to Drive Results

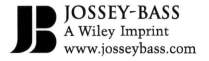

JOSSEY-BASS
A Wiley Imprint
www.josseybass.com

⟶ National Storytelling Network

The National Storytelling Network (NSN) began in 1973 as the National Association for the Preservation and Perpetuation of Storytelling (NAPPS). Over the years the group has become the premiere organization for thousands of individuals, groups, and organizations in the United States, advocating for storytelling in multiple disciplines and its effectiveness as a tool and an art form. Members range from beginning storytellers to platform performers who have won Grammy awards, and also include individuals applying storytelling in business, health care, education, and special events.

NSN's vision, "A world enriched through storytelling," is pursued in a variety of ways. The organization produces an annual conference, supports special interest groups (SIGs)—including the Storytelling in Organizations SIG—and several discussion groups, publishes a magazine every two months, and bestows honors such as the Circle of Excellence and Lifetime Achievement awards to top-ranked performers in the field. It promotes Tellabration!—a worldwide storytelling event the Saturday before Thanksgiving, supports the annual National Youth Storytelling Showcase, and funds storytelling projects around the country through grant monies. In addition, NSN co-owns the National Storytelling Festival, held annually the first full weekend in October, where more than ten thousand people enjoy performances from more than forty professional storytellers.

NSN's services are designed to improve the quality of storytelling at all levels and in any arena where storytelling can make a contribution.

To learn more about NSN, please visit www.storynet.org, e-mail NSN@storynet.org, or write to the National Storytelling Network at 132 Boone Street, Suite 5, Jonesborough, TN 37659. We look forward to hearing from you!

NATIONAL
STORYTELLING
NETWORK

Published by Jossey-Bass
A Wiley Imprint
989 Market Street, San Francisco, CA 94103-1741   www.josseybass.com

Jossey-Bass books and products are available through most bookstores. To contact Jossey-Bass
directly call our Customer Care Department within the U.S. at 800-956-7739, outside the U.S.
at 317-572-3986, or fax 317-572-4002.

Jossey-Bass also publishes its books in a variety of electronic formats. Some content that
appears in print may not be available in electronic books.

Cartoons in "Cartoon Story" in Chapter Three ©Narrativity Ashraf Ramzy/Gerben Valkema
2005.

Library of Congress Cataloging-in-Publication Data

Silverman, Lori L., 1958-
   Wake me up when the data is over : how organizations use stories to drive results /
Lori L. Silverman.
      p. cm.
   Includes bibliographical references and index.
   ISBN-13: 978-0-470-48330-5
   1. Industrial productivity. 2. Communication in organizations. 3. Storytelling. I. Title.
HD56.S485 2006
658.4'5—dc22   2006022818

FIRST EDITION
PB Printing   10 9 8 7 6 5 4 3 2 1

Contents

To North—whose personal courage has inspired me.

To people who are searching for ways to make organizational life more engaging.

─⁓─ Foreword

This book shatters a long-standing pattern. Volumes that are edited, whether as collections of articles or as anthologies, are enormously difficult to do. The quality of the papers is uneven, they are not well knit together (the sum is not greater than the parts), coherent philosophies and concepts are lacking, and the reader is left with too many disconnected ideas or conflicting opinions. By the end, readers are not sure what to think or next steps to take. Worse yet, these edited volumes do not sell because of these shortcomings.

The contributors Lori Silverman has worked with, their seminal contributions, and the way she has woven all together into a wonderful and meaningful package for us make a distinct break from the same-old, same-old. Lori worked tirelessly to create a consistent voice and pattern to each chapter while not reducing the contributions to milquetoast. In this work you will find clear, consistent thinking, concepts that weave the chapters together, lots of meat, and clear direction for anyone who wants to bring storytelling into core business activities. Readers will not only walk away understanding why storytelling is so powerful in organizational life, they will also begin to take those steps necessary to follow the examples and advice from the companies and contributors found within these pages. We no longer need justifications for why storytelling is important for organizations. Today, we are ready for more—more detail, more experiences, more insights, and more specific results. That is what this book provides: practical experiences from the field to guide you on your way to using stories and storytelling effectively in your organization.

Lori and fourteen contributors interviewed more than 140 people from more than seventy organizations around the world about their work with stories within their own organizations. These for-profit, nonprofit, and government organizations not only share their experiences, processes, and learnings, they also provide hard-core results gained through their story work initiatives. Parts One and Two cover tactical and strategic business issues that organizations grapple with every day: serving customers, engaging employees, building teamwork and leadership, branding, strategic planning, changing culture, and managing finances, to name a few. Here you will find the nuts and bolts of how stories and storytelling are being used in organizations. There is no fluff here—simply real-world knowledge and tangible, quantifiable outcomes.

Part Three brings it all home by delving into lessons from story pioneers, insights from those conducting research on storytelling in organizations, and an examination of themes that emerged from a study of the story applications covered in this book. In the last chapter Lori presents a model for those who want to bring stories and storytelling into their organizations. Not only is this a significant contribution to the field, it will also help organizations chart a course for using stories effectively in myriad ways to achieve results. This book will soon become required reading for anyone wanting to access the power of storytelling within organizations.

I trust you will enjoy reading how story work has a place center stage in organizational line activities. I know I have. And I am certain that the material provided here will motivate you to immediately start working with stories and experts in the field to generate powerful outcomes for your organization.

KAREN DIETZ, PH.D.
Executive Director
National Storytelling Network

⟶ Preface

Stories are like viruses. They are contagious. Tell a story to someone and you will get one back in return. This is what I experienced in fall 2003 as I gave numerous radio and television interviews to promote *Stories Trainers Tell: 55 Ready-to-Use Stories to Make Training Stick,* a book I coauthored with Mary Wacker. During interviews, I was asked to talk about the benefits and pitfalls of storytelling, the most outrageous stories I had ever heard, and how leaders could bring them into organizations. In return, on breaks or after the interviews were finished, on-air personalities would frequently share at least one example of where stories had made a difference in their personal or work life. Often, this was followed by a question: Can stories be used in marketing? Can they work effectively on a shop floor? How could they be used in sales and customer service? While I was able to provide examples from my consulting work in strategy, organizational change, and performance improvement, I was hungry to learn more.

My desire led me back to books on storytelling in organizations that I had previously reviewed—books by authors such as Stephen Denning, Peg Neuhauser, and Annette Simmons. Browsing magazine and professional journal articles got me a few more examples, but not many. So I joined the National Storytelling Network and started attending meetings of the Storytelling in Organizations special interest group. Whenever I heard names of people doing work in the field, I would call or meet them to find out more about their efforts and what they were learning. Their comments led me to attend events at the Smithsonian Institution and through Golden Fleece. Yet I still was not satisfied. Something was missing.

Not one to wait for examples to materialize, I decided to find a way to scour the planet for examples of how story was being used in a variety of business disciplines. Knowing I could not do this work alone, I approached Karen Dietz about partnering with the National Storytelling Network. Together we approached Jossey-Bass with a plan to collaborate with individuals who were applying stories to workplace needs in a worldwide search for new examples—examples that had not previously been published or brought to the forefront of the storytelling industry. Our collective efforts took us fourteen months to complete. The fruits of our work are housed in this book.

HOW THE BOOK WAS DEVELOPED

Through the membership of the National Storytelling Network, and the research efforts of fourteen contributors, and colleagues in the field, organizations were identified that consciously and purposefully use stories in specific business disciplines or applications. In addition, individuals doing active research in the field of storytelling in organizations were pinpointed. A total of 171 people were interviewed, representing eighty-one organizations around the world. Contributors used a set of topic-specific questions to query these individuals. Specific examples of story use are provided by seventy-two organizations. These organizations run the gamut of for-profit, nonprofit, and government entities. While many are internationally recognized, several are locally based.

In addition to gathering examples of how story is being used within these enterprises, contributors collected specific stories and activities. These are interspersed throughout each chapter. The "Five Sides of Story" model, presented in Chapter Fifteen, was developed based on the findings described throughout the book.

PURPOSE OF THE BOOK

The conceptual whys and hows of what makes story work as a communication approach have been covered in several books and articles provided in the Suggested Resources section. This book does not present or replicate this work; it goes a step further to highlight how organizations are currently using story to drive results.

The main purpose of this book is to increase the visibility and influence of story work in organizations, specifically its practical application to a variety of business disciplines—such as marketing and market research, finance, customer service, and project management—and business needs related to topics like organizational change, building teams and teamwork, and dealing with difficult issues. Specific examples outlined in the book provide myriad tools and techniques that organizations can model and adapt to their settings. The stories given by interviewees are meant to enhance and provide specificity around real-life examples. Activities presented here are those that have been used in organizations featured in this book.

For individuals and organizations to consciously and purposefully bring story into their workplaces, this book also presents a spirited discussion on research in the field of storytelling and a model for the strategic use of stories. These chapters are also meant to spur further conversations and research in the field.

WHO THIS BOOK IS FOR

The primary audiences for this book are individuals who are interested in moving organizations to a higher level of performance and enhancing how they personally interact with others in the workplace. This includes business owners, executives, and senior leaders; middle managers and first-line supervisors; members of cross-functional teams, project teams, self-managed teams, and natural work groups; and those contributing in staff functions such as project management, organizational development, training and development, human resources, marketing, public relations, and corporate communications. Outside organizations, the audience includes external consultants in the fields of management and business, organizational development, coaching, marketing and public relations, and career planning; as well as faculty at universities and colleges specifically providing courses in narrative, folklore, and organizational storytelling that offer programs in business, communications, organizational behavior, marketing, public relations, and the like.

HOW THE BOOK IS ORGANIZED

This book has three distinct parts. Part One focuses on how stories are being used in daily work functions and issues people face on a day-to-day basis. Part Two addresses the application of stories to an organization's strategic functions and challenges. Part Three provides advice and research results to move stories into and across the organization so their use becomes deliberate and integrated throughout the business. The Suggested Resources section at the end contains a comprehensive listing of materials related to story work in organizations as of December 2005.

Chapters One through Thirteen are structured in the same manner. The themes described in each chapter were identified directly from the interview content. This information is followed by a presentation of the results that organizations have correlated back to their examples and topic-specific pointers on story use. Chapter Fourteen is also organized based on the content from interviews with those who have conducted research in storytelling. Chapter Fifteen is structured around a five-pronged approach for bringing stories into an organization. This model grew out of a synthesis of the content presented in Chapters One through Thirteen.

HOW TO USE THIS BOOK

Start reading with whatever topic captures your attention. The book has been written so individual chapters stand on their own and can be read out of sequence. Consider reading specific chapters with colleagues in your community or within your organization and setting aside time to discuss the approaches covered in them and how they might be applied to your work. The activities presented here can be used in meetings or training events, and a few are applicable to individual work. Unless prior copyright approval is received, the stories in each chapter are to be shared orally rather than reprinted.

Please note that the full title and credits of everyone interviewed for this book can be found in Appendix 1. Some of these titles and credits have been shortened in the text for the convenience of the readers.

Introduction

Sylvia L. Lovely

The world is undergoing changes that are radically altering the landscape of our lives. As a leader I have experienced many of these alterations through my varied professional roles—as former interim executive director of Kentucky's Office of Drug Control Policy; as founder of the NewCities Institute, a national nonprofit organization that encourages citizens to actively help their cities thrive in the twenty-first century; as executive director and CEO of the Kentucky League of Cities (KLC), a nonprofit association providing myriad services and legislative advocacy for more than 370 member cities throughout the state; and as co-owner with my full-time lawyer husband of Azur, a restaurant in Lexington, Kentucky.

It is one thing to acknowledge the vast changes we face, yet quite another to find effective ways to master the challenges they bring, especially when feeling overwhelmed is the norm.

TAKING THE QUANTUM LEAP INTO A NEW ERA OF BUSINESS

While previous eras—known commonly as the hunter-gatherer, agricultural, and industrial ages—each lasted for centuries or even millennia, recognizable eras are now coming at us with blinding speed by historical measures. The Information Age focuses on people's intellectual abilities as the key to organizational success. This is true in numerous areas in my organizations—from the persuasive thinking that brings success to KLC's legislative advocacy to innovative approaches in marketing, research, and community-building methods that characterize the NewCities Institute.

While the Information Age still carries considerable influence, a number of observers believe it will last only a hundred years or so and is already giving way to another era that carries many names: the Conceptual Age, the Experience Economy, the Creative Age, the Dream Society, and the Existential Era among them. Whatever its ultimate label, this new era is defined by the realization, born of quantum physics, that consciousness itself can create reality—that our dreams, emotions, intuition, creativity, and such aspects of spirit as Carl Jung's collective unconscious are forces of far greater importance than previously recognized. Quantum theory, which suggests the universe is about elements affected and defined by their relationships to each other, marks a sea change in the scientific view of how the universe operates, a change that is leading to new philosophical approaches and practical operations in everyday life—including the potential these relationships hold for business leaders focused on bolstering the bottom line.

In essence, this leaves you and me—and the organizations in which we operate—straddling two ages while having to meet the fundamental needs that arise from each era.

CHALLENGES OF THE INFORMATION AGE

While the Information Age and resulting knowledge economy have enhanced organizational performance and emphasized cultivating talented people, some unresolved issues remain. Most organizations have not addressed how to share knowledge effectively among employees. Without changing age-old systems in which departments and business units habitually operate in isolation and leaders cling to a brittle hierarchy that impedes information flow, knowledge workers often have insufficient knowledge to make key decisions and take effective action.

The result is reduced potential and productivity, which has caused many organizations to seek overseas labor to reduce costs and rely on technology to accomplish tasks faster than the humans they replace. While these strategies might bring greater profits, they are only temporary bandages. Without developing a cohesive, dedicated, and informed staff that has a clear idea of the company's vision and goals, businesses can easily become the organizational equivalent of dinosaurs—stuck in the mud, doomed to extinction.

CHALLENGES OF THE CONCEPTUAL AGE

The Conceptual Age we are entering also raises issues that are becoming more apparent with each passing day. The first—connecting people at all levels of organizational life into a comprehensive tapestry—is not just a fanciful notion. It is a fundamental element for survival.

This need for strong connection is no small matter. A Northwestern University study of a hundred organizations in the U.S. media industry in 2005 found that satisfied and engaged employees—including those who do not interact directly with customers—are significant factors in increasing profitability. The Gallup Organization has produced similar findings. In numerous studies since 1979, Gallup has polled about three million American employees. Finding three levels of employee involvement—engaged, not engaged, and actively disengaged—Gallup research has determined that by far the greatest contribution to an organization's success is made by engaged employees, while the performance of the organization is markedly reduced by actively disengaged employees. Here is the significant wake-up call: Gallup found only 29 percent of the U.S. workforce is engaged, which is far lower than estimates made by most chief executive officers and chief learning officers.

It is no accident that quality of life—a second issue of the new era—is a key factor in how a mobile workforce of the "best and brightest" chooses to live and work. As more and more baby boomers retire, there will be a period where the smaller Generation X population will not be big enough to fill all jobs. This will eventually subside with the maturation of Generation Y, which is actually more numerous than the baby boomers. However, there will be major challenges filling key jobs in the interim, making the need to recruit and retain key talent more critical than ever. I am particularly conscious of this as it will be critical for Kentucky cities, where the U.S. Census Bureau projects the state's sixty-five-and-older population will increase 79 percent by 2030.

Are business leaders recognizing the importance of these quality-of-life desires? An Accenture learning survey of CEOs conducted in 2005 revealed that they are making a palpable shift to a softer approach and demeanor. People concerns were foremost, demonstrated by the need to attract and retain talented and skilled staff. Second on their list was shifting organizational culture and bolstering attitudes following a spate of downsizing and cost cutting that had made life difficult for employees.

There is also a third issue to attend to in this new economy. In *The Dancing Wu Li Masters: An Overview of the New Physics,* Gary Zukav says, "Quantum mechanics shows us that we are not as separate from the rest of the world as we once thought . . . that the rest of the world does not sit idly 'out there.' . . . The ideas of the new physics, when wholly grasped, can produce extraordinary *experiences.*" This too has implications for organizations. In my work, for instance, having stronger connection to and having an impact on the experiences of my customers (that is, city officials) and other key stakeholders (legislators, the media, and the public at large) helps us better understand their perspectives and find the best avenues to persuade them and find common ground—not to mention compromise.

Daniel Pink, in *A Whole New Mind,* suggests that as the Conceptual Age fully takes hold, it will prompt a need to offer "something that satisfies the nonmaterial, transcendent desires of an abundant age." Pink envisions a world in which abundance will satisfy most material needs and leave people more focused on the aesthetic, emotional, and spiritual aspects of living. He asserts that this will require leaders and employees who emphasize such qualities as people skills and emotional intelligence and who possess creativity and imagination.

GOOD-BYE, SECURITY BLANKET; HELLO, NEW IDEAS AND APPROACHES

None of us can avoid these emerging issues. In a world of rapid change and technological advances, leaders must find new ways to connect with their people and their customers and constituents. This is no easy task. It requires a willingness to abandon the security blanket of old-school thinking and be open to new ideas and innovative approaches. While it does not require leaving everything behind, the trick is to keep what still works and incorporate it in a new environment built around relationships, new and flexible forms of organizational structure, and more attention to the experiences embraced by customers.

These changes all cry out for a new approach to communication. Alan Deutschman in *Fast Company* magazine cites a study that found that two years after having heart bypass surgery, 90 percent of patients did not maintain the healthier lifestyles they had been urged to adopt. Given such resistance in the face of potentially dire consequences, how then to get people in an organization to change? Deutschman went to Harvard Business School professor John Kotter for the answer. In studying organizations in upheaval, Kotter found the central issue was never strategy, structure, culture, or systems. Rather, it was changing people's behavior—mostly by speaking to people's feelings, even in professions focused on quantitative measurement and analysis.

Enter stories. Facts inform, but stories resonate. Facts can be filed away. Stories inspire. Stories connect us in profound ways that go beyond mere intellect and get to the deeper currents that move us to reflection and inspiration. They can impart values, vision, and ideas. When vital information and visionary thinking merge with storytelling, the result is an emotional connection with the facts *and* the intended impact. Hearing that drug prices are skyrocketing is one thing, but consider the difference when it is the story of a grandmother who must choose between paying for life-sustaining drugs or buying food.

Stories help us see how we are far more alike than different. Through them we can appreciate the human condition (and yes, the human comedy), as they show us how we share the same foibles and fears and hopes. Top executives and managers who sincerely desire to lead better can build trust and rapport with their people when they apply stories to their own experiences and to behaviors they are asking others to adopt.

Most important, stories can teach us significant lessons in both business and life. The irony is that the twenty-first century's most needed means of communication is one of the most ancient. Native Hawaiians call it "tell story." Joseph Campbell spent a lifetime underscoring it as the power of myth. Egyptians told it with hieroglyphics. And prehistoric people conveyed it with drawings and figures painted on the walls of caves. Despite its universal attraction, the use of stories in businesses, nonprofit organizations, and government is only now beginning to be recognized as a way to address the joint challenges arising from the Information and Conceptual Ages.

STORIES ARE THE KEY TO PERSUASIVE COMMUNICATION

For me, developing a systematic way to use stories began around 1995 in a discussion with the mayor of Burkesville, a small town in southeastern Kentucky. A former army general, the mayor listened as I marveled about the many colorful, interesting, and gifted elective officers I met through my role with KLC. I had this sense that the stories they told about choosing a life of public service could do far more than help the public understand government and government leaders. Such stories could build trust and the genuine connection and tolerance for opposing views that is necessary for democracy to flourish. But for all the stories that intrigued me, I had no time to reflect on them, much less write about them. The mayor offered a simple suggestion.

"You might be busy, but take the time to carry index cards and write down the vignettes of those you come into contact with," he said. "You'll return to those cards someday, and they will be more valuable than you realize."

Keeping those words in mind, I was amazed at how my ears became more attuned to stories that had been right under my nose. I found myself writing them on scraps of paper or napkins—anything, really.

Several years later, in 2001, my mother was diagnosed with an illness that would claim her life. During the six months of her illness, I canceled my busy schedule and sat many hours alongside my father at her bedside. It was there that I heard their stories, many of them new, some of them old, but each with a depth and detail that was not present before. Not long afterward I remembered all those stories I had written. I read them again. They came alive in a way I had not fully appreciated before. It was then that I realized the stories of our lives form the basis of all we are and do.

I have gone so far as to incorporate the use of story into KLC and NewCities Institute policy—by assigning a database for their collection, hiring a writer to develop them in various formats, and disseminating them throughout our work in the field, to underscore the value of the insurance products we sell and the training we conduct, and everything in between. By using true stories, we breathe life into issues that otherwise might seem too remote to solve anytime soon. This makes our concerns more vivid to the media and general public and inspires local leaders to work together and speak with one voice on bills of vital importance to them, helping convince lawmakers to pass needed legislation. My staff and I also have been able to foster a greater feeling of community among disparate groups of leaders in cities large and small. The result has been increased sales in the insurance and financial services we offer to cities and a huge increase in the direct participation of city leaders who either go to the state capital or make phone calls and send e-mail to their representatives when General Assembly is in session.

I formed the NewCities Institute to revitalize people's participation in meaningful citizenship—and to underscore the importance of connecting to our sense of local place even as global influence increases. It is the product of my hearing numerous stories of despair and frustration among both officials and the citizenry—stories of how individuals felt they could not make a difference and stories of mayors who felt caught up in day-to-day demands with no time to impart a vision for the future or develop a game plan to cope with the onslaught of change.

Azur, meanwhile, was founded as much on the idea of creating community and connection as it was a place to have excellent food. (Whoever coined the word *eatertainment* has it right.) Even in the restaurant business, story again plays a major role. Restaurants, after all, are places where people seek to be with others as much as they are places to eat a meal. As owners, we hang out there quite a bit and talk with our customers—as do some of our workers when appropriate. Our customers are particularly enamored of the stories of how six "guys" from vastly different backgrounds came together to go into the restaurant business, including how our two chefs both worked in New York City, arrived in Lexington for widely differing reasons, and by chance met each other by taking positions at Azur. Through some marketing and word of mouth, these stories give our restaurant an edge in a business of razor-thin margins.

STORY IS POWER THROUGH WHOLE-BRAIN THINKING

Lest all this seem too light and fluffy, with stories floating around in some ambiguous ether populated by group hugs and tired parables, keep in mind the secret is to integrate right-brain qualities of imagination and innovative thinking with left-brain analytical thought. The real goal is a *whole-brain* approach. Only because right-brain functions have been relatively overlooked is the emphasis now on cultivating our creative and intuitive side.

This new world we are living in serves up a paradox. Even though technological marvels allow us lives of great convenience and opportunity, they also threaten to isolate us from each other. Stories help bridge the gap. In a world that increasingly emphasizes relationship building, clear communication, and a strong sense of community—be it in a city, an office, or a marketing campaign—stories are essential. For organizations that seek to stay ahead of the game, the time to act is now. Those who learn the power of story and apply its principles are those most likely to succeed.

Wake Me Up When
the Data Is Over

PART ONE

How Organizations Are Using Stories in Day-to-Day Operations

S tories and storytelling have a rightful place in people's everyday work—no matter what their role in the organization. The first chapter, "How Can I Help You? Service with a Smile—and a Story!" by Susan Stites, covers how stories can help instill a customer service philosophy, improve service during the sales process, develop long-term customer relationships, and foster internal customer service. It also addresses challenges faced when using stories in these ways. Marcy Fisher's chapter, "Put Your Money Where Your Mouth Is: Unleashing the Power of People Through Stories," also speaks to building connections— but from an internal perspective. In addition, it shows how stories and storytelling can convey tribal knowledge, influence company practices, and bring forth the value of specific initiatives, departments, and the whole organization. Strengthening relationships is again brought out in "We Need More *We* and Less *Me*: How Stories Build Teams and Teamwork," by Susan M. Osborn, Ph.D., M.S.W., and Marcy Fisher. Key here is the impact of stories on visioning the future, enabling trust, support, and mutual respect, and reframing perspectives.

Anyone can exhibit leadership within an organization, which means development in this area is all-important. In the chapter titled

"You Get What You Give: Leadership in Action Through Stories," Lori L. Silverman talks about story use in mentoring staff, passing on leadership and life lessons, communicating strategic information, shifting people's behaviors, and building employee engagement. Conveying critical information and communicating and capturing lessons learned are two themes brought out again in "Are We On Track? How Stories Impact Project Management," by Denise Lee. The chapter also covers stories and storytelling in preparing for and initiating projects. The impact of stories on financial management is demonstrated explicitly in "Who Said Money Is Everything? Story Is the New Currency in Financial Management," by Alicia Korten and Karen Dietz, Ph.D. This piece addresses the use of stories in moving from financial crisis to financial health, building a financial base with donor and foundation grants, and garnering support for social change initiatives.

The theme of change, which is a part of each of these initial chapters, is the primary focus of "We've Never Done It This Way Before: Prompting Organizational Change Through Stories," by North McKinnon. Topics covered relative to story use include the role of leadership in mobilizing change, co-creating a vision and road map for change, overcoming resistance to change, and respecting heritage while moving forward.

CHAPTER ONE

How Can I Help You?

Service with a Smile—and a Story!

Susan Stites

When Sharon Love, owner of Incredible Pets, teaches customers how to care for their pets, she tells them a story. Terry Nicholetti, sales trainer and account executive for the *Washington Business Journal,* tells stories when teaching potential subscribers how to enhance their sales. Sandy Johns, Lands' End learning and development manager, uses stories to train customer service representatives. Craig Hunt—"Catfish Hunter," on-air personality for KYGO-FM, a Denver-based country music station—creates stories to connect to his listeners. Tracey Briggs, communications representative for Orlando Regional Healthcare, finds and writes *Healing Stories* about employees, patients, and their families.

Why are these people and their organizations using stories to develop exceptional customer service? "It just makes sense," says Love. "Which would you rather hear? A bunch of facts and figures about customer service or a story? People will remember stories long after they've forgotten the facts."

INSPIRING THE USE OF STORY

According to Jackie Johnson-Caygill, director of Lands' End Business Outfitters Contact Center, the retail company's rich storytelling heritage came from its founder, Gary Comer. "When the company was small, Gary recognized that stories would help people understand Lands' End and its values." Sandy Johns adds, "He always said, 'Take care of the customers and the rest will take care of itself.' When employees followed his advice, he would tell stories about their efforts and the positive results. This inspired employees to maintain a single-minded focus on the customer."

Comer also encouraged employees to tell stories to customers. "Gary asked them to discuss their own experiences with Lands' End products," says Johns. "He wanted them to talk about what they liked, how they used it, and how they cared for it. Customers had more confidence when products they ordered had the approval of a trusted employee."

For Sharon Love, using stories to develop good customer service at Incredible Pets came out of necessity. "We have three stores and thirty-five employees," she explains. "We don't have time to put employees in a classroom and teach them customer service. Individual store managers must train and coach. Because retail is a social environment, we found that storytelling just happened. It was the way people shared what they knew. Over time, we realized the most valuable learning came from the stories that managers and veteran employees told about their experiences with customers."

Stories about customer service can result from deliberate actions on the part of a single individual or arise naturally from employee experiences. Regardless of how they originate, if these stories are to support customer service, a philosophy must be in place first.

INSTILLING A CUSTOMER SERVICE PHILOSOPHY

Love uses stories to orient new employees to the store's customer service philosophy. One story, "Kitty Crates," on page 5, demonstrates several important customer service principles.

"First," says Love, "this story shows that employees have freedom to make whatever decision is necessary to ensure a customer, or a potential customer, is happy. It also allows us to show employees we support them even if we would've handled the situation differently.

KITTY CRATES

Contributed by Sharon Love

One day, some children were playing outside when they found some abandoned kittens. They wanted to help the kittens, but had never owned any before and didn't know what to do.

Being close to Incredible Pets, they went into the store and asked for a cardboard box. The clerk explained that a cardboard box would never hold the kittens and proceeded to take two brand-new crates from the shelf. She gave them to the children along with a new water bowl and some towels. Because the clerk was concerned that the children might not care for the kittens properly, she spent time teaching them what to do. The children took the kittens home, then returned the supplies to the pet store.

That should have been the end of the story. The clerk simply did what she needed to do to help.

However, many months later the children told a friend about the kittens they rescued and about the nice lady in the pet store who helped them. That friend happened to be my niece. I was pleased but surprised to hear the story—the clerk had never told me about it. When I asked about the incident, the clerk said, "I didn't think it was anything special. I was just doing my job." In my mind, not only did this clerk do a great job in making potential customers happy, she also created a ripple effect when the children spread the word about the pet store to others.

In this instance, the clerk could've given the children a couple of used crates instead of new ones. There is always a chance to talk later about what could have been done differently. The story also demonstrates the *ripple effect* of customer service. If we provide outstanding service—give customers something to talk about—they will talk about it to others and attract more business."

Tracy Storck, assistant store manager, learned the company's customer service philosophy in this way. "When my managers trained me, they used stories to teach me how to handle a variety of situations. I learned our return philosophy by hearing stories about how they were handled. I also learned how to handle challenging customers."

Now Storck uses these same stories when she trains employees. "The stories keep the subject interesting and fresh. And employees are more apt to ask questions when the problem is in the context of a story." Storck continually learns from these stories every time she tells them. "Each story contains many lessons. Every new employee interprets them differently."

Jackie Johnson-Caygill voices a similar sentiment regarding stories at Lands' End. "Our philosophy is simple: Guaranteed. Period. To show we really do mean what we say, we share stories about employees who have taken the authority to do whatever is required to make a customer happy. When they hear about Nora Halverson, who sent her husband's set of cuff links to a customer because the ones the customer ordered were on backorder, they understand the extra efforts our people extend to serve our customers."

Martha Johnson, manager of the 55PLUS Program at Orlando Regional Healthcare, a group of not-for-profit hospitals, describes how the organization instilled customer service through story. "I was asked to join the hospital-wide customer service initiative, an intense strategic undertaking. Across the country, hospitals were experiencing a decline in customer satisfaction. Our hospitals were no exception. Our first step was to conduct a survey to see how employees felt about their jobs. We discovered most people were proud to work in our hospitals, but many felt their jobs had changed. There was too much red tape, too many interdepartmental issues. We knew that to improve customer service, we would have to change the culture."

To accomplish this, they first developed a service statement: "We are here to serve when it matters most." Johnson soon discovered employees had a slightly negative reaction to the word *serve*. "They saw the word as menial, subservient." To overcome this, Johnson turned to stories. "I met with people and talked about the meaning of their work. I asked them to share the reasons they went into health care. Once they remembered why they chose this profession, they overcame their resistance. Their own stories helped them understand what it meant to *serve*."

A clearly stated customer service philosophy is a prerequisite to identifying and sharing stories that support it. Without it, there is no way to know if the appropriate behaviors are being reinforced consistently throughout the organization.

IMPROVING SERVICE DURING THE SALES PROCESS

Terry Nicholetti joined the *Washington Business Journal* to improve sales and customer service. "We found that some people weren't buying or renewing subscriptions because they lacked the time to read the paper," says Nicholetti. "And even if they did subscribe, the papers got lost in piles of other materials."

One of Nicholetti's most successful customer service initiatives was the development of a free seminar on using the newspaper as a sales tool. "With this seminar, we not only build positive relationships with current and potential customers, we also teach them to build positive relationships with their own clients. A key component is storytelling. I've always told stories in my seminars, primarily to gain attention. But it didn't take me long to learn that when people hear stories, they become engaged."

Going a step further, Nicholetti gets attendees to use stories with their own customers. "I have them define their customers, and then I take them on a tour of the newspaper. I encourage them to find stories relating to their current and potential customers." She challenges them to go beyond simply reading the articles they find. "It's the story behind the story that counts. When you know something about someone and what they are going through, you can better serve their needs. In the most fundamental way, you know their story."

Nicholetti emphasizes that salespeople who know their clients' needs are more likely to gain their trust. "With their trust," she adds, "you can help them write the end of their story by offering products and services that address their needs, their problems."

Joan Fletcher, owner of Winning Ways, Inc., a consulting and seminar firm, vouches for how well Nicholetti's approach works. She has completed Nicholetti's class and now team-teaches with her. "Terry's class opened my eyes," says Fletcher. "It never occurred to me to think of newspaper articles as stories. Now I understand that my job is to figure out what my customers' stories are. What has happened to them? How is their situation unique? How does their story relate to my business or something they might need?"

Sondra Singer also believes storytelling is a powerful sales tool. Singer, a certified radio marketing consultant, sells advertising for KYGO-FM. "Advertising, if done well, *is* storytelling," she explains. "Once you know what a customer's products and services are, it's the salesperson's job to help the customer construct a story that will compel others to buy them."

Singer believes product endorsements are an important storytelling tool. "A typical radio commercial is presented in third person—it's not personal," she points out. "But a product endorsement is a firsthand testimonial—a story told directly to the listener by a trusted on-air personality. It's a more intimate way to sell a product."

Singer says Craig Hunt, "Catfish Hunter," one of the station's popular on-air personalities, is an excellent spinner of product endorsements. His effectiveness stems from two well-developed skills. "First, he has outstanding customer service skills. When he develops an endorsement with a client, he goes out of his way to use the product and note its features and benefits—he won't accept an endorsement unless he believes in the product. As a result, he develops trust in two important constituents. The client trusts him to give a heartfelt endorsement, and the listener trusts that the product he's talking about is as good as he says it is.

"But that trust, that product knowledge, isn't enough," continues Singer. "Craig also has a knack for talking about the product using interesting and colorful stories. It's theater of the mind. Craig takes his experiences with the product and paints a picture. His stories are the context for the call to action."

Organizations that use stories in their sales process have two powerful advantages. First, by hearing customers' stories, they can better determine and fulfill their customers' needs. Second, when they use stories to tell customers about their products, they build trust, an essential ingredient in long-term customer relationships.

DEVELOPING CUSTOMER RELATIONSHIPS

Lands' End teaches employees how to use stories to develop long-term customer relationships. As Anne Hore, director of employee and customer communications, notes, "Every customer sales representative is trained to listen to each customer and build a relationship. Their goal is to provide a lasting experience that makes each customer come back. And they do!" As a result, Lands' End has compiled booklets containing stories that demonstrate how each employee goes the distance for customers.

"These booklets are useful in helping people understand what Lands' End is all about," says Johnson-Caygill. "When customers receive the booklets, they get a glimpse of everything we are willing to do. When employees read the stories, they see the many ways in which other employees have gone to great lengths to make a customer happy."

If you ask Lands' End employees which story is their favorite, you get varied answers. Kelly Ritchie, senior vice president of employee and customer services, likes the story where a distant customer casually mentions to an operator, "Stop and visit if you are ever in town," and the operator actually pays the customer a visit. Johnson-Caygill recalls the team of employees who took an unexpected trip to Las Vegas to deliver attaché cases after the first shipment was incorrectly embroidered.

However, the one story they all love to tell is "Pre-Wedding Jitters." "It's a great story about relationships and trust," says Sandy Johns. "Look at how much this customer had at stake, and yet she trusted us on her wedding day."

For Johns, the story booklets are valuable tools for training customer service representatives. "First, they serve to remind employees

PRE-WEDDING JITTERS

Contributed by Lands' End

One Friday when Ruth Lang was working the third shift in customer sales, she received the strangest but most fun call ever. A customer called and asked if Ruth would call her at 5:00 A.M. EST. She was staying in a mansion turned hotel that did not have a wake-up service. The next day was her wedding day and she was afraid that she and her sister would oversleep. Since she had been a loyal customer of Lands' End, she knew she could count on us to help in any way. Of course Ruth couldn't turn her down and agreed to call her. When the bride-to-be answered the phone the next morning, she said she and her sister were sure Lands' End would come through. They said they were exhausted but that the day was going to be beautiful.

From *Lands' End at Your Service: The People, the Stories, the Traditions.* Dodgeville, WI: Lands' End, Inc., 2000, p. 3. Reprinted by permission of Lands' End.

of their freedom to act on behalf of the customer. Second, we use individual stories to illustrate key learning points."

Johnson-Caygill adds, "The Las Vegas story illustrates we're all human and that mistakes happen. But these mistakes give us the chance to recover in a spectacular way. In reality, who wants to have that kind of mess-up? Who wants to go to Las Vegas at the last minute? But employees are empowered to make these kinds of decisions and the recovery gives great customer service."

"There's something much more essential that we want employees to learn," adds Ritchie. "As important as it is to tell the stories that are in our history, it's even more important to create new stories. Every time a customer has a problem, a need, or a request, we want employees to use judgment and creativity to meet the need. We want them to use their personalities to create their own stories—to become a part of the legend."

KYGO-FM also creates stories to build relationships with radio listeners. The station has a "live and local" philosophy, which means programming is targeted to appeal to the Denver audience. No prime-time program is syndicated.

"Our program director, Joel Burke, is a master at knowing our listeners," says Sondra Singer. "He often assigns new on-air personalities a playful variation of their real name. This gives the station a character of liveliness and fun. It's how Craig Hunt became 'Catfish Hunter.'" On air, Paul Donovan is also known as "The Professor" because of his penchant for waxing intellectual with the music. "Detour Dave" announces traffic from his helicopter. Steve "Mudflap" McGrew is the station's nationally known comedian, who in his spare time plays guitar in a country band.

Each on-air personality is free to develop a unique rapport with listeners. Catfish uses his "Catfish Diaries" to connect with his audience. "I just go on the air and talk about my daily adventures. Sometimes I'll tell them about a visit with my mom, other times I'll take a current event and embellish it, make it funny."

Catfish also has on-air rapport with "Dewey from Louisville," a small community southeast of Boulder. Dewey adds a story-like quality to the show. "Dewey calls in and we banter on the radio," says Catfish. "He's always unemployed and his sister dances at questionable venues. We talk about topical stuff and Dewey gives his comedic take on it. The listeners love Dewey. Many think he's real, but he's actually from Atlanta."

"With the 'Catfish Diaries' and 'Dewey from Louisville,' I try to create one or two memorable moments per shift, something the listeners will remember, an insight they will ponder. I like to find a good odd thing that sticks. Who knows? I'm now thinking of getting a dog and naming him 'Flash.' Then I can come on the air and tell my stories of 'Fish and Flash.'"

Singer adds, "We like to extend the fun by interacting with our listeners and getting them to tell us their stories. For example, we sponsor an event called 'Take the Plunge.' Listeners write stories telling us how they fell in love and why they want to get married at the water park inside Six Flags Elitch Gardens. Each year, we pick the best stories and sponsor a big wedding. Our advertisers provide the cake, flowers, pictures, a certificate for the wedding ring, and the reception and honeymoon. Morning air personality Jonathan Wilde, who is also a minister, becomes the 'Right Reverend Johnny Wilde' for this event. He puts on his best preacher voice and performs the wedding ceremony at the top of the water slide. Once the couples have spoken their vows, they 'take the plunge' down the slide. Portions of the wedding are aired the next morning and the morning personalities recap the event. It's a community effort and everyone buys into the story."

Orlando Regional Healthcare also captures both staff and customer stories as a way to develop customer relationships. Tracey Briggs says, "Our stories touch customers in several ways. First, they highlight our compassionate care, which brings comfort to patients and their families. We compile our *Healing Stories* into booklets and put them in waiting rooms so people can read about the nurse who taught the new dad how to change a diaper or the doctor who came in on his own time to check on a patient. This brings peace to a family going through a difficult time.

"Our stories also validate the patient's experience. People are surprised when we ask them to share their story. They are honored that someone feels their experience is significant enough to capture in a story. *Healing Stories* convey the message that our patients are valuable. Sharing their stories provides ordinary people with ordinary means a way to give back to the hospital that helped them."

Finally, Briggs explains, stories provide inspiration to patients: "The reason people are in the hospital is often surprising and never comforting. We need to find ways to comfort them. Reading *Healing Stories* about people who have experienced similar ordeals and had amazing healing experiences right here in this very hospital inspires them with faith and hope."

Both internal, staff-driven stories and stories from customers play an essential role in building long-term relationships. Whether they are shared orally, as is the case at KYGO-FM, or in writing, as Lands' End and Orlando Regional Healthcare have done, they can create a bond of loyalty between the organization, its employees, and customers.

FOSTERING INTERNAL CUSTOMER SERVICE

To inspire staff, Orlando Regional Healthcare uses stories to enhance internal customer service. "When you share positive stories that highlight what employees have done, it motivates other team members to follow the example," says Briggs. "Recognizing team members in a story acknowledges them for doing an outstanding job and inspires them to keep it up." "The Hurricane Story" is an example.

This story illustrates how staff adjusted their routines to help the hospital prevail, even as other businesses closed. When employees see the extraordinary lengths the hospital is willing to take to accommodate them, they are more willing to do the same for each other.

The same is true at Lands' End. To enhance internal customer service, it has an "all hands on deck" policy during the holiday peak season. "No matter where you work, everyone sets aside four weeks to

THE HURRICANE STORY

Contributed by Orlando Regional Healthcare

Dying branches hung precariously in the air, caught by the trees that survived both Hurricanes Charley and Frances, when the news arrived that Hurricane Jeanne loomed off the coast. *Could Central Florida withstand another blow?* Anxious feelings returned as everyone once again made preparations—buying gallons of extra water, searching for generators, and stocking up on nonperishable groceries.

As with the two previous hurricanes, restaurants closed their doors, shops boarded their windows, and employers sent their workers home. Central Florida closed, except for a few essential services—police, firefighters, hospitals—the everyday heroes that guard the safety of the community. As residents gathered around their battery-operated radios to listen to storm updates, Orlando Regional Medical Center (ORMC) team members chose to set aside personal concerns to provide much-needed medical care.

Windows shook. Trees fell. Power lines snapped. But the storm could not match the strength of spirit within ORMC. Patients arrived injured from the storm or from debris cleanup with broken arms and legs, wounds from power tools and falling branches, to find care and compassion awaiting them.

As days turned into weeks, Central Florida worked to restore power and normalcy. Businesses remained closed, yet ORMC continued to serve around the clock. With schools and day-care centers closed, medical staff brought their children to work. ORMC corporate staff put aside normal duties to care for [them]. They read stories, rocked babies, played games, and changed diapers, giving parents peace of mind . . . so they could concentrate on patient care.

Corporate policies bent with the trying times, allowing employees to cash in vacation time for much needed home repair costs. Team members covered for each other when they needed extra time to repair the damage to their homes. Even a special team member Disaster Relief Fund was established to provide assistance to those worst hit.

Central Florida's most severe hurricane season in 40 years shook the foundation of the community, but only served to strengthen the resolve of the dedicated ORMC team. Team members developed a stronger bond with each other and the community.

As George Geans, manager of spiritual care, shares, "Our team members are living proof that we don't just care *for* our patients, we care *about* them as well."

From *Careholders' Report 2004.* Orlando, FL: Orlando Regional Healthcare, 2004. Used with permission.

help out, either on the phones or in the warehouse," explains Anne Hore. "This means that everyone—regardless of their position—has a chance to work side by side to serve the customer."

"It's an opportunity to get new stories," adds Diane Huza, call center manager. "When my hands are 'on deck,' I want people to grab me and tell me what's happening. I want to know what's going well and what's not. This is often the time when I hear new stories."

"The experience is great for everyone," says Hore. "Employees get firsthand experience working with customers; it builds team camaraderie, helps with our holiday staffing, and we all get new stories to share throughout the following year."

A key to enhancing internal customer service is deliberately seeking out and retelling stories that showcase employees helping each other and the organization supporting them in their work. These stories can energize and motivate staff and reinforce collaborative working relationships.

THE CHALLENGE OF USING STORIES IN CUSTOMER SERVICE

The most prevalent challenge these organizations encounter is getting employees to come forward with their stories. "Sometimes, we don't hear about something an employee does until long after the fact," says Lands' End's Johnson-Caygill. "We hire people based on their ability to treat people with dignity and respect. When they go out of their way to help a customer, they don't think it's any big deal. They're just doing what's second nature for them."

Internet customer service specialist Nora Halverson, the employee who loaned a customer her husband's cuff links, demonstrates this. When asked why she sent the cuff links, her response was simply, "We weren't using them. Besides, if I have something and somebody needs it, they can have it. It didn't even matter to me if the customer sent them back." (For the record, the customer did return the cuff links after the backordered ones arrived.)

Orlando Regional Healthcare's employees are equally reticent. "People believe good customer service is a part of their jobs—they just don't see themselves as heroes," remarks Martha Johnson. "They don't tend to come forward with their own stories. We have to go out and find them."

That is exactly what these organizations are doing. Says Johnson, "I started by walking around and asking people for stories. I also posted requests on the intranet. It's important to train managers and leaders to be on the lookout for stories." When Tracey Briggs took over the *Healing Story* initiative, she built on this work. "I look for stories in letters that we receive from patients. Then I call and ask them to share their stories. They are always impressed that someone read their letter and that their thoughts mattered. I also look for stories from their families and team members."

Lands' End implemented a *Legendary Customer Service Award* to draw out employee stories. Still, employees shy away from submitting their own. In Halverson's case, it took three different leaders to get her to share her story. "I just wasn't comfortable bragging about myself. However, I was given lots of encouragement from all three of my leads—Paul Berg, Steve Peterson, and Greg Gorsline. Greg was the one who finally submitted the story." To Halverson, that was the end of the story. It took one further question for her to offer a final piece of information: "Yes, I did win the award."

Getting employees—and customers—to tell their stories is a challenge, but people will come forward if organizations reach out and demonstrate their willingness to listen. Regular encouragement and positive outcomes can aid in this.

THE RESULTS TELL ALL

All five organizations have experienced benefits from story use. However, each has a different way of measuring success.

For some, it is financial. Says Tracy Storck of Incredible Pets, "We measure our customer service by how well we are doing monetarily. If customers keep coming back, we feel that our approach is working." At *Washington Business Journal,* Terry Nicholetti points out, "Since I've started doing seminars, I've increased my subscription sales each year. When I give a seminar, between 25 percent and 50 percent of the attendees subscribe."

At KYGO-FM, Sondra Singer proudly describes the many awards the station wins. It is consistently recognized for excellence in programming, including the National Association of Broadcasters' coveted Marconi Awards for Large Market Station of the Year and Country Station of the Year in 2004.

Amount and type of feedback are key indicators for Joan Fletcher, Craig Hunt, and Lands' End. Reflects Hunt, "I've only had my 'Catfish' nickname for two years, but I can tell you that I've gotten more feedback by being Catfish for two years than I got in ten years being simply Craig." For Fletcher, "My seminar evaluations always say 'Tell more stories,' so I know the method works." Jackie Johnson-Caygill refers to the Lands' End letter board—a wall that contains letters from satisfied customers—for results. "We know our efforts are working when we see these letters from all our satisfied customers." In fact, the effort works so well that in 2004 the company received more than 1,130 positive letters or e-mail messages from happy customers.

Lands' End and Orlando Regional Healthcare also measure success through customer satisfaction surveys. "If we are getting good ratings, we are comfortable attributing our results to our training and development methods," explains Diane Huza of Lands' End. "These methods include storytelling." At Orlando Regional Healthcare 90 percent of people completing a customer satisfaction survey say they would recommend the hospital to others. "Since 2003, we've seen our patient satisfaction increase by a score of two points. This is considered very good," comments Martha Johnson. She attributes this improvement to all the hospital's customer service initiatives, including stories. "People were reluctant to accept the changes we were proposing. When they started hearing the *Healing Stories,* they got on board."

To this, Tracey Briggs adds changes she sees in patient attitude. "When I interview people, they often describe their experience in four steps. One: I didn't want to have surgery. Two: I needed surgery. Three: I had surgery. Four: I didn't want to go home. When we make this big a difference for even one person coming in to have surgery, I believe our customer service efforts are working. Our *Healing Stories* are a huge part of that effort."

LESSONS FROM THOSE
WHO ARE DOING IT

What can you do to capitalize on what these organizations have learned? Try these techniques:

- To help employees internalize your customer service philosophy, have them tell stories about why they chose their profession.

- Assume employees are already telling stories about how they handled customers. Find ways to bring out these stories (including your intranet) and acknowledge them. And train managers and supervisors to be on the lookout for them.
- Share stories about outstanding customer service to inspire others to provide similar service.
- Identify key learning points for customer service training. Then find stories that reinforce them.
- Encourage employees to provide such outstanding service that they become a story themselves.
- Sponsor contests that reward the best customer service stories.
- Publish and share your stories with customers so they become part of your organization.
- Use media articles about your customers to learn their stories.
- Encourage customers to share stories about their experiences.

By using these story techniques in customer service, you will be able to more quickly and easily relate key philosophies and practices to your employees. In the long run, your employees will be able to connect more closely to their customers and help deliver exceptional service to them.

Special Thanks

Thank you to Susan M. Osborn for her connection to Incredible Pets and to Kelly Ritchie, who generously made time, space, and people available for interviews at Lands' End. Special appreciation to the National Storytelling Network, whose broadcast e-mail requests uncovered the *Washington Business Journal*, KYGO-FM, and Orlando Regional Healthcare.

CHAPTER TWO

Put Your Money Where Your Mouth Is

Unleashing the Power of People Through Stories

Marcy Fisher

—◊◊◊—

Organizations are turning to stories to enhance their investment in people. Take enterprises like Information Resources, Inc., the world's leading provider of enterprise market information solutions; BMC Software, Inc., a leader in enterprise management; Rush-Copley Medical Center, a hospital providing the highest-quality health care in an efficient manner; Motorola, a recognized global technology leader; and BP, one of the world's largest energy companies.

Why are they moving in this direction? For Gordon Peterson, vice president of organizational effectiveness at Information Resources, it is strategic. "Storytelling allows us to put our business situations, culture, and employee actions into a context that allows staff to practice global interactions within the company in a low-risk way," he says. "Strategic initiatives in any organization can be achieved by using story to align, train, inspire, coach, and orient your leaders," adds Laura Folse, vice president of exploration & production technology for BP.

FROM ACCIDENTAL USE TO A MANAGEMENT APPROACH

Leaders happen upon story in different ways. Laura Folse says, "I'm from the south. It's part of my heritage and a natural way to communicate with people. . . . Yes, even us heavy technology folks." She adds, "Until recently, I'd never thought of story as a management tool." Because Folse experienced the benefits of story, she uses her natural storytelling abilities to connect with employees. She models these skills when she motivates and coaches her eight hundred technical people.

Modeling natural storytelling abilities is also visible at the top echelon of Motorola. "Our new CEO led us into using story. He's a natural storyteller," reports Orlando Ashford, vice president of human resources strategy & organization development. "The CEO has conducted numerous town hall meetings telling the story of where he sees us going," he notes, adding, "A side benefit of the [CEO's] formal use of story is [staff's] reflection on what's been said. They often turn around and retell the story they've just heard."

In both organizations, leaders are receiving help to excel as storytellers. "[At Motorola] we're training leaders on [storytelling] due to the effectiveness and fun associated with using story to establish corporate direction," comments Ashford. And Stephanie Moore, vice president of human resources' Exploration & Production Technology, says, "Some of our storytellers work with an external coach; some even participate in theater and improvisational groups to hone their story skills. This is a big change. I believe it's based on Laura's use of story."

There are many ways to discover the benefits of stories and to learn how to tell them—through personal experience, hearing them modeled by others, and formal training. No single approach appears optimal. What matters is how stories are being used to convey important messages.

FORGING A CONNECTION

Stories forge numerous connections. "Stories link people to a concept or topic by connecting their heads, hearts, and hands," comments Armida Mendez Russell, head of global diversity and inclusion at BMC Software. She explains how this affects her work: "Diversity management is people management. It's change management. We want employees to lead the charge for change and be energized and passionate about making diversity and inclusiveness happen. Our goal is to weave diversity into the ethos of the organization. Because of the connections stories [make inside people, they] play a critical role in the change process."

Laura Folse of BP expounds on this. She often speaks on the concept of good leadership using "The Story of Leo." "Telling 'The Story of Leo' enables me to use imagery to describe servant leadership in a way that emotionally resonates with people. When I've tried to describe [this concept] with unemotional bullet points, it didn't have the same impact. Each time I tell the story, people instantly understand what it means. [They] can [also] continue to interpret its meaning [over time]," she explains. Stephanie Moore concurs. "You can see people engage with the story. . . . Some even have that childlike, wide-eyed focus. I see it evoke emotional connection," she says.

Folse and her staff regularly employ stories that connect people to concepts. She gives an example: "When we think we have a technological breakthrough, we can give all sorts of scientific and technical data or provide the same information in a story with the technical data involved. Stories help our highly technical people convey technically difficult concepts in an understandable and compelling way to non-technical people so they are able to carry the message forward."

Because stories enable myriad connections that evoke change, Orlando Ashford, from Motorola, offers a caution: "Use a story and people understand on an intellectual and feeling level how they, as individuals, will be impacted. You must decide [beforehand] how and if you want to use story to translate a word picture to this level of

THE STORY OF LEO

Contributed by Laura Folse

Once, a small group of people decided to take a journey to the East on a quest to experience this mystical place and to meet some spiritual leaders of the area. As part of their preparations, they enlisted the services of a sherpa named Leo.

Each day, Leo helped them plan the journey. He'd warn them of the hazards along the way, as well as the beauty they were likely to find. Each morning, Leo prepared their breakfast and, as they embarked on the next part of each trek by foot, [made sure] that each person's pack was prepared and everyone was capable of carrying the weight they were assigned. As they made their way through the forest, Leo kept a watchful eye on the group. If anyone strayed from the path, Leo would very gently direct [them] back.

Each night, Leo helped the travelers find a good resting place—a suitable place to pitch their tents. He prepared dinner and [made sure they all had soft spots to rest their heads]. As the journey grew longer and more difficult, the travelers began to question themselves and wonder if their quest was complete folly. On these nights, Leo would very gently sing them to sleep.

One morning the group awoke to find Leo gone. He'd gone without a word. Without Leo, the group became disoriented and lost its will to move forward. The group wandered aimlessly for days and people began fighting among themselves. It eventually disbanded, gave up its search for the great gurus, and went home.

Many years later, one member of the group decided to once again go in search of the great Eastern gurus. But, as time wore on, he became lost in the forest and feared a repeat of his previous quest. After a few days, he was found by a group of monks. When he explained his driving quest to meet a great leader from the East, the monks offered to take him to meet their leader.

The man was escorted to a monastery and taken into a large room where a group of monks were sitting in a circle. Although the men all looked similar, one had an aura of calmness and wisdom that suggested he was the leader. The traveler staggered forward and extended his arms to embrace that which he had been seeking for so long. As the monk rose to meet him, the traveler recognized the monk as his former servant, Leo.

Based on H. Hesse and H. Rosner, *The Journey to the East.* New York: Picador, 1956.

understanding. Storytelling is a powerful tool, not to be used in a cavalier manner."

Armida Mendez Russell of BMC Software cites an example that demonstrates this caution: "I once told a story about a person who had an odor. I didn't do a good job of constructing the story. It came off as though I was labeling an entire ethnic group as smelly people. It was awful." What did she learn from this? "[You] must think through the story, its lesson, what you want to achieve with the story and the unintended consequences of the story's construction."

Well-constructed stories provide the imagery people need to picture a situation and themselves within it, thus provoking an emotional reaction and providing a vehicle to connect their feelings to their thoughts and actions. These connections can align people around a concept, goal, or new behavior and foster change. This level of impact implies an obligation: Story use needs to be conscious and purposeful and considerate of those who hear it.

CONVEYING TRIBAL KNOWLEDGE

Because she wanted to make sure that "warmth, humanness, and connectedness—traditional values of the nursing profession—were not lost in this high-tech world," says Shawn Tyrrell, MSN, CNAA, CHE, vice president of nursing services at Rush-Copley Medical Center, she encouraged her nursing staff to embark on a story initiative. "I'd used [stories] before so I knew [they] would work." Tyrrell also had a second need she was hoping stories could fulfill: "[I] work within a hospital building that is ten years old. In [my] hospital the traditions from our hundred-year-old [parent hospital's history] could be lost. These traditions include the wisdom that is part of the [organization's] DNA that intuitively directs nursing staff to do the right things. In our case, doing right means making a difference in the lives of our patients."

Jodie Beverage, a registered nurse in the operating room, explains what happened. "The process started out slow and small. I asked staff for stories about their work. We started sharing them in staff meetings. Then I encouraged them to request stories from patients using [the phrase] 'tell me about yourself' instead of asking a series of questions," she says.

Beverage also models story use in response to staff inquiries. "Nurses often ask, 'Did you ever have this happen to you?' They might be seeking technical information or emotional support. I respond with a story to answer their questions," she explains. Why does she do this? "My grandparents told lots of stories. To this day I can remember their vivid details. I wanted to have the same effect on my peers."

Communicating traditions through stories began with nursing staff, and is expanding within the organization. "It's spreading to other departments [such as] physical therapy. One doctor is using stories as part of his grand rounds. He told me he's able to teach residents about medical issues, information acquisition, and humanizing the medical experience," says Tyrrell.

Knowledge at Information Resources is conveyed in leadership orientation. "Storytelling [through] a case study is used with our directors and [executive] leaders in their week-long on-boarding process. It's based on a real story with actual data. The story sets the culture and business context and provides leaders with a sense of what interaction is like within the company," explains Gordon Peterson. Adds Kevin Yates, director of learning solutions, "Selecting the right story was natural. We used consultants to ensure we got the story [structure] right. They facilitated our collection of input for the story, showed us how to be creative, and added large doses of fun and realism.

"What wasn't natural was the execution of our story," says Yates. "We originally thought we could select any executive to come and tell [it]. We quickly discovered in practice sessions that there's an art to telling stories that have an impact. Success requires a good story and someone comfortable telling it."

The story was used in a variety of ways. Yates explains, "We were creative in how we used story as part of the instructional design. I looked for a way to create a learning sandwich. We sent the story out as prework. And participants heard it in the training program. Then we used it again to follow up and reinforce learning achieved in the program." Peterson elaborates on the follow-up: "We gave participants an assignment that required them to do homework. Then they used the Internet to share their new findings and reinforce their learnings— they interacted with each other in real time, which showed them how much easier it is to learn with a rich story as a base. The learning sandwich deepened learning and the experience."

Using technology to convey story via the Internet was powerful. Comments Yates, "We needed to connect senior leaders over long distances. The use of story and some new technology allowed us to do both." Peterson adds, "A well-written story about the internal workings of the company with global participation created a realistic learning environment. We look forward to using it in other distance learning programs."

Every organization has the need to communicate tribal knowledge—the wisdom to do the right things. This knowledge, whether relayed through oral or electronic story sharing, helps employees and leaders quickly assimilate into the organization, remember critical information, and ultimately make sound decisions.

IMPACTING COMPANY PRACTICES

Commonly held stories reinforce company practices. Ashley Fields, director of organization development & diversity at BMC Software, explains. "BMC uses stories to illustrate its actionable beliefs in respecting other cultures and values. For example, we choose not to make major communications on Friday because the work week is Sunday through Thursday in our offices in Israel," he says. Where are these stories told? "In each quarterly management briefing and all-hands meeting our senior leaders, especially our CEO, Bob Beauchamp, tell stories exemplifying company values [as well as stories] illustrating staff retention, employee recognition, and customer experiences with sales and marketing."

Fields provides another example. "There are countless stories of people [successfully implementing] our flexible work scheduling policy. [One story involves] a senior male manager based out of his residence due to a dual career situation with child care considerations. He covers a large geographical client group and, at times, another one as well. When not 'on the road,' he does a lot of work during evening hours when his wife has returned home and their child care times are less restrictive. This is mutually advantageous to him and his colleagues in the United States because it corresponds to their daytime hours."

Armida Mendez Russell speaks to the impact of these stories: "People are able to see diversity is about more than race and gender. Once people hear them they can discuss their reactions and thoughts about the situation and how it affects each of us over the long term." Fields adds, "People have greatly appreciated the sensitivity management has gained through listening to and [retelling] these stories."

Motorola is also reflecting on company practices, a result of the CEO's story about future organizational direction. Orlando Ashford notes, "We're in a transitional time in our company and are engaging people in discussions to understand what we want to keep and what we need to change. [For example], we're having online chats about our values. We've collected story examples about our values in action and we're using them around the company." He comments on why stories are necessary in shifting times: "A business in transition needs to have threads that hold people and groups together in a special way. Over time these story threads are woven together to create the new cultural fabric."

Stories that organizational leaders choose to communicate can shape the business practices that are embraced and reinforced inside their enterprises. Thus, selecting those stories that will be told cannot be taken lightly. It is also important to listen to the employee stories that result from embodying these stated practices.

REALIZING VALUE ON MANY LEVELS

Communicating the value proposition for a human resources initiative, the department, or an entire organization is critical in today's changing marketplace. In past work experiences, Armida Mendez Russell has used stories to drive value at an initiative level. "Story helped convey a business case for diversity: increased sales because of a stand on gay rights and understanding that an English name for a new product won't positively translate in a foreign country. These are just a couple ways business cases played out because of stories that were told. It sometimes means taking a risk."

And she practices what she preaches. She crafted the story "A Risk Well Worth Taking," on page 26, based on a prior work experience where the business case for the company's involvement in a public event came under fire.

Armida Mendez Russell uses this story when subjects seem too risky to tackle. "I've used it in formal training and organizational meetings and informally [when] coaching [individual] leaders who appear to be apprehensive about an issue," she adds.

Communicating the value of the Human Resources Department can also occur through stories. At Motorola, "Story allows us to demonstrate the value proposition that Human Resources provides in a variety of areas, from aligning our entire organization to training. We share our stories and listen to those from others that demonstrate why human resource activities are much more than just transactional activities," says Orlando Ashford.

Since 2000, Rush-Copley Medical Center has used stories to reinforce its organizational value proposition. "Our values are based on a promise to our patients—the promise of comfort, responsiveness, safety,

A RISK WELL WORTH TAKING

Contributed by Armida Mendez Russell

Sitting here, thinking about my work as a diversity consultant with Fortune 500 organizations around the business case for diversity over the last nineteen years, makes me reflect on one of the major risks a client, American Express IDS, decided to take several years ago. A request came in from the gay and lesbian network in the company, to allow them to march in the Gay Pride Parade wearing their company shirts. Management had quite a heated discussion. They were concerned about customers and community reaction and possible repercussions to the company. Nevertheless, management held firm in supporting their employees.

We went through a business analysis to decide what to do. To no one's surprise, supporting this request was high risk. One of the long-tenured leaders suggested that we look at our stated values. "If we followed our stated values about people, integrity, and honesty, what is the right thing to do? We are leaders and we must do what is right especially when the risk is high." We all agreed that the company's values supported participation in the Gay Pride Parade. The approval was given.

It was a beautiful sunny Minnesota day—a perfect day for a parade. The requesting group marched in the parade wearing their company T-shirts. They were filled with pride and joy having the honor of representing their company in this celebration of their lives.

The company got many negative calls about its representation in the parade. Short term, the company lost some business and received hate mail. However, in the long term, a commitment to diversity produced a new market niche and focus: The substantial gay and lesbian buying community that had not previously sought out the firm but now considered it a preferred provider of financial services because management had the courage to act based on the stated corporate values.

Nothing comes without risks. Staying true to your core values is always the right thing to do. Most times it pays off, both emotionally and financially.

> Management sure was right about living the values. It is easy to state one's support of diversity. It is a different level of commitment to act on it.

compassion, and partnership—and is embraced by the caregiving team. It reinforces the goal of offering the best experience possible while in the hospital," says Shawn Tyrrell. To make good on this promise, nursing staff documents and relays stories about patients who have affected them and vice versa. "The stories help staff celebrate how they've made a difference with kindness, humor, touch, prayer, and critical thinking," points out Jodie Beverage. Tyrrell adds, "We gather stories from nurses and from patients. We share these stories with new nurses to allow them to feel and hear how we achieve a warm and caring environment."

Initially, Tyrrell encountered pockets of resistance. "Nursing staff felt it was bragging to tell their stories," she explains. Beverage notes, "Many nurses said, 'It's just my job.' Or, 'This is just another management flavor of the day.' Once stories began to be published in a monthly newsletter and in the annual publication, *Extraordinary Care: A Collection of Stories from the Nurses at Rush-Copley Medical Center,* people got into sharing their stories. It was a turning point." Tyrrell adds, "They let go of resistance when they saw the power of nurses' stories from different parts of the medical center."

Beverage's Bachelor of Science completion program assignment was to write three stories about her work. "I took one of them, fleshed it out, and submitted it to Shawn. She put it in an annual publication," Beverage says. A synopsis of it is on page 28.

"Now other nurses have me review stories they're writing for future publications. Helping others connects me even more to staff and patients I will never get to meet," says Beverage.

Value is a difficult business concept to communicate. Stories are a vehicle for expressing the business rationale for human capital initiatives and an organizational promise to care for people—and collecting data on and relaying the value of a human resources function. Because evoking these stories may not be easy, providing examples can jump-start the process.

DISCOURAGEMENT & DEPRESSION:
TURNING IT AROUND IN THE OPERATING ROOM

Contributed by Jodie Beverage, RN

Ross's name jumped out at me from the long surgery schedule for the day. He had been to our department many times over the last six months.

On the day of the procedure, I was the circulating nurse. Ross arrived late in the Day Surgery Unit from the nursing home where he resides. This was not the first time I had cared for him, but I did not expect him to remember me. He was alone, lying awkwardly in the bed, his gown barely covering his legs. I could see the loosely bandaged right foot with a shape that gave hint to the missing digit. He looked irritated and uncomfortable. I introduced myself as I nonchalantly pulled the blanket to cover him. As I approached the head of the bed, I offered my hand. He looked me up and down, rolled his eyes, snorted, and turned his head away.

I offered to help him adjust his position. He grunted, "It doesn't matter." With a little persistence, he allowed me to get him into a more comfortable position. It was going to be a few minutes before I would take him to the OR, so I brought him a warm blanket and a pillow to place under his right leg. My actions met with mild protest. "Seems like a lot of fuss for nothing." Though I did notice the furrow in his brow loosen.

When I transported him into surgery, he commented, "If I have to." I asked if he wanted the surgery and if the surgeon had explained all his options. He stated he knew and to "just get it over with." When we entered the OR he howled, "Why does it have to be so damn cold in here?" I started to tell him, but cut myself short to get him some blankets from the warmer, noticing he was not listening to my explanation.

After he was transferred to an OR bed, he commented on seeing us all again in a few weeks when this procedure fails to stop the advancing gangrene in his foot. "You'll be hacking off more of my leg soon enough." I tried to reassure him that although that was possible, all of us were hopeful the procedure would be a success. He replied, "Yeah, right. Then how else would you guys make a living?"

The statement stung. I was taken aback. I tried to explain that the whole surgical team would rather be out of a job. He just stared blankly at the ceiling as he was anesthetized and intubated. I continued to hear the tone of his words repeating in my head.

The procedure was quite long, which gave me an opportunity to learn more about this discouraged old man. Looking at his records, I noticed his admit date to the nursing home was just a few weeks earlier. I mumbled aloud the facts while watching the surgeon and his assistant in anticipation of any special needs. As I reviewed the notes, I noticed Ross had a different primary care physician than [for] his last surgery. I also noted his pain medication was not given often, especially at night.

I started to ponder my findings. Why the change? What was his pain level? Was he experiencing side effects from the pain medication? What about his sleep pattern? Had he been evaluated for depression? What was his nursing home discharge plan? I asked about his discharge planning and was told others would handle it. My hands were tied. I spoke to his doctor about my findings, asking that he assure me they would be acted on. I also prayed this intervention would make a difference.

Two weeks later, I saw Ross's name on the surgery schedule. I was not involved in his case, but wanted to see how he was doing. When I found him, it set me back again, but this time with a smile. He had an upbeat and lively demeanor. I asked how he was doing. He smiled and said, "Better." He said the doctor was "just cleaning up some" today, not amputating. I complimented him on how good he looked. It was obvious he was doing better. He was clean-shaven and had a fresh haircut. He said he was in a senior center apartment and had to look good for all the women that fuss over him. I told him it was nice to see him, and the next time I saw him I hoped would be at Jewel or Wal-Mart, not the hospital. He just smirked and said, "This place ain't all that bad."

(Continued)

I gave a smirk back and winked, "I guess not." When I looked at his chart, I was pleased to see he was back with his original doctor and on an antidepressant. My hands were not as tied as I thought they were. The difference is [that] kindness, prayer, humor, touch, and critical thinking can make a big difference, one person at a time.

THE MORAL OF THE STORY: VALIDATION

There are many ways to use stories to enhance an organization's investment in its people. What results can organizations achieve from their efforts?

Stories improve the speed of message deployment. Orlando Ashford of Motorola tells this story, which he heard from a colleague: "Over coffee, his group [Learning and Development] was talking about what his organization would be in the future. Suddenly, these individuals were constructing a story about where they were going to take the group. They even drew a picture of their story. They constructed their future state much more quickly than they were ever able to do using their old methods." This speed has also improved Motorola's ability to establish its new business direction. "Using story allows us to get a message to the organization. In most cases about 80 percent of the folks get it quickly. That's a great return on investment," he adds.

Laura Folse of BP echoes this result: "I work with very technical people who speak in technical language. Taking techno-speak and turning it into a story—a visual experience—has helped my organization communicate benefits and needs to the people who make financial decisions. This has cut the amount of time we spend [making ourselves] understood in meetings."

Because stories engage people, they further organizational goals. "We're trying to establish servant leadership in our organization. The use of story by our leaders certainly role-models this desired outcome," says Stephanie Moore of BP. She adds, "When I can get a connection to better than 80 percent of my audience, I'm delighted." Kevin Yates of Information Resources has seen similar results. "Story keeps learners engaged and therefore reinforces concepts, even over long distances. We have senior leaders asking us to continue the use of story—live and electronically. I cannot ask for better results," he says. Gordon Peterson adds, "We're still assessing the long-term advantage for the use of story. We've planned a three-month pilot using e-learning and we plan to incorporate storytelling as a part of [it]."

Stories also bring an organization's core values to life—a significant benefit for BMC Software. "Our core values highlight diversity—they're our corporate DNA. Story lets us make that DNA visible to all. This is how we're embedding them into our organization," says Armida Mendez Russell. Ashley Fields adds, "There's no need to measure [its impact]. It may feel like an act of courage to use story in an organization because there are no numbers. In your gut you know it's working; you see the look on people's faces. What more validation can you ask for?"

Ultimately, stories can improve staff retention and the bottom line. After introducing its story initiative in 2000, Rush-Copley Medical Center saw turnover of nursing staff drop, on average, from 25 percent to 15 percent. In the operating room, nursing staff turnover went from 35 percent to below 5 percent. Is this all due to storytelling? "No. But it's a big part of our success. Rush-Copley has been recognized nationally. We believe that story played a part in this success," reports Shawn Tyrrell.

WORDS OF WISDOM

How can your organization achieve the same types of results as these enterprises? Consider incorporating these lessons into your practices:

- Encourage people who can tell stories to share them. Slowly grow the skill in others to ensure authenticity in telling the story and congruence between the tellers and the messages they are presenting.

- Have a clear idea of what you are trying to accomplish by telling a story. Take time to think through the structure of the story, its lesson, and what you want to achieve.

- Consciously select those stories that will be used to explicitly communicate organizational practices. Continually listen to the stories that result from people exemplifying these practices.
- Be inclusive in the process of relaying tribal knowledge through story, whether orally or electronically. In this way everyone will obtain the wisdom to do the right things and make the right decisions.
- Find ways to make it comfortable for staff to share stories that relay the value of human capital initiatives, the Human Resources Department's work, and the organization's mission.

To enhance your organization's investment in people, heed Laura Folse's advice: "Just do it. You need only to don the ancient robes of a storyteller to be able to connect with the heads and hearts of people within your organization."

Special Thanks

A special thank you to Lisa Schumacher, vice president of sales and marketing at Wisdom Tools, for the contact to Information Resources, and to Irene Stemler, president of Creating Spirit, for the referral to Rush-Copley Medical Center.

CHAPTER THREE

We Need More *We* and Less *Me*

How Stories Build Teams and Teamwork

Susan M. Osborn, Ph.D., M.S.W.
Marcy Fisher

When Governor Arnold Schwarzenegger appointed Dennis Boyle as director of the four-thousand-staff California Department of Social Services (CDSS), it had been leaderless a year. Boyle faced budget cuts, staff loss, reduced services, increased workloads, fewer benefits, and declining motivation.

Kembrel Jones, Ed.D., is associate dean for the full-time MBA program and assistant professor in the Practice of Marketing at Emory University's Goizueta Business School. His problem in spring 2000? "The institution did not appear in the top thirty of any major business school ranking," Jones says.

The Web Strategy and Operations Team at AARP Services, Inc., was mandated to redesign the Web site the organization maintains for thirty-five million members. The predicament? Complete the project in one year amid organizational changes and phenomenal growth.

St. Andrew's United Church needed revitalization because of "a maturing population, declining membership, and tight financial times," says Alan Shugg, a congregation member.

The Ginger Group Collaborative, a network of consultants across Canada who study complex human systems, faced several dilemmas.

"Do we have the energy and vision to stay together? Is it time to get into business?" reports Kate McLaren, a founding member and organization development consultant.

What do these organizations have in common? They addressed their respective team challenges through stories.

STRENGTHENING RELATIONSHIPS

For successful teams, leaders need strong relationships with people and effective working relationships among them. This was true for Dennis Boyle at CDSS. Because of myriad issues, four months after his appointment, Boyle launched quarterly leadership forums for his hundred-member management team. The first forum covered expectations, priorities, goals, and relationships. "I told my story . . . about growing up in California thinking I'd be a rancher and about my Navy experiences. I talked about who I am, what's important to me, and how I came to be in my current position. Then I told a mission story and emphasized the importance of the department's mission— to help build stronger families—and by doing so, building a stronger community, a stronger California, and ultimately, a stronger America," says Boyle.

Was this effective? According to Michelle Schmitt, program manager, Office of Professional Management Development, "Whether you're a branch chief doing a disability evaluation program or running a personnel operation, there was something you remembered— that made you have rapport and identify with him as your leader. It was clear from subsequent feedback that people appreciated Dennis's stories and wanted more."

The second leadership forum addressed purposefully using stories to build a committed team. Boyle opened it by telling the story "Robbie Tries to Communicate." Then managers attended a two-hour workshop on using stories to establish rapport and trust, coach employees, deal with adversity, empower people, solve problems, and catalyze change.

Boyle says, "I told this story to demonstrate the importance of persistence in communication. Never assume people understand your message the first time—and never give up if someone doesn't understand you the first time you try to communicate."

Schmitt reflects on Boyle's stories: "Teaming is . . . why Dennis uses stories. He wants to create a personal bond with his management team

ROBBIE TRIES TO COMMUNICATE

Contributed by Dennis Boyle

My wife and I have an African gray parrot named Robbie. Like other gray parrots, Robbie has the IQ of a three-year-old, the personality of a two-year-old, an amazing vocabulary—about a hundred words—and grasps emotions such as anger, happiness, surprise, and sorrow.

One day when we were cleaning house, we put Robbie in his cage outdoors near the back fence. Not long after, we heard a strange sound. Thinking it might be a cat, we ran to the sliding glass door to see what was going on.

What we saw amazed us both. There was a blue jay perched on the fence near the cage. Robbie was doing his best to initiate a conversation. After mimicking the sounds of a variety of different birds, Robbie resorted to English. He started with "Hello." Then he progressed to, "Hello . . . want some?" Finally, in desperation, he said, "Hello. Want some . . . beer?"

and to leverage it to communicate skills, lessons, and operational information. He's creating a common language and goals for the team to use and relationships within the group."

Collaborative and caring relationships also matter at Goizueta Business School because servant leadership matters. "In the second semester we focus on the culture of teams and organizations. We emphasize the importance of stories and passing them on to keep myths and legends alive," says Kembrel Jones. To this end, in the classroom Jones tells "Welcome, Joy," a story on page 36 about student camaraderie.

What resulted from this story? According to Molly Epstein, Ph.D., assistant professor in the Practice of Management Communication, "Each class creates its own identity; the 2003 class was the first to embrace fundraising and charitable work. The story of how it raised money to send a classmate to Africa to see his baby daughter became a rallying cry for giving back to the community. It presented the largest class gift ever to Emory University—over $100,000. The 2004 class increased that amount by 60 percent. Because of this story, MBA students have taken ownership of fundraising and produced results

WELCOME, JOY

Contributed by Kembrel Jones, Ed.D.

Three years ago a man from a small village in Nigeria came to Goizueta to get an education and better his life. He left his wife, who was eight months' pregnant.

At the end of September he received word she'd given birth to a baby girl whose name was Joy. He sent a most amazing e-mail message to everyone in his class about how overwhelmed he was and how he wanted to share his happiness with them. He mentioned he didn't have pictures but as soon as his wife sent some he would share them. He added that, when he went home in the spring, his daughter would be a year old and he would take pictures and be happy to share those, as well.

He sent the message on a Thursday. Over the weekend his classmates put together $4,000 to send him home for the Christmas holidays. They said, 'We can't have you not seeing your daughter for a whole year!'"

topping anything that's ever happened at Emory." Jones adds, "We have dozens of stories that highlight how everyone steps up and takes care of people."

In technology projects, relationships are critical too. The Web Strategy and Operations Team at AARP knew this walking into the organization's Web site redesign initiative. "We don't make widgets; we make relationships with our members," says Liz Kelleher, manager of client services.

How did the project start? "We used classical tools to create a strategy, followed by feasibility and usability testing that told us we needed to redo the entire Web site—over a dozen major channels, more than a hundred sections, and over six hundred pages. We had to overhaul the technology underpinnings and underlying content management system, plus create fresh code," Kelleher explains. Challenges surfaced. She adds, "People said, 'Why this long? Why this level of effort?' Leadership said, 'You're going to need a much bigger team.'"

So Mike Lee, director of client services, and Kelleher worked with fellow managers and AARP leaders to reorganize the team and bring on new hires. Kelleher notes, "People got new positions, titles, and reporting relationships. That's a lot of change." Soon after, she engaged a consultant to help the team develop its story. She explains what happened: "'Living a Success Story' was the title for the four-hour retreat. We started with individual storytelling around, 'What am I doing here?' People created pictures to connect to their [team] role and what success would look like for them." This occurred, she said, because, "When you're endlessly innovating, you must be able to see your own story line. [For example], I try new things, some of which succeed, some of which fail, lots of which are risky. Through this I learn that failure is necessary to success."

The team's historical story was merged with these individual stories. Kelleher notes, "We told each other [about] the Web team's early days—how it started, who was there, changes it had gone through, and how the team got to where it is today. [From all this], we created 'Living a Success Story'—a visual time line. Years were marked out from 1996 to the future. . . . We [even] made cartoons [to depict] 'happy team,' 'happy clients,' and 'happy bosses.'"

How did the retreat aid the team? "This session allowed us to get beyond our fear of failure. Sharing our personal background gave us the ability to overcome conflict, frustration, and barriers with ease. Without storytelling we'd never have achieved this," says Kelleher. Lee concurs: "As a group we heard each other's stories and reflected on each person's journey. This enabled us to bridge the difficulties and stresses of a year-long project."

Sharing personal stories—by leaders—fosters stronger ties between the leader and the team and among team members. Telling and capturing team and member stories can alleviate fears and bridge the gaps brought on by conflict and stress, thus strengthening bonds between people who work together each day.

VISIONING THE FUTURE

Visioning stories build cohesive relationships and the possibility of a new future. To restore vitality, St. Andrew's United Church needed a new story and a core group to embrace it. "We held a church board retreat. We thought it important that the congregation have tangible goals and action plans to move forward. It [became] clear members needed to be consulted on possible futures to avoid feeling the board had already made a decision," says Alan Shugg.

He explains what happened a few months later: "A team of facilitators ran twelve focus groups; 120 people conversed about what brought them to St. Andrew's and what kept them here. Then we asked about their preferred future and what would be involved in getting there." Soon after, this feedback was presented to the congregation. The Reverend Dr. Geoffrey Wilfong-Pritchard, the church's minister, engaged people in dialogue. "I asked everyone for their vision of the future and how we could carry this to the next level," he says. From this input he drafted a future story. Then he tested it.

"I assembled the facilitators, told the story, and asked: 'Do you like what the congregation in the story did? How did they do it? What would stop us from doing the same thing?' Then I asked, 'What barriers did people face? How did they overcome them?' Finally I asked, 'How do you make it your story?' with the idea that, if facilitators made it their story, they'd be excited and committed to moving it forward," Wilfong-Pritchard explains. Afterwards, facilitators explored how to tell the story to all congregants and engage them in discussion.

Weeks later, at a Sunday service, Wilfong-Pritchard presented the "Talking to the Future" story. Over lunch, congregants responded to three follow-up questions. From this, five goals were identified. "The conversations we had about the story were remarkable. A tremendous amount of energy was released and mainstays of the congregation took up the charge," he says.

What has changed? Wilfong-Pritchard reports, "We're not focusing on problems or lack of resources. We're saying, 'Here's what it could look like. How do we get there?' If somebody can imagine it, it can happen. It takes away the sense of fear and failure." Shugg adds, "The main advantage of story is the ability of people to take ownership."

How to depict its vision while exploring its future is also an issue the Ginger Group Collaborative addressed. The network, begun in 2000 by three organizational consultants, had grown to fifteen members. "After four years we were at a turning point," says Kate McLaren. To decide whether to create a formal business venture, the group convened a weekend retreat. "We invited a consultant/painter to bring collaborative painting techniques to help us have conversations we were finding difficult," adds McLaren. According to Marilyn Hamilton, Ph.D., CGA, a Ginger Group affiliate and meshworker, "Because we get together twice a year, trying to maintain momentum and clarity about what we're doing is always a challenge. This was a way for us to go beyond words and create a picture of the story that was unfolding."

Hamilton describes what occurred at the retreat. "People shared [their] personal brilliance. This set up the opportunity to engage in image-making representations around our intentions." Then everyone began painting in response to the questions, How do I see my world? and Where am I at? "In silence, for five minutes, we painted the stories of our lives at that moment in symbols and images. Afterwards we talked about our paintings. It was individuals telling their stories," says McLaren.

"In a second round," she adds, "each of us began a painting that responded to, 'If Ginger were a garden of paradise, what would it look like?' We painted for one minute. Then we moved to the painting on the left and painted for another minute. Then we went on to the next paper. At the end, each painting was a collective vision, yet each was very different. We'd created all these group visual stories that led us to a vision for ourselves."

Deeper understanding emerged through conversation that followed about the metaphors embodied in the paintings. McLaren notes, "We might not have had commitment to keep building this network if there hadn't been [a] breakthrough in our sense of purpose and identity. Painting got us out of our cognitive, explanatory, analytical head-space. We didn't start with narrative but a story emerged from the process." Hamilton adds, "Building on that story, we've learned to work together. We broke through a lot of blocks. Now we know each other's strengths and capacities."

Both oral and visual story techniques can be used to flesh out an organization's vision. To be effective, these approaches must honor individual contributions and energize people as they work collaboratively to forge a new future.

ENABLING TRUST, SUPPORT, AND MUTUAL RESPECT

In any team, enabling trust, support, and mutual respect between members and with those outside the team is key to its success. This is true even in a student environment.

Goizueta Business School is named after Robert C. Goizueta, who fled Cuba with a wife, three children, and $40 in cash in 1961. As Kembrel Jones reports, "Goizueta's story boils down to the uniquely American idea that a young immigrant could come to this country with nothing but a good education and [experience] as a chemist, and thirty years later lead one of the world's best enterprises."

When Goizueta was CEO of the Coca-Cola Company, its stock market value went from $4.3 billion in 1981 to $180 billion in 1997. Goizueta donated $1.5 million to the university's business school in 1979 and became an Emory University trustee in 1980. In 1994 the business school was renamed in his honor; his values are ingrained in its practices. Jones notes, "We show a wonderful video of Mr. Goizueta's life at the opening convocation of the school. The story says a lot about who we are and what we're trying to do."

Jones also uses personal stories to underscore the values of trust, support, and mutual respect. During Welcome Weekend, he shares an incident from his own graduation called "The Cry Story" to bring them to life.

"I cry every time I tell that story," says Jones. "Everybody in the audience cries, too. I only tell it once a year. I want people to know the spirit of this place." He adds, "When prospective students hear this story they remember it. Many decide they want to come to Goizueta."

THE CRY STORY

Contributed by Kembrel Jones, Ed.D.

Each year Emory University gives an award for university service to one student from the current class, a class of approximately thirty-five hundred undergraduate and graduate students. When I graduated in 2000 I won that award. I was the first business school graduate to win it.

About thirty thousand people were assembled for the ceremony. They called me to the front and the president of the university talked about what I'd done for the school.

About halfway through his speech he got to the part where he recognized my family. They'd come from Alabama and were sitting in the front row. As he said, 'I would like to recognize Kembrel's family,' my parents stood up. At the same time thirty thousand people said, in one breath, "Ah. . . ." I looked up to see that my entire class had also stood up. They just automatically said, by their actions, "We're part of Kembrel's family."

While video and oral stories about trust, support, and mutual respect abound at Goizueta Business School, the Web Strategy and Operations Team at AARP used another approach. It created a tangible story representation—a hard-hat tour—to reassure people when its Web site redesign project neared completion, a year after its inception.

Mike Lee explains the rationale. "The 'hard-hat' metaphor is based on taking a mayor through a building before completion to assess progress and get an appreciation for the amount of work that goes on. We don't have that for the Web. People see the Web as one or two clicks of a screen full of content. Rarely do they see more than four or five pages of a site. So the [real size] is difficult to discern," says Lee. What audience did the team hope to reach? "We had new leadership arrive in this division [during the project] and a lot of diverse groups interested in the Web site," notes Lee.

Lee describes how the idea came to life: "We converted a meeting room into a construction office. We put up hazard tape and placed orange cones with blinking lights in the hallways." Adds Liz Kelleher, "We created a narrative storyboard with project artifacts, including designs for key pieces of the site, side-by-side comparison charts of how the site looked in the past and how it'd look in the future, and a time line that reminded people of the steps."

Finally, the open house hard-hat tour day arrived. "We gave people hard hats with the project logo on them," says Lee. Shares Kelleher, "Team members talked clients through the steps of what happened. [Even] the chief communication officer—the principal stakeholder and sponsor of the project—and the CEO of AARP Services attended."

And the results? "Leadership declared the Web site design a success. Clients got a sense of excitement and anticipation around its launch," Lee reports. "It reminded people that when the redesign goes out it doesn't mean we stop work. As in any new construction, there's a punch list of fixes afterward." Adds Kelleher, "Top leaders were reassured it's going to happen and it's going to be great. This was much more effective than reading a project plan."

Trust, support, and mutual respect are cornerstones for effective teams. These behaviors can be role-modeled through videotapes or the oral telling of stories. They can also be embodied in visual representations and team artifacts.

REFRAMING PERSPECTIVES

The expectations we bring to a team can differ from the ones we need for success. Kembrel Jones acts on this distinction at Goizueta Business School. "When [students attend] orientation, I let them know the way we operate, why we operate this way, and why they're expected to operate within this realm," says Jones.

How does he do this? "A picture comes on the wall showing a group of women from an African country, standing in line in the desert with vases on their heads. This little trickle of water is running out of a rock. They're waiting to gather water to carry back to their village. I say, 'Somebody tell me the story about this picture.' Then we develop a story about where these people live, their living conditions, what they're going through, and how little they have."

Jones adds, "Afterwards I show a graph depicting the five quintiles of wealth in America. The point is everyone will make the minimum amount in the highest quintile when they leave here."

Jones then merges these messages. "I say, 'Put the two stories together. The moral is: We're privileged human beings. We're not going to moan, whine, or complain while we're here. Every time you get ready [to do so], walk to the nearest water fountain and get a drink. You're not standing in line in the middle of the Sahara desert waiting to get water after walking ten miles from a village that has no power. If you come to us with a complaint, bring a well-thought-out solution and we'll listen to you.'"

In addition to expectations, sometimes the present situation needs reframing, as demonstrated by the Ginger Group Collaborative. Notes Marilyn Hamilton, "For one day we engaged with a client in Nova Scotia. This organization had been working to help [employees] re-story their careers and capacities. Because of funding cutbacks, they needed to shift."

How did the Ginger Group proceed? She explains, "We reframed their capacities by holding an inquiry circle. People went on a silent walk [outdoors] and brought back something that spoke to them about the organization's potential. When everyone returned we co-created a collage composed of objects from nature and shared our interpretations of [it]. In their interpretations, people received insight about where the new opportunities were." The collage permitted people to share their stories. She adds, "This [approach] allowed them to raise the issue that was causing a block and identify their strengths.

They left with an appreciation for how they had something many organizations could use."

Kate McLaren offers advice when using activities like this: "Think about what you're tapping into—the most raw version of somebody's story. It could be their hope for the future or fears about the present, or what they love about the present. A facilitator needs to be very open and pose questions that leave lots of space for people to reflect and debrief."

Because stories can tap into emotions and the essence of people, they have the ability to reframe expectations and shift reality. To be effective, these uses require ample time for dialogue and reflection.

BENEFITS OF USING STORIES TO BUILD TEAMS

Each organization embraced stories as a way to overcome challenges. How effective were stories at addressing them?

At the California Department of Social Services, Dennis Boyle had to unify a year-long leaderless management team and overcome budget cuts, staff and service reduction, increased workloads, and fewer benefits. "This was the opportunity," recalls Boyle. How did stories help? Michelle Schmitt says, "We brought the team together, managed through all the barriers, and began to create a legacy for CDSS." Boyle adds, "Within days of announcing my retirement, people stopped me and shared the impact my stories have had. My Robbie stories have penetrated the entire organization and communicated the motivational value of relationships and sharing." Story use has traveled outside the department, as well. Boyle says, "I know of at least two other directors who are using story to successfully communicate with their organizations."

Will this impact continue? "Many organizations tend to brush aside past leaders and their accomplishments. For the first time we have a legacy given to us by Boyle: stories in an easily understandable language. Dennis was right when he said, 'There's no better way to communicate an idea or lesson. People remember and repeat the information, sometimes for years,'" notes Schmitt.

Thanks to storytelling, Goizueta is now rated as a top business school. Kembrel Jones reports, "In the top three major business school rankings over the last five years, we're the only new school to crack the top twenty. In 2004, the school was ranked first in leadership by *Business*

Week. The marketing program was ranked tenth by the *Wall Street Journal.* Board [GMAT] scores have gone from 620 to 680; nobody else has increased sixty points in five years. A significant amount of this success is related to our use of story."

This success has filtered to students. "Because students are learning to use stories, they're placing in every single case competition they enter," notes Molly Epstein. The impact of stories goes further, she says: "Students represent themselves and communicate more effectively in job interviews." Jones adds, "Recruiters comment on how one of our students will be invited back for a second round of interviews for every nine students from other schools. They remember what our students say and want to hear more." There is more. "Since we instituted storytelling," notes Jones, "one hundred percent of our students get internships. Full-time job placement has gone from 60 to 70 percent. In 2005, it'll be in the nineties."

How did AARP do? "We needed to reorganize the team and launch a new Web site within a year. Through story use we were able to bring long-term and new employees together into a single team to build and launch the site faster and with less pressure from leadership," reports Liz Kelleher. Mike Lee adds, "The hard-hat tour helped leadership see, hear, and feel our progress. They told us that when there were delays or problems they knew what was going on and how hard we were working."

Success continued after the Web site went live. Lee notes, "Normally, when you have a new Web site design, there's a dip in traffic for days or weeks because people feel disoriented if the design changed a lot. Although ours changed greatly, we didn't experience any drop in traffic." He explains why: "We were able to update and debug the program quickly with high-quality work. The bridges built between disciplines, various knowledge bases, and [people's] backgrounds made this possible." The Web Strategy and Operations Team formed these bridges by embracing a story approach throughout the project.

St. Andrew's United Church is beginning to see results from its story. Its challenge was to revitalize amid an aging and declining membership and tight finances. Wilfong-Pritchard reports, "Out of the future story, we have a new commitment to get more engaged in small group ministry, an initiative started a few years ago that stalled for a lack of a coordinator. People now have a sense for what small groups can do. We have a coordinator and a commitment to get rolling." He adds, "We're initiating a new Saturday night worship service once a month for six months to see if we could offer it weekly. We've also reinstituted a worship committee that's been dormant for ten years. The story helped shape the mandate of the committee and the start of this new worship service."

Wilfong-Pritchard provides a more important outcome for St. Andrew's: "There's dawning awareness within the board that we need to do stewardship differently. For years we've told the congregation what the budget is and how near or far we are from reaching it. This hasn't been entirely satisfactory for the board, staff, or congregation. The board is coming around to the idea that people won't commit to a budget as much as they'll commit to a vision. Our story helped the board and congregation see what we could be. We now have a new stewardship program called 'Welcoming Tomorrow.'"

Did the Ginger Group Collaborative address its issues through story? "A shared purpose evolved from the Ginger Group retreat. The resulting story provided direction, clarified roles, increased mutual trust, and promoted camaraderie," Marilyn Hamilton reports. Kate McLaren concurs: "Out of this discussion emerged a deeper understanding of what this group can be—more profound than our original idea. Our purpose is emergent—a natural design, not a business plan. We're creating our story." She adds, "Since the retreat, we've continued to experiment with painting. Profound knowledge doesn't just come from our heads; it also comes from our hearts."

What about involvement? "Ten consultants attended the retreat. They've stayed involved," reports McLaren. And the collaborative is evolving. Hamilton notes, "Ginger West is growing. Three consultants [recently] joined. The western node now has affiliates from Whidbey Island, Washington; Abbottsford, Victoria; and from Whitehorse, Calgary, and Edmonton." She adds, "The affiliate node in Ottawa meets regularly to learn about complex systems and how this theory works with a real system, namely social services for people who are homeless or at risk of becoming homeless."

BRINGING STORY TO YOUR TEAMS

Using stories to build effective teams requires sparking creativity and collaboration. Here are some ideas on how to make this happen:

- To create connections and establish rapport, the stories you tell must be heartfelt, genuine, and honest.

- To achieve organizational impact, directly tie story lessons to expectations, priorities, and goals. Otherwise the story will be an empty anecdote that people soon forget.

- Avoid storytelling by edict. When introducing story to a team, explain why you want to use it, where you hope to go with it, and how the narrative will be used.

- Have team members share their own stories—dreams, aspirations, fears, and failures. Be aware that some may be moved by this way of working and others may not. Help them safely grow their storytelling skills.

- Use stories about the team's history to provide context for where the team has been relative to where it is today and where it will be in the future.

- Be inclusive when creating a story about the team's future. Everyone has something of value to add.

- Search for themes and patterns across stories as a way of creating a team vision and shared meaning.

- Consider varied methods for evoking and embodying stories— from sharing orally to painting to experiential representation and symbolic images.

- Allow ample time for reflecting on and debriefing stories, especially if they are being used to shift perspective. Create powerful, provocative questions that tap people's creativity and emotional energy and move them to deeper meaning.

Using stories can transform a group of people into a team. A team focused on the collective whole. One that can address any challenge given to it.

Special Thanks

Thank you to Thom Haller of Info Design for the connection to Liz Kelleher at AARP; to Glory Ressler of Avalon Consulting & Associates for the link to Linda Naiman of Linda Naiman and Associates, who suggested Marilyn Hamilton and Kate McLaren of the Ginger Group Collaborative; and to Alicia Korten of Renual, who suggested contacting Geoffrey Wilfong-Pritchard at St. Andrew's United Church.

CHAPTER FOUR

You Get What You Give
Leadership in Action Through Stories

Lori L. Silverman

"How can leaders maintain trust?" asks Jim Concelman, manager of leadership development for Development Dimensions International, Inc. (DDI). "Storytelling is a means for doing so." According to Ralph Schwartz, director of leadership and staff development for Wisconsin Department of Natural Resources (DNR), "It also communicates credibility effectively." Bob Merchant, vice president of manufacturing & planning for Coors Brewing Company, a business unit of Molson Coors Brewing Company, asks, "How do you humanize yourself as a leader? By not talking about the issue at hand. It's easy to come across as dictatorial. Use a story. People will actively engage and remember it." Ray Wierzbicki, senior vice president of enterprise customer service in the Enterprise Solutions Group at Verizon, says, "When people remember a story, they remember its intent."

"Leaders must shift their leadership style to use story. They need to move from *control* to *caring*," explains Kimberly Cuny, director of The University Speaking Center at the University of North Carolina at Greensboro (UNCG). By equipping leaders with skills in storytelling and story use and altering their behavior, these five organizations find their leaders can mentor staff more effectively, pass on leadership lessons, communicate strategic information, shift behaviors, and build employee engagement.

MENTORING STAFF

Developing leaders is critical in today's work environment. Stories can play a powerful role in mentoring people as they move into leadership roles.

"In 2001, we started identifying top talent throughout Molson Coors—people with high potential. We now form two Mentoring Circles® a year—fifteen peers per group across the organization meet two hours every other week," notes Vonda Mills, vice president of global people development. Flo Mostaccero, vice president of technical services and business process development, Coors Brewing Company, was a participant and is now a mentor. "In the group, we talk through topics people want to discuss—integrity, communications, and leadership. As mentor, I start each session with a personal story related to the day's topic that participants can glean something from. Afterwards, anyone can ask for mentoring by saying, 'Here's my situation.' Everyone then tells a story around it," Mostaccero explains.

"Through stories people learn from life experiences versus an expert telling them what to do. It leverages experiences in a safe environment where people can network and build relationships," says Mills. According to Mostaccero, "The group imparts knowledge, not me. They know the organization's culture. Frequently I walk away with as much as participants, allowing me to better deal with difficult situations and to communicate effectively in a relationship-based company."

Similar to Molson Coors, Verizon also has formal mentoring groups. Lee Brathwaite, vice president, Verizon Real Estate, has worked with several. "I share stories about my encounters with people. For example, I had a ninety-minute train ride into New York City with rude people everywhere," he says. "After I got off the train, I walked to Starbucks and held the door open for a woman. Ten people rushed in ahead of her. No one said, 'Thanks.' When I left, I said to her, 'Have a good day' and walked to work. When I got to the elevator, she was there, too. We talked about the Starbucks experience and introduced ourselves. I discovered she's the secretary of a vice president I'm meeting with later that morning. I think, 'Whew. What if I'd been upset and rude to her? What would she have said about me to her boss? My reputation would've been sullied.' I tell people, 'You never know who you're interacting with.'

"Participants learn the power of storytelling by sharing their experiences, too," he continues. "Early on they talk about very personal, negative work experiences where they need help—how to maneuver through the organization or handle a bad time with a supervisor. Over time, these stories switch to successes—getting a promotion or a lateral job move."

In his organization within Verizon, Ray Wierzbicki mentors more than a hundred associates, first-level supervisors, and vice presidents one-on-one each year. "People want to know what got me to the next level in my career. I talk about the journey and tie my experiences to their challenges. Instead of saying, 'Have you tried finance or IT?' I have them look inside themselves," he says. He also solicits stories. "I ask, 'What makes you skip to work?' If you love what you do, you'll perform well and enjoy doing it. I also coach them on how to share personal stories about their church, community, or condo association involvement so their bosses can see the whole person." How does this benefit him as a leader? "I meet very talented people and learn about my own organization through people's stories."

Wierzbicki's "skip to work" technique has a toehold elsewhere. "At my town hall meetings I've established a 'caught skipping' award. Throughout the month, my team and I look for examples of people 'skipping' in their jobs. At the meeting I recognize these individuals, provide a token of appreciation, and ask them to share their story. This is always a highlight," says Karin Hurt, director, Verizon Partner Solutions.

Forty-six undergraduate student employees at The University Speaking Center at UNCG also use stories to mentor and acknowledge skills. "Our student employees are campus leaders. They offer one-on-one tutoring on oral communication skills to their peers and teach communication and speaking skills," reports Kimberly Cuny. "All employees complete a three-credit training class before working at the center. During the course, students shadow current staff. They use stories to teach each other back in the classroom. Depending on what time of day students shadow, they might not see much. By sharing experiences they learn what to do or not do if they're in similar situations."

How does this training get used in mentoring? According to April Reece, manager, "If I see a client using self-deprecating behavior, I take time to tell a story about how I've messed up. In situations where clients have storytelling class assignments, I'll help them draw out a story because they often don't know where to start."

Cuny also mentors employees through stories. Reece explains, "I had a problem relating to one coworker—I'm rather reserved and found her offensive. Kim shared a similar situation she'd encountered. It helped me understand what was happening and how to fix it." Cuny notes, "I have to believe in April to tell her a story and listen differently. I have to take in everything she says before I form a response. The story I told April won't help everyone; it's the depth of the relationship that makes a difference in how stories are selected and received."

Using carefully selected stories in mentoring allows leaders to learn from others' life experiences. When coached to share their own situations as stories, leaders learn the power of story firsthand.

PASSING ON LEADERSHIP AND LIFE LESSONS

Every leader has lessons to share with others about leadership and life. How can these be brought forward?

Ralph Schwartz explains, "In 2000, DNR created a yearlong Leadership Academy to develop leaders from high-potential employees. The academy's development team selected storytelling as the most effective way to deliver a common message and understanding to any audience. In the communication module, storytelling is introduced as a presentation technique [and] participants share a personal story. They also have twenty opportunities throughout the year to present to the group, using story, analogy, and metaphor. [Additionally], they use stories when developing a 'stump' presentation on, 'What does leadership mean to me.'

"One facet of the Academy is an individual project," Schwartz adds. The project, led by Bruce Neeb, government outreach supervisor, West Central Region, involved capturing stories. Neeb says, "In my area we were losing many senior management and staff to retirement. So I decided to undertake an oral history project that featured John DeLaMater—my mentor and a supervisor for thirty-two years before retirement. First, I distilled ten leadership competencies from [several organizational documents]. Then I asked people who knew John to identify times when he exemplified the competencies. Together we

CHANGING JOBS

Contributed by John DeLaMater

I was very anxious to move up in the organization. But I got frustrated because I competed for a couple of exams I didn't get. As you know, we are all our own harshest critics. So I thought if I couldn't get promoted in forestry, I'd look for another way to get promoted. I competed for an area land agency job and I got it. It was in Green Bay [Wisconsin]. I went over to Green Bay and as I started to undertake the duties of being an area real estate agent, I realized there was something missing in my work life. I started to realize that I'd taken that promotion for all the wrong reasons. And I was not happy. As you know, you need happiness in your job life or it can be pretty miserable.

I called the area supervisor, Dave Jacobson, from a motel room. I was in the process of looking for a place to rent and bringing my family over from Grantsburg. I said, "Have you filled my old job yet?" He said, "No." I said, "Geez, I would like it back." There was silence. Then I heard, "Well, we got rid of you. We don't want you back." And I thought, "Oh, no." So I said, "Well . . ." And he said, "Is this an official request?" I said, "Yes it is." So he said, "Well, I'll get back to you as soon as I can."

Then I called my wife who had everything we owned packed in boxes sitting there ready to be moved two days from the day I made this call. I said, "I may not have a job with the State of Wisconsin but I just can't live here and do this job. I'll be unhappy and consequently we'll be unhappy." I still remember her crying. It was both a happy and a sad time. But we got through that.

I learned from then on that I had to focus my energies on [forestry] promotions—I just wanted to move upwards. You shouldn't go after something just for the money. Never take a job for the wrong reasons.

identified thirteen stories that I captured [from him] using a broadcast-quality CD recorder so staff could listen to them while traveling in state-owned vehicles." One of DeLaMater's stories is on page 51.

"Initially, I produced twelve cassette and twelve CD copies that were distributed to each Division of Forestry bureau director, regional leader, and area leader, and to the Forestry Training Center. I included a flyer announcing the recording's availability, a checkout log, and a memo explaining the project [that] asked recipients to listen to the recording and share it with others," Neeb recalls.

While leadership and life lessons can be relayed after leaders depart an organization, leaders can also transmit lessons through stories on a daily basis. "There are more than 150 people in my [part of the] organization. How do I make communication exciting and engaging for them?" asks Sheryl Riddle, senior vice president of consulting services for DDI, a midsize human resources consulting firm. "Since people are less likely to leave if they're engaged with a leader, I tell personal stories on voicemail and in person. I've worked on some signature stories—stories about great development successes, challenges I've faced with people who've worked with me, and from my personal life." "Honest Is as Honest Does" is one of them.

"I use this story with senior teams to focus on integrity and honesty. I also solicit feedback, recognition, and lessons-learned stories to share in leadership meetings," Riddle says. "To use stories, you need a culture without a lot of fear—one that's not excessively hierarchical, where everyone has an equal voice."

Training on story structure and use helps leaders to present information in the form of story and to identify the best story prompts to use when soliciting them from others. To integrate stories effectively into ongoing communications requires leaders who are willing to create a culture to support this behavior and who take time to pass on important lessons.

COMMUNICATING STRATEGIC INFORMATION

Because we live in an uncertain world, communicating organizational strategy, vision, and values and aligning people around them is a necessity. How are leaders achieving these outcomes through stories?

"We put top talent at mid- and frontline levels through a year-long leadership development program. [Part of what] they focus on is bring-

HONEST IS AS HONEST DOES

Contributed by Sheryl Riddle

I was just a teenager. It was your typical Saturday night and my girlfriend and I were going to spend the evening babysitting together. The couple that entrusted their children to us said just one thing before they left, "Do not go out on the terrace." You see, we were in a big apartment building on the twenty-third floor.

As soon as the kids fell asleep, we grabbed some sodas, pretzels, and of course went out onto the terrace. We started throwing pretzels off the terrace for fun and our pretzels hit some other folks down a few flights on another terrace. Oops. We turned and fled back into the apartment. My girlfriend easily stepped through the open glass terrace door. And me? Well I went through the closed part of the glass door. Shattered glass was suddenly at my feet. And I had a very significant wound in my leg. I bent down, cupped the wound to protect the white carpet, hopped into the bathroom, got a big towel and my friend called her parents because mine were not home. I was transported by car to an emergency room in Hackensack, New Jersey.

Over a hundred stitches later, back at home, my parents asked, "How did this happen?" I said, "Gosh, well, gee, golly, I was in the living room and I just tripped and fell through the glass door." "Hmmmm, interesting," said my parents. Then with that little look that only parents get they said, "Why was the broken glass on the inside?"

And so I learned as a child, "Deception is something that is more easily seen through than a terrace glass door."

ing the [organization's] vision, strategy, and values to life," notes Vonda Mills. According to Cathy Krause, program manager of global people development, "Participants are asked to prepare a story to reinforce these concepts using a five-step approach that [involves] identifying the message, selecting and developing a story that reinforces it, determining when and where to tell it, and soliciting feedback on the message through practice." Mills points out, "The power is in the practice. You also must formalize the storytelling process." Krause adds, "Be deliberate about giving employees structure to tell their stories—they need help. They want to send a clear, specific, and inspirational message."

Pam Gardner, manager of sales productivity, was deliberate in bringing storytelling into DDI and giving leaders tools for its use. "I brought story into the organization because of a problem: How can we differentiate ourselves in the marketplace on big opportunities and from the competition through our relationships with customers? Two things make a sale: building trust and mitigating risk for potential clients. Technical differentiators are minute in our industry," she points out, adding, "Because I believe you must train on story in the context of a business application, it touched the most people to bring story in through client-facing jobs. We brought in a consultant to train the operating committee on story and then took it to a weeklong event with about three hundred leaders from sales, consulting, and our solutions group."

According to Bob Rogers, DDI president, "When our associates make presentations, I always ask, 'What story best makes your point; and why do you want to make that point?' I encourage delivery and salespeople to use stories because it breaks down barriers to trust and quickly establishes rapport." Gardner adds, "All new people with client-facing jobs now get training on where and how to use stories through a course on competitive selling and weeklong training in three major solution areas. We've also added a yearly *Hip Pocket Stories* booklet that includes success and implementation stories, cross-referenced by industry and solution."

Using stories strategically does not stop there. "A few years ago we discovered our three strategic priorities weren't clear to everyone," says Rogers. DDI has a thousand people between its headquarters and more than seventy-five offices in twenty-six countries worldwide. To address this, he continues, "I began sharing stories. Every other Friday afternoon through voicemail, I tell two short good-news stories per priority: increasing client impact, increasing market advantage, and leadership and selection dominance. There's at least one international story every time. Having me say or read them makes an impact. We also post these stories on a Web site."

How does he obtain stories? "Marketing canvases our field personnel. I get twenty or more to choose from [every two weeks]," he notes. How have these stories touched Rogers and the organization?

"I hear about client impact—which I use elsewhere—and about tremendous consulting work. Plus, I get trends and patterns from the data. For example, I saw that one of our services was being very successful and that we were doing well against a competitor in this area. So, I asked people, 'Can we do more against this competitor?' The new stories show we're having success."

Like DDI, Verizon offers training to help leaders communicate strategic information through stories. "We developed an in-house workshop, 'Leaders Growing Leaders,' for the Customer Service Executive Team to learn about a structured approach to communicating key messages around our seven strategic values," says Karin Hurt. "First, each participant picked a value and found a story about it from their personal life. Then they practiced their stories in small groups, provided feedback to one another, and worked to identify the main ideas of the stories. The executives then took these stories back and used them strategically in their communication with employees across the organization. We also provided a Web site where teams throughout customer service shared success stories around our strategies and values. The teams were rewarded with tokens of appreciation and the strongest stories were communicated across the organization."

Scott Watson, a watershed supervisor at West Central Region, DNR, is also interested in using stories to communicate values. "[Through the Leadership Academy] I wanted to demonstrate the value of public waters. I interviewed more than thirty people—from students to artists, water-dependent business owners, people with homes and seasonal cabins on water, recreational users and [others]—to discover personal stories that embody how they connect to and value public waters. More than a hundred stories were gathered on conflicts over water use, forestry connections, pressures that exist on water resources, and personal and emotional connections to water, specific rivers, and ownership," he explains. "Then I shared these stories with others. [For example], I used one to explain to a person why a regulation, which restricts the individual from doing something, is important to protect a value. It helped the individual relate to that value in a personal way."

Formalizing the storytelling process, having leaders practice telling stories and giving them story tools, aids them in applying stories when communicating strategic information. Finding innovative ways to share stories that highlight strategy and values spurs aligned behaviors and stories in return. Strategic issues can provide impetus for bringing the approach into an organization.

SHIFTING BEHAVIORS

Whether they face an organizational change or problem situation, people often need to shift their behavior. Stories can facilitate these conversations.

"Two years ago in Verizon's Potomac Region, which provides telephone service to customers in Maryland, Virginia, West Virginia, and Washington D.C., positive customer experiences weren't being shared. The skills needed to identify and re-communicate them were rare to nonexistent. Negative customer stories got immediate broadcast internally. So we had to figure out how to spin negatives into positives to reinforce the right behaviors," outlines Dennis Metzger, manager, Workforce Development and Performance Management, Network Services Group.

"[To change this], an initiative called *Service Culture* was created to impact behaviors of five hundred managers and fifty thousand employees that provide daily service. The Service Culture core team set up three major development activities. First, the management team was trained on how to recognize extraordinary customer service experiences. Second, the team attended a session on appreciative inquiry to learn how to put a positive spin on extraordinary experiences. Third, a storytelling helpful hints document was developed to assist them in capturing, recording and re-telling positive stories. Today, managers look for positive experiences—what went right."

A cultural issue also stimulated the use of story at UNCG's University Speaking Center. "We had a problem with staff members bending over to get their mail and showing their underwear while doing so," reports Kimberly Cuny. How did she address the situation? "I shared a story from pop culture with the whole staff via e-mail one night," she says. "Don't Be a Bob" was a success.

"The problem immediately went away," Cuny notes. "We work in an environment of care. Care means you take the time to tell stories— it's less *me*-oriented. It's not one-upping each other." According to April Reece, "Because of our culture, people realize these stories are meant to help, not harm you. Through stories we learn about each other as people [and] can be honest, be ourselves, and share with each other."

Finding just the right stories to shift staff behavior within a culture of caring can bring results. Sometimes this means replacing negative stories with positive ones; sometimes it means leaders' reflecting on what they have witnessed or their own experiences.

DON'T BE A BOB
Contributed by Kimberly Cuny

When I lived in New Jersey there was a Sharpie marker television commercial running in the New York City market. In the commercial, a reporter roamed the streets of the city asking folks about how they use their Sharpie markers. The last person interviewed is a man bent down, hard at work over a hole in the sidewalk. The viewers first see this man from behind where the top of the band on his briefs reads "Bob" (presumably in Sharpie). Next, the viewers see the reporter put his microphone in the man's face as he asks, "So Bob, what do you use your Sharpie marker for?" The man replies, "Bob, who's Bob?"

While this is funny to the viewer (and I laughed hard each time I saw it), from the man's perspective this is a sensitive situation. I bring this to the attention of all center employees because we had our share of Bobs when I started working at the center. Since our mailboxes are on the floor, a few folks have been seen showing their briefs, boxers, thongs, and bikinis to the rest of us when bending over to reach the boxes. After asking a few folks how best to deal with this issue, I decided to move forward with the advice I got on Friday.

I suggest that we all adopt the following behavioral modification:

When retrieving mail from boxes (or putting mail into boxes), let's all try to remember to either sit on the floor or kneel.

If we all adopt this change, we should have no more Bob-like situations.

This message is not intended to cause anyone hurt. I am simply interested in what is best for all of us. As such, I want our public space to maintain a professional atmosphere and to save all of us from future Bob-like embarrassment.

Please don't be a Bob!

BUILDING EMPLOYEE ENGAGEMENT

Getting employees to engage is a pervasive issue. How can leaders use stories and storytelling to address it?

"At DDI we advocate the technique of 'sharing thoughts, feelings, and rationale.' When this technique is used, story becomes embedded in it. A leader who uses storytelling to disclose something [personal] and transmits the communication sincerely gains trust, commitment, and empathy from others. These individuals know their leader has their best interest in mind," explains Jim Concelman.

This is exemplified at Molson Coors. Bob Merchant describes it in these terms:

> We've taken top leaders in my organization through training on building employee engagement with stories. They're taught how to tell, use, and listen for stories, glean things from stories, and repeat them in team meetings. I encourage them to practice telling stories—you have one chance when you're in front of people to get your message across. When Pete Coors, co-chairman of the board, tells stories, his manner isn't prescriptive. It's informative. You reach your own conclusion and get to buy in; you partly own the idea. When others in the organization re-use these stories, the organization becomes more communicative. A full-time communications manager also captures stories in print for our monthly *Golden Brewery Business (GBB) YOU* newsletter. We weave stories into topics that have business significance.

Lee Brathwaite practices these principles with his real estate staff at Verizon: "I do town hall visits with local management teams and work groups in Washington, [Texas], and [Pennsylvania] to champion them and the value they add. These are hard-core, vociferous, seasoned managers and doubting-Thomases. I ask, 'What's on your mind?' There's no force-feeding. No PowerPoint. No selling them on a rainbow."

"They share stories—about the challenges in getting things done and issues with operating budgets and system requirements. I listen and take notes. Through their stories, I learn how they interpret what they were told and assess whether we did a good job of communicating initiatives," Brathwaite says. "I share stories to show I understand their issues and about groups that found a way to resolve similar situations to get them to help themselves. Over time, people with experiences contrary to the naysayers are starting to speak up," he adds.

When leaders share their thoughts and feelings, and the rationale for them, stories come naturally. The key to engaging employees is communicating these stories in a way that allows them to draw their own conclusions. Hearing employees speak their thoughts and feelings through stories—and acknowledging them—shows a leader has their best interest in mind.

HERE ARE THE RESULTS

UNCG's University Speaking Center, Verizon, and DDI concur. Kimberly Cuny reports, "Story is a natural part of the way we work." Karin Hurt adds, "Today, stories and storytelling are embedded in the way we do things every day." Pam Gardner says, "Stories are now a standard way to talk about things in our business."

Cuny adds, "Through stories, we created the environment we set out to create—a center run by student leaders. They make their own decisions and learn from trying new things." April Reece says, "We have feedback forms for every consultation and workshop we do. The feedback shows our stories help."

According to Ralph Schwartz, "DNR's Leadership Academy participants report using their 'stump' story to open all of their talks with stakeholders and to demonstrate benefits of environmental work." Bruce Neeb continues, "Two years after the pilot project, John DeLaMater's recordings are still being used by the Forestry Bureau." Scott Watson adds, "The public waters project has clearly demonstrated that using people's stories is an effective way to communicate the value of public resources and can be used to enhance, supplement, or even replace the voice of a regulatory person."

Like DNR, Verizon is getting positive results from training and by capturing stories. "Training feedback at various sessions tells us storytelling is well-received," Hurt notes. "Leaders at the values workshop found many opportunities to apply their learnings. An interesting side benefit was the team-building effect as people disclosed more of themselves through their stories." Dennis Metzger says, "In the Service Culture sessions, a light bulb went off for people. Good service means good results; everyone is happy. The most effective enabler is repeat positive customer experiences. Positive stories are where we want to be."

"You can feel the results of town hall meetings," Lee Brathwaite points out. "Employees and management have a better handle on our direction. There's increased energy and pride, people feel engaged in issues versus resisting them, and they now ask questions." According to Ray Wierzbicki, "Stories enable me to be creative in communicating my message and capture more information holistically about where the business is going. Look at all our metrics—they're going in the right direction."

Molson Coors Brewing Company sees results in its metrics, too. Bob Merchant says, "Story has increased communication effectiveness. All indicators on our four buckets of measures are going in the right direction. Costs have significantly decreased—about $15 to $20 million a year in terms of costs of goods. There's decreased absenteeism and improved employee engagement scores. Employees feel they're part of the business and are on equal footing with management." Flo Mostaccero adds, "The business side profited because it showed leaders how to use storytelling to balance relationships with getting results. Personally, stories allow me to be more effective at driving change." Vonda Mills says, "Storytelling has improved the retention of top talent because they learn from and are supported by others through stories."

At DDI, "Overall, storytelling has made people more effective in dealing with clients," Bob Rogers points out. "Today everyone knows our top three strategic priorities. Each leader gets twenty-four hours of training a year; stories are integrated into it. We also encourage stories in normal interactions with clients." Pam Gardner reports, "Before, technology was number one. Today, providing value to clients is number one. We're closing more big deals and effectively incorporating stories into proposals."

MOVING FORWARD

Leveraging stories through leaders has significant benefits. Here is how your organization can apply what these five organizations have learned:

- Create a culture that supports the use of stories—one where everyone has an equal voice, people care about each other, and the group operates without a lot of control, fear, and hierarchy.
- When bringing the story approach into an organization, attach it to key business issues.
- Formalize the storytelling process and teach it to leaders. Provide a variety of tools to aid in its implementation.

- Develop formal programs for story sharing among leaders.

- Have leaders take the time to share personal and organizational stories in a nonprescriptive manner that relates to the topic at hand and to fully listen and acknowledge people's stories without judging them.

- Use a structured approach to capture stories from leaders. Put thought into the story prompts. Find multiple vehicles for relaying them to other leaders and employees.

- Give leaders the opportunity to practice the stories they plan to tell and to obtain feedback on them.

When organizations give their leaders the training, time, and tools to affect story use in the organization, both they and the leaders benefit. When leaders use this approach with their employees, the results are evident. You get what you give.

Special Thanks

Several individuals helped identify organizations for this chapter. Many thanks to Julie Manhard and Ellie Gilfoyle of The Mentoring Company for Molson Coors Brewing Company, to Annette Simmons of Group Process Consulting (author of *The Story Factor*) for DDI, and to Susan Stites of Management Allegories for the Wisconsin Department of Natural Resource—and her support.

Mentoring Circles® is registered in the U.S. Patent and Trademark Office by The Mentoring Company.

CHAPTER FIVE

Are We On Track?

How Stories Impact Project Management

Denise Lee

P roject management is evolving. "Today there's more science, discipline, and literature on the best ways to run a program," explains Martin Davis, a program manager at the National Aeronautics and Space Administration (NASA) Goddard Space Flight Center. According to W. Scott Cameron, global process owner-project management for corporate engineering at Procter & Gamble Company, "The tools have changed. Being in touch with team [members] is far more robust. As soon as you push the button on the computer you get a response."

With these shifts, stories are entering project work. Robert S. Frey, senior vice president of knowledge management and proposal development, RS Information Systems, Inc. (RSIS), uses project success stories to grow the business. Why use them? "Stories [help] engineers who like numbers, data, and facts to engage, pay attention, absorb information, and learn. They can relate to them. When they see numbers they add them up and challenge the speaker. If they hear a real-life story, it's hard to argue unless you argue with the interpretation of the lesson learned," explains Anastasia Walsh, two-way communication program manager at Lockheed Martin Space Systems Company. Major Dan

Ward, a project manager in the Information Directorate at the U.S. Air Force Research Laboratory, notes, "Project management comes down to the ability to tell a story." In addition, Cameron adds, "Stories make our work thought provoking. [They] make project management real."

PREPARING FOR PROJECTS

Are stories useful in project management training? At Procter & Gamble, W. Scott Cameron's organization partnered with the Global Engineering Learning Solutions Department to have senior project managers train junior project managers. "Expert practitioners share knowledge about their experiences in stories to make learning more pertinent. It's a conscious strategy," reports Cameron. According to Andrew R. Poole, manager of global engineering learning solutions, "We developed a new five-day training class. [Before they attend], we expect project managers to have [baseline] knowledge or get it via Web-based training. For example, [they know that] when creating a cost estimate you shouldn't overestimate. [In] the classroom, the storyteller says, 'Let me tell you a story about a situation I was in where a high cost estimate caused high spending.' The stories make it real."

Stories are also generated in training, Poole explains. "We'll ask learners, 'How many of you have experience with underestimates causing overspending? OK, Tom, I see you have. Would you be willing to share your experience?' Tom says, 'Yes. This is what happened to me.' You get stories being told from learners."

In addition to stories being used to train project managers, project management success stories can play a role in gaining approval of project proposals. At RSIS, "Twice a year, the organization convenes three-day off-site meetings with seventy-five project managers from across the country. [They're] tasked to present their particular program," relays Robert Frey. Where real storytelling takes place, he says, "Is in informal evening discussions. There's a wonderful exchange of success stories." How does he capture them? "I take notes. When I need more information, I go back and interview the person. After interviewing hundreds of people I've found that most don't know what they know. They know a whole lot, but they don't know how to package what they know and give it back."

"A Powerful Proposal Story," on page 64, is a story example that RSIS uses internally. It models the format used for all prospective client proposal stories.

A POWERFUL PROPOSAL STORY

Contributed by Robert Frey

During the course of many face-to-face meetings both this year and last, we listened carefully to the strengths, constraints, and future direction of your organization's operational environment. We recognize that tomorrow's enterprise success factors have changed from technology-centric ones to those premised upon "business plus planning," "business plus security," "business plus enterprise architecture," and "business plus capital planning."

This is precisely where Mr. Bill Williams, our team's fully accountable, on-the-ground program manager, will be of significant benefit to your organization.

Three years ago, Mr. Williams spearheaded a team of 135 technical and business-savvy professionals who faced the challenge of optimizing the return on investment (ROI) of one critical defense agency's information technology (IT) portfolio. And that was only one of [many] challenges. Another was that this agency's IT assets were geographically dispersed throughout four states in the southeastern United States.

With tremendous enthusiasm and endurance over the course of two years, Mr. Williams and his management team worked hand in hand with their government counterparts to increase ROI by 8 percent and drive total cost of ownership (TCO) down by 11 percent. In fact, Mr. Williams and his team worked 65 percent of all weekends and holidays during that time to ensure that all performance requirements were fully met.

Was our customer pleased? The 99.9 percent award fees are solid evidence that they were. Because Mr. Williams's role on that highly successful contract is now complete, he will bring to bear his passion, programmatic knowledge, and people leadership skills to support your important program requirements and your Agency's mission.

By the way, Mr. Williams and his core management team received a Group Achievement Award for their outstanding support of our defense customer. But Mr. Williams was not

there the day the award was made. He was on site in
Charleston, South Carolina, making sure that an extensive
IT asset inventory process was being conducted in accor-
dance with FAR 45 and with new DoD property management guidelines.

Why that level of programmatic oversight? Because property management takes on added criticality in an operational
environment with aging, hard-to-replace, and extremely
expensive equipment located across thousands of square miles.
You can look forward with confidence to this level of above-
and-beyond customer care. Expect it. We will deliver it.

Frey coaches on story use in proposal presentations. "[I] translate
the narrative proposal into a graphic slide presentation and then
coach [project managers] to get in front of federal government evaluation boards," he explains. "It's about building trust and emotional
connections—making project managers believable and real by having them tell stories about their experiences."

Frey assisted Rick Stalnaker, director of NASA programs for RSIS,
on developing his story. Stalnaker says, "Bob coached me on my résumé
for a proposal. [It] turned into a collection of stories rather than dates
and institutions. It painted me as a successful leader—a person who's
accomplished a lot—much more than what you'd expect on a résumé."
He adds, "We won [the project]. Storytelling lent credibility."

Stories can prepare project managers to lead projects effectively.
Specific stories about project experiences can be evoked from trainees
and shared by experienced project managers in training. In project
proposals, well-thought-out success stories are beneficial on an individual and organizational level.

INITIATING A PROJECT

Relationships are vital to project initiation activities. W. Scott Cameron
of Procter & Gamble knows this well: "When I took a new assignment, I scheduled one-hour one-on-one join-up meetings with lead

personnel on the team and their hierarchy. During one meeting, the person informed me how pleasantly surprised she was that I'd scheduled [it] as few individuals took the time anymore. I was shocked. I was taught that establishing a one-on-one relationship with team members is critical to project success."

Following this encounter, Cameron spoke with a mentor. He says, "My mentor indicated his predecessor had conducted few join-up meetings. Again, I was shocked. I realized a negative trend was emerging in our fast-paced, schedule-driven, 500-e-mail-per-day, cell-phone-ringing, 24/7-communication, multi-tasking work lives: *no face time!*" He crafted a story about his experience and shared it with project managers across Procter & Gamble. Andrew R. Poole read it. He notes, "He could have [written], 'Every time you start a new job you must have join-up meetings for three reasons: blah, blah, blah.' He didn't start out that way; he told a story. You're engaged. You say, 'Where's he going with this?' Then, boom! You're hooked. You have the realization just like he did." Cameron believes his story has increased company-wide awareness about the importance of join-up meetings.

Imagine what happens to relationships if you are asked to restart a project because your predecessor performed poorly. Martin Davis from NASA shares this story widely to communicate his learning. "Three 'project managers' were to solve a problem. One guy was managing the project. Another guy, from the parent contractor organization, was helping him. I was from the customer, the funding agency. So I felt I was in control. They weren't doing a great job of working together [when I took over]. [One day] I saw elephant rides being given at a nearby strip mall. It hit me. The three of us need to get on that elephant [together]," Davis says, so he dragged his two fellow managers down to the mall. Did it work? "Sure it worked. There's a picture to prove it. Afterwards, we worked more closely and moved beyond our differences."

In project initiation, a project vision is as important as relationship development. For Major Dan Ward, "Leadership is the ability to tell a story . . . to craft a vision that makes sense to people, that gets them on board." However, he notes, "We're talking about people who're technically skilled. They want leaders to say, 'Hey, let me talk about where we're going with this [project].'"

Ward's colleague, Captain Gabe Mounce, lead engineer in the Information Directorate, U.S. Air Force Research Laboratory, elaborates: "When you're trying to lead a group of people, especially technical folks, it's sometimes hard to get them to understand exactly what you're trying to get at, where you're trying to go. That's where a leader has to [use] a story. That way people better understand what you're trying to do."

Building solid relationships and communicating a project vision are critical in project initiation. Stories about real-life experiences provide the hook to alter project manager and team member behaviors because they engage people and help them understand expectations.

CONVEYING CRITICAL INFORMATION

Can stories convey quality challenges, project updates, and solutions to problems? At Lockheed Martin Space Systems Company, Anastasia Walsh notes, "We have explicit, rigid processes and procedures because we build satellites, rockets, and other defense-related technologies that have to work. Processes don't cover some of the tacit knowledge that [occurs] between [processes]. We've been using storytelling to transfer [it]."

For example, Walsh employed stories in a collaborative project with the Quality Assurance (QA) organization. "The president asked me to influence the reduction of mishaps. Not that we have a lot, but any at all is a big problem. I began working with QA on how it passes on information about near misses and discovered QA reports were technical," Walsh says. Arthur L. Major, director of system safety in Product Assurance & System Safety, adds, "The report would say, 'We were on step 36B of procedure XYZ and somebody turned the wrench the wrong way. It resulted in. . . .' We were having trouble communicating this information in usable form to the workforce."

Walsh suggested stories to overcome this challenge: "I use a story model that says, 'Once upon a time, suddenly, luckily, and happily ever after.' [Today,] Quality Assurance tells the mishap using a story format that talks about what happened—the crisis, what was recognized or realized about the situation, and how it was stopped or fixed," she explains. Major adds, "Our lead-in words are 'There we were' doing a test and something happened. Or 'There we were' doing a crane operation and a wire got jammed." He adds a caveat: "Stories are written so they're ambiguous. People's feelings get hurt if they think you're talking about them."

Have stories made a difference? Major notes, "About 250 people a month—executive management, program and project management, and system safety and test people—[get the report]. In the past, we issued reports and never got feedback. Since we went to this approach, we're gradually getting feedback; they want to know what happened. People don't care that the wrench weighed two pounds or that it came within six inches. All they care about is, 'I dropped a wrench and it almost hit something.' That paints a picture in their mind about the engineering details." Major explains why this feedback is critical: "Some people say, 'Gee, that happened to me too.' They want to connect with those who experienced the problem. We connect [them] because they don't know each other. That has never happened before."

Major Dan Ward also communicates key information through written stories. He incorporates them into articles for Department of Defense (DoD) journals. He describes an example: "One article used punk rock as a metaphor for program management principles. You wouldn't expect a band like the Ramones to be a good example for a DoD program manager. It is. Instead of a boring list of principles, I used an engaging story to keep things lively and interesting." Consequently, Ward receives e-mail from readers. "[People] say, 'That was neat.' [Often I] find out, 'They solved a problem that I've been working on for my project.' I'm able to leverage this. We've built connections— many times we're able to collaborate on stuff directly related to my job," he adds. How important are these connections within the Air Force Research Laboratory? Captain Gabe Mounce says, "We're trying to figure out ways to get folks to talk to each other and collaborate if they're not working on the same type of project at the same time, so they can reference something that somebody else has already done to help them." For Ward and Mounce, sharing stories is the answer.

Stories can also communicate progress. At Procter & Gamble, W. Scott Cameron asks project management staff to write stories "to explain [to] management what they're doing or what they've done [on a project] and why. I call them b-l-u-r-b-s." Why do this? Cameron says, "People are inundated with data. [Using stories] separates you from others. How do you get somebody's attention in an e-mail or telephone conference? You start stamping out your story."

Arthur L. Major at Lockheed Martin experienced what happens when these stories are told: "I had to brief senior management on what I was going to do to reduce mishaps and near misses. So I convened a team; Anastasia was a member. She coached us on storytelling." He adds, "The coaching I got wasn't to preamble them with, 'Now I'm going to tell you a story.' I wove it into the presentation like I would a dry line. It flowed. Anastasia helped weave [several] stories into my presentation." And the outcome? "As I gave the presentation—which in the past, would've been very dry—I told stories. I saw executives lean forward, put their pens down, look at me, and listen. Their behavior changed because I changed the way I presented." The executives then approved the continuation of his mishap and near misses approach for the next year.

Critical project information conveyed through stories orally and in print has the power to influence decisions and shift mind-sets because stories capture attention in ways that pure data cannot. Being conscious of the structure of the story and how it is told will increase the effectiveness of the message.

COMMUNICATING AND CAPTURING LESSONS LEARNED

When a project ends, it is important to examine, capture, and share learning experiences. Major Dan Ward does this through stories he presents. "With the National Geospatial Intelligence Agency's School for Leadership, I spend a couple of hours telling stories about project management successes and failures—from my past [and] research I've done. Interesting stories include the development of the bazooka in World War II," he explains. The text on which Ward bases his bazooka story presentation is on pages 70–71.

Ward comments on the story's impact: "Until you hear it you think, 'Any kind of weapons system development is going to take three years,' because it usually does. As soon as we say, 'No, it can be done quicker, cheaper, simpler, and easier. Here's an instance when it was done that way,' the realm of possibility expands. People are more willing to step out and try something if they hear it's been done before."

Along with oral sharing of lessons, organizations document stories. At Lockheed Martin, Anastasia Walsh manages a program to improve employee communication that includes capturing stories. "We coach project managers and capture their stories on videotape—stories that people tell about other employees they admire or who've done something that [embodies] the values [of] Lockheed Martin. [They're] collected and put on our internal Web site for internal communications," she says. Arthur L. Major adds, "These stories are a great way to communicate and transfer knowledge. People don't know they're being taught."

Developing the Bazooka

Contributed by Major Dan Ward

Early in World War II, the U.S. Army contracted with General Electric (GE) to create a hand-held rocket launcher. GE had a mere 30 days to design, build and deliver several thousand units. Today we know the weapon as the Bazooka, and its introduction gave American infantry the unprecedented ability to fight against German tanks and pillboxes. This new weapon changed the battlefield significantly, and contributed to the eventual Allied victory. The story of its development is an intriguing example of the Radical Elements in action.

Naiveté: The belief that something can be done which has not been done before

In an unusual example of military naiveté, the Army believed this incredibly aggressive approach was workable and acted on that belief. Major George Thomas told GE, "We said thirty days and we meant it. We're going to make that deadline."

Once the bazooka was designed (in a single day) and production began, "The workers refused to admit the deadline was impossible." That is very nearly the definition of naiveté! The first test gun was made in four days—another "impossible" feat. The final units were delivered with eighty-nine minutes to spare.

Monomania: Single-minded and enthusiastic focus on a Big Goal

The aforementioned 24-hour design session could only be pulled off by a talented monomaniac who was able to focus with enthusiasm on this secret weapon. That individual was James L. Powers, a GE engineer. The production team of 400 people was similarly dedicated, "refusing to take time out for anything more than a sandwich."

> Such dedication cannot be found among workers who do not care about what they are doing. These workers did not make such sacrifices because they were highly paid; they did it because they had a common goal and were dedicated to a single Grand Purpose.
>

At Procter & Gamble, W. Scott Cameron watched as Alexander Laufer, Ph.D., conducted a research project about how project managers managed projects in the mid-1990s. "Alex pushed the envelope when he asked project managers to tell and write stories. [They] thought, 'What do I have to offer?' [Then], they all wrote great stories. The stories aren't dated. They're [still] great stories," he explains.

In 2000, Dr. Laufer moved to a similar project at the NASA Academy of Program and Project Leadership (APPL), where he started *ASK Magazine,* a print and Web-based publication featuring stories from project managers. Dr. Laufer recruited Cameron to write. Not one to waste an opportunity, Cameron brought back his stories. "I sent my *ASK Magazine* stories to people within Procter & Gamble. The feedback was very positive: 'These stories are great.' 'This was a good thought-provoker.' Nobody said, 'Quit sending me these stories.' [In fact], the list of people of people wanting to receive them grew," Cameron notes.

Consequently, in 2003, Cameron added stories to an existing quarterly publication. He explains, "We've taken the twenty stories I've written, plus other *ASK Magazine* stories, and improved the quality and content of our newsletter, *Capital Management Express.* Project managers and others in the engineering community contribute stories. Then we put the newsletter together and post it on an internal Web site. It's helped us effectively communicate successes and learnings within a big global company to our project managers for their use and potential application."

At NASA, Martin Davis knows the power of lessons-learned stories in his work. He participated for five years in the APPL knowledge-sharing program. At one APPL Master's Forum, a three-day conference, Davis encountered a practice he thought he could use. "When Linda

Rutledge from the U.S. Air Force spoke about her [organization's] procurement process, I thought, 'I've got a lot of procurements coming up on a new project. Maybe we could learn something. [One of her staff] came and talked to my people. We garnered several ideas. One item required an exception to the procurement regulations. NASA Headquarters said, 'Go try it.' We presented it at Goddard and Headquarters to the head of procurement. They agreed to let us use this new practice," he says. And the benefits? "We saved a good month and a half in procurement activity over what we've done before."

Davis has also written stories for *ASK Magazine*. The excerpt below from "A Good Man Is Hard to Find" describes a fundamental project management issue.

Davis's colleague, Sandra Cauffman, assistant director of the Flight Programs and Projects Directorate, shares her reflections on *ASK Magazine* stories: "I pass down the stories. I remember what I read and retell the story or I hand out the magazine for someone else to read. I always want it back; I have a shelf full of them."

Because RSIS also knows the staying power of stories, the organization logs them electronically. Robert Frey explains, "We're documenting

A GOOD MAN IS HARD TO FIND
Contributed by Martin Davis

Every project has its stories. The ones we usually want to tell are the outright success stories—but the ones we also need to hear are the "things we did wrong and should have known better."

The Compton Gamma-Ray Observatory (CGRO) was the heaviest astrophysical payload ever flown at the time of its launch in April 1991. Working on CGRO, we accumulated our fair share of that second breed of story. I'll share [one] here:

The One-Person Syndrome
The Energetic Gamma Ray Experiment Telescope used light pipes to measure time-of-flight. These were simple pieces of

plastic, bent and glued together, and this appeared to be an easy task to accomplish. The catch here is that the task appeared easy.

It was known to the engineers that only one person had been able to complete this task successfully so that the light pipes worked optimally. Unfortunately, this man was about to retire, and an attempt to procure the light pipes from another source failed. Only by appealing to the man to save the project and the Center's reputation did he agree to hold off his retirement to finish the work and to train a replacement.

It was much the same way when it came to a contractor who made the photomultiplier tubes for the science instruments and who used only one of their assemblers to make the tubes. The specifications were quite rigid, and the one assembler who knew how to make the tubes had a success rate of just 40 percent.

CGRO needed more tubes and this one man was on vacation. The project office put pressure on the contractor to keep the production line working. The contractor reluctantly agreed.

Ten tubes were pushed through the manufacturing process and the yield was zero. What the one man did working at an identical station with identical parts is not known, but CGRO lost time and the contractor lost money. They informed us that from then on we should wait until their one man was available. We agreed.

What do these cases say to a manager? Project life is rarely as simple as it seems. Make sure you find out how difficult the work is—and if told only one person can do the job, no matter how "trivial" that work might appear to be, pay careful attention to the situation so that you know that one person will be there when you need him or her most.

From M. Davis, "A Good Man Is Hard to Find." *ASK Magazine,* December 2003, 15, pp. 12–15. Copyright © 2003, U.S. Government as represented by the Administrator of the National Aeronautics and Space Administration. No copyright is claimed in the United States under Title 17, U.S. Code. All other rights reserved. Used with permission.

and putting success stories into a business development knowledge base—stories related to supporting nationwide customers, solving issues, cost savings, and schedule control." Rick Stalnaker has contributed several. His favorite? "The Americans with Disabilities Act, Section 508, requires Web site accessibility by people with handicaps. So I hired a blind student for the summer through United Cerebral Palsy to navigate each site we've developed. She wrote a report and we implemented a few changes. We told this story [and won an important contract]," he explains.

Careful thought went into the knowledge base design. Says Frey, "We slice and dice success stories across projects, technical disciplines, and programmatic issues." Does it benefit RSIS? "When we want to build a diagram that shows we've been able to provide cost savings to different clients, we can search for it. [It] allows us to develop proposals with the best materials and the latest and greatest success stories. Frankly, it's the keys to the kingdom."

Currently, the most prevalent use of stories in project management is sharing and capturing lessons. While stories can be documented in print or electronically to aid in their future retrieval and use, hearing stories orally can inspire a project manager to reflect on possible project improvements.

THE RESULTS

From preparing and initiating projects to conveying critical information and communicating and capturing lessons, stories make a difference in project management. Robert Frey notes, "Over the last six years, RSIS won 67 percent of the proposals it's pursued. IT industry average is about 35 percent. We're nearly two times what everyone else in our market space is doing. . . . We'll close 2005 with $360 million. Effective, customer-centric storytelling in proposals and oral presentations is a key contributor to our company's successful seven-year growth trajectory."

Martin Davis of NASA knows the financial value of sharing stories. "When Sue [from Glenn Research Center] called, she said, 'I read your [ASK Magazine] article. I have a completely different project and this is my problem.' We talked about the way I solved mine, and how it might be tailored to hers. She implemented some changes, resulting in cost savings," he says. Later, Sue wrote an article where she estimated saving $500,000.

Listening to stories also benefited Davis through procurement changes made on his project—where cycle time was cut by a month and a half. RSIS experienced this benefit, too. "We now [build proposal prototypes rapidly] using the business development knowledge base to draw upon the best proposals and practices, success stories, and lessons learned throughout the company. We're much further ahead during the development life cycle," Frey notes.

At Lockheed Martin, Anastasia Walsh awaits year-end results on the mishap project. "In the first ten months we've seen a dramatic drop," she notes. Arthur L. Major concurs. "[We're hoping that] by year-end we'll have reduced mishaps by 76 percent. We've increased [reporting of] 'near misses' by 39 percent, which is great news. People are willing to contribute. They could easily brush it under the rug and report it as 'nothing happened.' We're becoming a learning organization using storytelling."

Procter & Gamble's training results improved through storytelling. Andrew R. Poole explains, "My training group thinks about training as a learning experience. We've designed all kinds of learning sciences into classes to create this experience; storytelling's one of them. Stories allow learners to connect with topics to better understand how facts and procedures create great results, enabling [them] to more quickly contribute at much higher levels. With staffing reductions, this efficiency gain is needed." He adds, "We regularly gather informal and formal level-three training evaluation feedback. Data show skill building resulting from classes where storytelling's a major component is much higher than [from] the bulk of other classes."

W. Scott Cameron has also seen results. "I train using stories from personal experience to accentuate points. This has caused my instructor rating to increase and allowed participants to engage in more discussion—they want to understand what happened in the story and why I handled [the situation] the way I did. [Afterwards], trainees comment on my stories and how they've grown to be more well-rounded project managers by better understanding how I reacted in certain situations, and that others—including me—have faced situations similar to those they currently face." Major Dan Ward gets results too. "After a recent [storytelling] presentation, one gentleman told me it was the most productive hour in six months. That's a fairly typical response," he says.

Ward's use of story is also assisting the Research Laboratory. "I'm on a mission to transform the organizational culture around me.

Storytelling sessions are powerful tools for casting the vision of what our organization could be like and recruiting people to help foster change. The result is a loosely connected informal network of hundreds of 'unindicted coconspirators' who're committed to exploring this vision and bringing it to reality," he explains.

Captain Gabe Mounce believes Ward is influencing culture change. "[Most articles] in the *Defense AT&L Magazine* are technical and dry. Ward's articles are all like a novel. [This] resonates with lots of people throughout the Lab. They're saying, 'Look at this guy with his ideas. Hmmm. I've got some crazy ideas. I'm going to throw them out there.' We don't have to write like this [or] communicate this way. We can be real people and talk to each other," he says.

Procter & Gamble's internal newsletter, *Capital Management Express,* has also made a difference. "People who write spread their influence. Readers want to discuss the story or talk to the writer to obtain more wisdom and knowledge. Their stories allow them to network outside their normal workspace to find better ways to achieve success," Cameron says.

HOW YOU CAN BENEFIT

Stories have value throughout the project life cycle. Here are ways to bring them into your project or the project management structure in your organization:

- Incorporate experiences from expert project managers into training through stories in a deliberate manner.
- Capture and document success stories for use in project proposals and project manager résumés.
- Use daily project management experiences as a springboard for crafting stories that will benefit other project managers in the organization.
- Consciously structure stories in a way that is effective for relaying information to technical people.
- Use stories to communicate the vision for a project and the project's status to executives and team members. Stories connect project managers who have similar issues, encouraging some who may not have routine contact to communicate with one another.

• Make it possible for project managers to tell best practice and lessons-learned stories to each other in a face-to-face setting. Oral sharing is optimal.

• Find ways to capture project stories in print and electronically so they can influence more people and be reused in other communication channels.

By incorporating stories in these ways, you make it possible to reap the benefits these organizations have experienced and keep projects in your organization on track.

Special Thanks

Thank you to Beverly Floyd from EduTech Ltd. for the time and effort she has given to this chapter.

CHAPTER SIX

Who Said Money Is Everything?

Story Is the New Currency
in Financial Management

Alicia Korten
Karen Dietz, Ph.D.

In the world of finance, storytelling plays a vital role. "You won't get someone investing time and capital with just facts. It takes more than numbers if there's a decision on the table. Attracting investors is about being a good storyteller," says Dan Hendrix, president and CEO of Interface, Inc., the world's largest manufacturer of modular carpet and a leader in the sustainable business movement. Dorothea Brennan, board member for Gaylord Hospital, a long-term acute care hospital, agrees: "Stories are vital for giving meaning to numbers. They provide context and capture people's imagination."

These two organizations used story to pull themselves out of financial crises. Other organizations using story to develop and relay their financial communications strategies include Alternatives Federal Credit Union, a community development financial institution; United Way of York County, Pennsylvania, a federation of local member agencies; and Spare Key, a not-for-profit organization dedicated to providing mortgage payments for families with critically ill children.

FROM FINANCIAL CRISIS TO
FINANCIAL HEALTH

"For fifty years Gaylord was one of the best-known and successful tuberculosis (TB) sanatoriums," Dorothea Brennan explains. "As TB started to be cured, the hospital moved toward stroke rehabilitation. It became known for traumatic brain injury, spinal injury, and sleep medicine. [Today], the hospital takes complex medical patients—people who have a number of health issues happening at once."

While maintaining a stellar health care provider reputation, the organization has not always been able to maintain equally rosy finances. According to Jim Cullen, president and CEO, "By 2003, on an annual budget of roughly $55 million, the hospital was losing [almost] $5 million a year. We were pulling millions of dollars from our endowment fund to stay alive. I told the CFO, 'We're staring into a very deep hole. We're at the end of our rope.'"

How did the organization tackle this crisis? "We instituted metrics-driven performance," Brennan says. "Metrics are monthly goals that define success such as the number of patient admissions in a month . . . and reduction in number of patient falls. When balanced together, these metrics provide a sense of how well the hospital is doing." Stories are then linked to these goals. "We told stories that helped line staff think about how to effectively meet these measurable goals," Cullen explains. Brennan adds, "We wanted them to think about how to increase revenue or make up for lost revenue through expense savings."

Chief Financial Officer Janine Ross recounts a story that showcases staff initiative, management responsiveness, and management and line staff collaboration—ingredients to Gaylord's financial recovery. "One housekeeper was cleaning out a room and wondered if she was throwing away things that didn't need to be tossed. She brought this to her supervisor and asked her what she [thought] should be thrown out and saved and whether [housekeeping staff] should start auditing rooms for what was being tossed," Ross says. The supervisor shared this question and idea with the director of nursing and the director of material management, who shared it with me. We agreed the audit was a good idea. So the directors of nursing and materials management audited several rooms [and] we got people to examine their areas. We tracked this through our financial improvement process and found unnecessary waste. Now all housekeepers train on what products to throw out. Because of this housekeeper's observation, question, and idea, the hospital is saving $30,000 annually."

While stories like these stimulated staff to demonstrate new behaviors and instigate cost-saving initiatives, these changes were insufficient. "The staff are wonderful care providers and very customer oriented. But most weren't aware of the hospital's budgetary needs," Brennan says. The hospital needed to transform its culture so everyone attended to patient care *and* fiscal responsibility.

To help transform its culture, the hospital started a "good stories" ritual. "Good stories are about staff members who take extreme measures to support Gaylord's financial, patient service, and strategic goals—actions such as nurses' taking extra patients, working extra shifts, and pitching in when others are on sick leave. These stories are personal and positive—and speak directly to what we're trying to accomplish," Cullen explains. "In addition to reviewing financial and program performance, part of senior management's weekly meeting is to tell good stories."

"Don't Lose That Patient!" is an example.

"After these good stories are shared, a senior manager visits staff in the stories to thank them," Cullen reports. Rick Serafino, administrator for Gaylord's Sleep Medicine Program, says, "When you thank peo-

DON'T LOSE THAT PATIENT!

Contributed by Rick Serafino

Our sleep medicine program had scheduled three patients to spend the night as part of a diagnostic sleep study. They were a family—a husband, wife, and son. The father called and asked, "Do you have a VCR?" We replied, "We don't." They responded, "I guess we'll have to cancel." To which we said, "Give us an hour and we'll get back to you."

We got on the phone with our facilities department and they delivered us a VCR. Then one of the physicians went to the video store to rent some videos for the patients.

We got those patients in. We knew we couldn't afford to lose the money.

ple, they realize these stories do get talked about." These stories are then relayed to staff. Cullen explains, "We convey information through storytelling in a way that helps people relate to their work, makes them feel appreciated, *and* is tied to organizational accountability and goals.

"We had laid off lots of people so morale was waning. We needed to hear good stories and to thank people," he says. "It can't all be negative [or] about numbers. It has to be about people pitching in to get Gaylord better financially."

Interface, Inc., also turned to stories after finding itself in a financial downturn. "We had about $57 million in revenue in 1982. We went public in 1983 and made several strategic acquisitions over the next five years. By 1988, revenue was at $500 million," Dan Hendrix outlines. "Then, in the early 1990s, the commercial market softened. During that downturn, we lost some credibility and our place as the darling of Wall Street, but the industry had lost favor too."

During this time, Interface started shaping itself as an environmentally sustainable company. "Ray Anderson, our founder and current chairman of the board, began talking about sustainability as a better business model. After he spoke at an investor conference in 1995, I got a call from an analyst who'd received a call from one of our biggest shareholders. Ray had decided to talk sustainability, not company performance. On behalf of the shareholder, the analyst asked if Ray was terminally ill! The shareholder thought that was why Ray was talking about a higher purpose. I said, 'No, he's not terminally ill.' I asked, 'What if oil was $100 a barrel? (It was at $18 then.) For an industry that is 80 percent dependent on petrochemicals, what would that high cost of oil be like for us?' This didn't resonate with Wall Street. No one in the industry was thinking this way. Shareholders were very skeptical," Hendrix explains.

Despite the backlash, Interface continued to deliver its sustainability story to shareholders. "We told the story of how Ray read a book, had an epiphany about the environment, and turned the company toward a new vision over and over in meetings and conferences. The story of oil at $100 a barrel, and why sustainability is a better way to make a bigger profit," Hendrix recounts. For almost five years, Wall Street's response remained unchanged. "They wondered if we were just a bunch of tree huggers and kept asking, 'How much does it cost?'" he notes.

"Wall Street didn't turn around until NeoCon 2003 when investors heard our competitors also talking about sustainability," Hendrix continues. "Our share price was going up as the carpeting market turned. Interface's sustainability story resonated with architects and designers who were buying our products. Suddenly there's a green movement and Interface has a nine-year head start. I'll never forget one analyst saying, 'I finally get where Ray was. What a visionary!'"

In addition to sharing its sustainability story with investors, Interface echoes this theme in product stories. "The Biomimicry Story" is one such example.

"To bring [shareholders and customers] on board, it was important to tell the story of biomimicry. We captured it on video and Power-Point," explains John Wells, president and CEO of Interface Americas.

THE BIOMIMICRY STORY

Contributed by John Wells

The head of product development was struggling with the company saying it was going to be sustainable by 2020. This person's thinking, "what the heck am I going to do? All my products are nylon!" [Nylon is made from oil.]

Then someone sends him a book called *Biomimicry.* It's about how we can learn from natural systems. He thinks about how nature makes one of the hardest ceramics at the ocean bottom with no waste while it takes us all kinds of energy and waste to make something equivalent. He asks himself, "How would nature design a floor?"

He sends a team into nature and the woods. They find in nature that there's no sameness. Every leaf is different in size and shape, but when they [lie] out next to each other on the forest floor there's beautiful symmetry.

This led Interface to develop a breakthrough product called Entropy—carpet tiles that can be laid in any direction on the floor. Because tiles don't have to match—they can be turned in any direction—there's no waste. This significantly reduced cost. The innovation led to an economic model for carpet tile never seen before. Suddenly the product became competitive with all kinds of flooring. Today Entropy is the number one carpet tile sold of all time!

According to Hendrix, "Financial institutions watch earnings. They say, 'Show me the money or we won't buy your story.' We have to keep telling our sustainability story—and backing it up with financial results—for investors to get it.'"

Alternatives Federal Credit Union is another organization that uses stories to overturn financial crises, albeit of a different sort. "We use stories to help people fix their credit and secure a loan. We help them create a different story about what money means. Money has meant something that is against them because they don't have it," says Joe Cummins, community development educator. Alternatives members often live paycheck-to-paycheck and are deeply in debt.

"We have a class called Money Wise® that focuses on [sustainable] behavior changes. The backbone of Money Wise® is tracking expenses," Cummins notes. "I got bored [teaching it] and thought about how to engage people in learning. So I brought story into the program."

One story he tells has a twist. "First I read a story—usually *The Little Prince*. [Although] it has nothing to do with financial management, it opens people's imaginations and gets their minds out of fear—money is stressful for them," he says. "Using your imagination allows you to dream. Dreaming creates the ability to change your story."

"I also tell my story around money—I was $60,000 in debt—to help them open up," Cummins explains. "Then everyone tells their story. Classes include lower-, middle-, and upper-income people, but their stories are the same—no matter how much people earn, they say, 'I thought I was the only single mom who couldn't get her act together.' Or, 'We have big incomes and don't know where our money is going,'" he notes. "As people share their stories, they feel relieved."

"We teach people to successfully track their expenses," Cummins says. "Willing participants share stories of how this technique helped them. Others hear these stories unfold. They connect to them and create their own stories." He gives an example: "We had a middle-class couple in class. The woman was a Wall Street financial analyst. She and her husband tracked how much cable television cost them and realized they didn't watch it much. So they eliminated it. There was a low-income individual in class who never had savings. He lived paycheck-to-paycheck. [After hearing the story], he said to them, 'You've inspired me. I've always had cable and decided to give it up. For the first time I have money in my savings account.'"

As part of a multi-pronged strategy to confront various financial crises, stories can help staff change their day-to-day actions to achieve organizational goals, position a company with shareholders and consumers, and help people transform their attitudes toward money and connect to personal financial power. By giving deeper meaning to numbers, stories spur institutions and individuals to financial health.

BUILDING A FINANCIAL BASE WITH DONOR AND FOUNDATION GRANTS

United Way of York County, Pennsylvania, is one of thirteen hundred locally managed United Way organizations across the United States. Like its counterparts, it secures donations that it distributes to local organizations and programs. "We fundraise with employees [across the county] by holding group meetings in the workplace. Seventy-three percent of our funds—almost $7 million—come from employees. We allocate most of this money to thirty-eight programs in other agencies," explains Robert Woods, executive director.

"[For several years] at group meetings, we had speakers [from programs we fund] talk about their agency for ten minutes. But their messages were dry—they were all about how many people they served and their annual budget," Woods notes. "I thought, 'We've got to do something here. We have to connect to employees' hearts.'" According to Deb Gogniat, director of major gifts, "Speakers were going over administrative details." What did the agency do? "We came up with the idea of storytelling as a way for people to understand what the numbers mean," Woods explains. Adds Gogniat, "We lined up a great storyteller [who] worked with our initial speakers to help them tell good stories."

Speakers learned to narrow a long story to its essential elements. "We need to net life experiences down into three-to-five-minute stories that set the stage, identify the right message, and capture what has the most impact," she says. What is the key to telling stories? "Practice, practice, practice. The best speakers hone their stories," Gogniat points out. Woods adds, "To build storytelling skills we offer speaker's bureau training to new people from the funded agencies. They tell their own story in mock demonstrations." Training does not end in the classroom. "[Our staff] attend speakers' presentations—we coach them afterwards. We also offer peer story coaching where speakers write stories and get them critiqued [by staff and volunteers]," Gogniat points out. "All our speakers are expected to attend this training. This shift has had a significantly positive impact on our campaigns."

"It took a while to [make the] transition," Woods continues. "Sometimes speakers are so connected with what they do, they automatically assume others are interested. For example, a speaker might think everyone wants to know the organization serves 3,280 people. But most people don't care. When speakers tell stories they find people interested in what they're saying. The audience pays attention. Then they're convinced. For those who won't or can't tell stories, we say, 'Look, you either learn to tell a story or don't come back. You've got to be effective. This is the only opportunity we have to reach people who can make donations.'"

Gogniat stumbled upon a story she has told potential donors. "When I started at United Way, I reviewed our giving list of $1,000 or more and

UNEXPECTED HELP

Contributed by Deb Gogniat

During dinner I said to my friend, "I'm surprised and pleased you're a Leadership Giver. As a new United Way staff member, I'm always interested in why people donate."

She said, "Well, I don't usually talk about this. [About fifteen years] ago, my mother, who was in her sixties, was suddenly missing. My family was worried and distraught because she couldn't be found. After two weeks the police showed up at the door with the worst news possible. A drug addict had hijacked my mother's car and murdered her. With the police was a representative from the Victim Assistance Center. I'd never heard of VAC and even if I had I wouldn't have thought I would ever need them."

She continued, "The police caught the person who murdered my mother. He did this for no particular reason and showed absolutely no remorse. VAC knew my family and I would need help through the emotional turmoil of having a loved one murdered and through the mechanics of the trial. They did this for us."

To this day, my friend still finds it difficult to talk about what happened to her mother. She was a donor to United Way before this incident. Afterwards, she stepped up her commitment and has been increasing her gift steadily over time.

was surprised to see my friend's name. One night at dinner I asked why she donates," she says. The story Gogniat heard is on page 85.

"I still get choked up when I share this story. It definitely gets the audience's attention," Gogniat says. Woods adds, "For storytelling to be effective it needs to be sincere. The stories need to be honest, have integrity, and reflect reality. [Otherwise] people will see through them."

Like United Way of York, Spare Key relies on stories to convey powerful messages to potential donors. Even the organization's name conjures up stories itself. "Everyone's been locked out of a house or car. Everything in life stops until they [find] a spare key. Our clients—who have critically ill children—are locked out of life while tending to their child. They understand the relief a spare key can bring," explains Patsy Keech, who co-founded the organization with her husband, Robb.

What caused them to start the organization? "Our son, Derian, passed away in May 1996," she says. "When we looked at the theme of his life, it was 'time.' To care for my child I took eight months' unpaid leave. But my paycheck was supposed to cover the mortgage. People stepped in to pay it. They purchased time for us to spend with Derian in the hospital. Spare Key makes mortgage payments for families [in similar situations]. Our son showed us what was needed."

Executive Director Kim Lovrich shares how she came to the organization. "In 2002, we had a critically ill child named Macklin. Within days of his birth, we were told he wouldn't live long. The last month of his life we received a Spare Key mortgage. Spare Key gave us time—we can never get that last month of Mac's life back again," she says.

"By using our personal stories in a PowerPoint presentation that has a clip of the *Oprah* show when Patsy and Spare Key received the Angel Network award in 2000, we connect donors and recipients to the organization's mission and the importance of our work," Lovrich says. "The presentation conveys messages more powerfully than simply stating facts and statistics. It makes our mission more personal and helps people walk in someone else's shoes." The technique is powerful. "At one presentation, within five minutes of ending, a woman gave me a $1,000 check," she reports.

Lovrich realizes these two stories enhance people's understanding of the organization's purpose. "The Keech and Lovrich stories [can't be] the dominant stories. [In the past] it's led to the misunderstanding that we only assist families with terminally ill children. But that's *not* our mission. Our mission is to support families of critically ill children," she notes. "Now we regularly tell other stories. Their diversity also helps people recognize the universality of these experiences.

"In addition, I've learned to be very respectful when soliciting and listening to stories in our grant application process. This creates validation and understanding. We always ask permission to use a family's story," Lovrich says. What advice does she offer others who use stories for fundraising? "Take into account all major stakeholders—donors, board members, and recipients. [When collecting stories] ask them about their impressions of the organization, how they got involved, and why they donate," she shares.

Stories exemplifying an organization's mission can help people see value in making a financial donation. Often these stories are about the teller's personal experiences, or about the impact an organization has had with the people it serves. While numbers often leave people cold, one well-framed story may be all that's needed to move an audience to make a significant financial commitment to a worthy cause.

GARNERING SUPPORT FOR SOCIAL CHANGE INITIATIVES

At Interface, when John Wells wanted funding to develop a new technology called Cool Blue, he reached for a story to convince his superiors. Cool Blue, a backing for carpet tiles, is made from waste materials such as piping and old carpets. "John's story sold senior management and the board on moving forward with the project. It opened people's minds," Dan Hendrix says. "If a traditional MBA student had presented a market analysis using only facts, we probably wouldn't have done it.

"When John started discussing Cool Blue, I was skeptical," Hendrix acknowledges. "It required a $5 million investment to make the most environmentally sound carpet backing at a time when we really didn't have money for it."

How did Wells gain executive support for these monies? "We created our own movie—a spoof on the original movie *Back to the Future*. We made it into a real story," Wells states. "I was Michael J. Fox. Another gentleman was the mad scientist. We had a DeLorean car that looked just like the *Back to the Future* car. Do you remember what they used to power their time machine—the flux capacitor? Garbage. We went back in time to tell people about Interface's evolution. Then we showed a picture of the flux capacitor. We threw cans and bottles and old carpet into it as part of our future story. The Cool Blue manufacturing process actually does this. You throw old carpet tile into this thing and it grinds it into little pellets."

"The [movie described] our history and legacy and how Interface had changed. It [captured] both good and bad times, right up to the present. Then it talked about the future," Wells says. "It put meat on the bones of our mission to be sustainable by 2020."

"The flux capacitor story helped people visualize our sustainability story," Hendrix adds. "John told it to our board of directors. After that, we got the go-ahead to make the investment. He convinced people even though we had little capital. People felt we couldn't afford *not* to do it." Wells concurs: "The story shifted dialogue away from 'it takes this much to make and this will be the payoff.' It showed this product could differentiate us in the marketplace."

Like Wells, Deirdre Silverman, director of development and community ventures for Alternatives Federal Credit Union, was challenged with garnering financial support for a social change concept: in her case, the community development credit union. "Community development credit unions are a hybrid between a financial institution and a not-for-profit institution. They focus on low-income people and populations other financial institutions won't work with," she explains. "It's hard to break even, let alone make a profit. This population is more expensive to help. They require more programs, [and they] may have higher loan default rates and lower savings and investments."

Silverman's job is tough. "My job is to bring in external funding," she says. "Explaining we're a financial institution as well as a not-for-profit with a community development mission is hard to make clear to people. The agencies we approach—government agencies, corporate foundations, and the like—often don't see why a financial institution should get funding. They assume we're making profits from our loans to cover our needs. But this money doesn't cover our program offerings."

Silverman turned to stories to solve this dilemma. "Through stories, people understand the types of changes we're trying to effect. [They learn] we're trying to improve financial situations for individuals and communities by funding start-up businesses and increasing home ownership." Here is one story she uses: "A man was staying at a homeless shelter I set up in Ithaca, New York. When we got our food delivery, he started organizing it. He said he hadn't seen so much food in years. Years later I ran into him. He'd cleaned up his act, gotten into one of our training programs, took our financial management class, and bought a home. When I tell people about his changed life, including our role in it, people understand what we do," she explains.

Alternatives also uses stories in its print media to reach members and potential donors. "Our annual reports feature real people and results. They're full of stories about how each of our programs has helped change people's lives. Using stories is the best way to communicate why it makes sense for others to partner with us," Silverman explains, but she adds a caveat: "There has to be a balance between stories and data. You can't give up the data entirely."

When social change initiatives challenge the worldview of individuals whose support is critical for success, stories can evoke a paradigm shift in them, thus garnering their financial assistance. These stories can come from real-life experiences or from movie or book dramatizations. In this way, stories can help stakeholders commit to taking the risks inherent in supporting a social change agenda, as well as help outsiders see a hybrid organization for what it is—an enterprise with a social mission.

THE OVERALL BENEFITS

Storytelling is one of several actions that brought Gaylord Hospital back to financial health. According to Jim Cullen, "The hospital made more than $3 million from operations in 2005. Since we were in debt, that means our turn-around [in one] year is about $9 million!" What was the impact on employees? "We gave everyone a $500 check. It created a lot of positive energy."

"Storytelling definitely impacted the bottom line," concludes Janine Ross. "It's a huge morale booster when someone other than your boss recognizes you through story—our turnover is down. We can rely more on employees when things get tough." Dorothea Brennan adds, "Story ensured consistency of care even [through] staff reductions. It's helped people focus on Gaylord's mission of patient care, which has led to financial results."

Interface's stories are also boosting the bottom line. "Institutional investors are beginning to understand our sustainability story," Dan Hendrix states. "In 2003, one large institution sent analysts to our plants. They later bought 10 percent of the company. That's about five million shares—in today's dollars that's approximately $70 million." According to John Wells, "Investment in Cool Blue was roughly $5 million. We forecast this process could account for up to 10 percent of our total production. Entropy led to the creation of the i2 product line. In four years, i2 sales went from zero to 40 percent of total sales, representing 40 percent of our margin dollars," Wells notes. Hendrix acknowledges, "Yet not all investors have been swayed by our story."

Storytelling revitalized United Way of York County's annual fundraising campaign. "In 2004, the number of employee meetings we hosted grew from 291 to 449 and 144 companies held meetings. Funds have increased steadily. Eighty-five [companies] had double-digit increases in donations," Robert Woods reports. "In addition, storytelling has affected how our staff views United Way. There's not a lot of turnover. People feel good about what they do and whom they represent in the community. Today, speakers tell stories and our entire campaign film revolves around stories."

For Spare Key, storytelling has also been a powerful fundraising tool. "In 2002, I was with a group of mortgage brokers. I had seven minutes to tell our story. When I was done there wasn't a dry eye in the place. Right away one company said they'd give us $2,000," Patsy Keech says. According to Kim Lovrich, "Tom Birch attended that meeting with a group of men. After Patsy's story, he says the men couldn't talk. He called Patsy and said he had to contribute in some way. Now he's chairing our board. Mortgage brokers have done numerous things to help financially. In 2005, the National Association of Mortgage Brokers raised funds for us on a national scale."

Lovrich reports more results. "In 2004, we had a formal event with a silent auction at a country club. We had permission to use five anonymous family stories at the event. At the end of each was the amount of the family's mortgage. Within forty-five minutes, donors had paid for all five mortgages," she reports. "From 2002 to 2004, our income grew by 30 percent annually. In 2005, we disbursed more than half a million dollars to more than five hundred Minnesota families."

Alternatives raised money, in part, due to the stories it tells. "[In 2004, we were] awarded $1.4 million from the CDFI Fund of the United States Treasury Department," Deirdre Silverman says. "Others providing [money] include the Federal Home Loan Bank, which supports our Individual Development Account savings program; Tompkins County Planning Department, which funds micro enterprise work with rural county residents; the New York State Credit Union League and the National Credit Union Foundation, which fund work with previously unbanked members; and NFCDCU's Bridge grant for our partnership with Summit Federal Credit Union in Rochester, New York."

There is more. "The Money Wise® course created financially responsible members [who] realize things can be different. This creates hope and hope stimulates change," says Joe Cummins. "Many graduates continue tracking expenses long after completing the program. I'll be at a bar and people will pull out their tracking sheets. They tell me how helpful it's been and that they're still doing it. One former participant told me she still remembers to make unconscious spending conscious, to make unexpected bills expected, to be aware that what's in her checking account isn't what she has available to spend until her next paycheck . . . and to differentiate between wants and needs."

ADVICE TO OTHERS

These five organizations have learned much about the ins and outs of using stories for financial purposes. Here are their insights:

- To obtain the most from storytelling, formalize the approach and tell stories orally.
- Use positive stories to reinforce behaviors needed to achieve cost savings and shifts in financial mind-set.
- Through stories, share results from the use of donated funds to secure additional monies.
- Highlight stories that directly relate to the organization's financial goals and mission.
- Balance storytelling with data—people may also want facts and figures.
- In addition to conveying facts through PowerPoint, treat it as a means to enhance stories by showing video clips and music.
- Ask permission to tell someone else's story. Not everyone will want their stories retold.
- To tell a story effectively, hire a professional storyteller to help shape the story and then practice it with others. Real-life stories need to be honest and come from the heart—but that does not mean you should not polish them for best effect.
- Search for new narratives so that one or two stories do not dominate or define the organization.

- Be creative in finding stories to use as metaphors to demonstrate a financial need or request.

Stories make numbers come alive. Storytelling plays a vital role in creating financial turn-arounds, building a financial base through grants and donations, and securing financial support for socially responsible initiatives. They add heart and soul to financial charts and projections. They are the new currency.

Special Thanks

A special thank-you to Amy Domini, founder and managing principal of Domini Social Investments, and to Marita Kenney, finance manager at Westerra Credit Union (formerly known as Denver Public Schools Credit Union), for helping identify appropriate contacts for this chapter.

CHAPTER SEVEN

We've Never Done It This Way Before

Prompting Organizational Change Through Stories

North McKinnon

———∿∿∿———

Constrained budgets and aggressive profit targets can fuel a constant radical organizational change. "I recall someone saying 'constant change is stability,'" says Pat Duran, senior business consultant for global operations strategy and planning at Hewlett-Packard. While often beneficial to the bottom line, change can lead to cynicism, complacency, turnover, and resentment. "Change is never easy. When radical change is necessary to survive, you can only go as fast as people are willing to buy in," points out Erik Shaw, president and CEO of FivePoint Federal Credit Union.

What do these leaders—along with others from Cerium Laboratories, LLC; Endevco Corporation; and Hewlett-Packard's Imaging and Printing Group (IPG) business unit—have in common? They use stories to successfully navigate change. "What I've discovered," says Clayton Fullwood, managing director, Cerium Laboratories, LLC, "is that storytelling addresses the typical complaint that people have about communication and change. It [provides] rationale for why change is essential."

THE ROLE OF LEADERSHIP
IN MOBILIZING CHANGE

Frequently, leaders must spearhead change. To shift the status quo performance prevalent in larger, slower-moving companies, leaders at Cerium Laboratories, a spin-off of Advanced Micro Devices (AMD), solicit and tell "Tar Pit Stories"—situational vignettes that capture operational efficiency improvements. How does Clayton Fullwood evoke them? "I'll ask, 'How are we working right now?' 'What's holding us back and keeping us stuck in old ways?' I'll also ask people to tell a story of a future image and describe it as real." What response does he receive from employees? "Initially, I'll get minor resistance like, 'Why can't we just keep doing our jobs the same way? Everything will be just fine,'" he says. But then people begin to see possibilities for themselves.

For example, Lynette Ballast, section manager, recalls telling the "Tar Pit Story" below in a management meeting.

"When employees tell a Tar Pit story, a paradigm shift occurs," Fullwood notes. It did with Ballast's story. "After our spin-off, old ways still lingered. In our new environment, [they] kept our growth 'stuck' in the past. . . . Many procedures appropriate for AMD became hindrances to our new leaner operation," Ballast says. The result? "A new direct purchasing process was created for non-capital expenses."

TAR PIT STORY

Contributed by Lynette Ballast

AMD uses SAP as its central purchasing processes technology. It's a lengthy process to order supplies through the SAP system. I followed the standard process of making the request through SAP, waiting for multiple approvals, and finally a buyer from the purchasing department placed a purchase order for the item. It took three weeks! I could have just gone direct to a vendor and had the order in a few days, but a direct purchase is not allowed by the AMD purchasing system.

This is a "Tar Pit" and it's holding us back! We need to be able to handle small purchases for supplies and small desktop equipment with a company credit card or a reimbursement process to sidestep these delays.

A purposefully used story can shift people from complacency into action. Erik Shaw provoked transformation this way: "In 1935, Five-Point Credit Union started as Texas Company Port Arthur Works Employee Federal Credit Union. It evolved into Texaco Community Federal Credit Union, the largest independent, not-for-profit financial institution in southeast Texas. All was fine until 1998 when Texaco sold its last interests in the local refinery and gas stations. While our Board of Directors recognized the marketing need to alter our name, it wasn't compelling," notes Shaw. Kristen Bellanger, senior vice president of operations, explains, "A name change [implied] loss of identity for many Board [members] and long-time credit union employees; the entire Board, except for one person, was either currently employed or retired from the Texaco refinery. The touching stories they tell about [our] history are linked to Texaco."

In 2004, the credit union acquired a "community chartered" status, allowing it access to five counties, making it possible to become a leading regional credit union. But the Texaco issue continued. "We discovered through focus groups that many people believed you had to be a Texaco employee to use our credit union even though [membership was] open to the general community long before. The name was limiting our growth," Shaw explains.

Soon after this realization, Shaw had a chance meeting with a credit union member. Their conversation, provided in "Is Our Name Telling the Right Story?" gave Shaw his lever for change.

"I had proof," said Shaw. "The name was keeping potential members away." He quickly engaged board members and staff with his airplane story. "The Board realized our growth could expand outside southeast Texas and possibly into southwest Louisiana, where the Texaco name could be a limitation," notes Bellanger. "We had to change. For us, this was about survival," Shaw adds. His story greatly impressed everyone, spurring them to craft a new name.

To instill change, a story can arise from a single leader or several working together. The latter happened at Hewlett-Packard during its merger with Compaq Computer Corporation. Before the merger, leadership of both organizations recognized the opportunity to leverage their strengths. "We envisioned a future story from a single choice point—'create one great company,'" says Jim Arena, director of strategic change, Merger Integration Office, adding, "[The office's] purpose was to conceive and develop the operating model, processes, and accountabilities for the new Hewlett-Packard."

Is Our Name Telling the Right Story?

Contributed by Erik Shaw

As I was flying home from a business meeting, I started making small talk with a fellow seated next to me. He asked where I worked. I told him, "Texaco Community Federal Credit Union." He said, "I'm one of your members."

I was delighted.

He said, "We live in Lumberton. With the new branch there, banking is a whole lot more convenient for us. We really like your service."

I saw this as an opportunity to learn more about the value of our name, Texaco Credit Union. I fired off three rounds of questions without a pause. "So, how did you join? Was it through an employer? How long have you been a member?"

His response? "No, we didn't join through our employer. My father-in-law used to work for Texaco." And then his words rang loud in my ears, silencing the drone of the plane's engines. "Isn't that the only way you can join? Work for Texaco or have a family member that does? That's what the name says, right? Texaco Credit Union."

A huge bright light bulb went off in my head. He was right. That is what the name says. If people don't know the truth, they'll assume you have to be a Texaco employee or be related to someone at Texaco. If I dispel that assumption now, I'll be able to see how he'll react. At least, he'll tell others that Texaco employment isn't required.

So I told him, "We're a community chartered credit union. You don't have to be affiliated with Texaco or related to anybody with Texaco to join. It used to be like that years ago, but that's not the case anymore. All you must do is live, work, or worship in any of the five counties we serve."

He expressed no confusion or questions. He took the explanation as fact and that was that. Except, telling one person at a time wasn't going to cut it for me.

The experience really drove home a strategic point. What you want to do is one thing, but what your name tells people is another. It was clear our name was telling the wrong story. It was time to give this name change some real consideration.

There were challenges to overcome. "The reigning belief was that two giant high-tech companies couldn't be successfully merged. Yet we had high-quality, passionate people throughout both companies who wanted to prove we could," Arena says. What approach to change was used? "To get people to join a major change they must feel they're creating something bigger than themselves. The key was crafting a future story of great success. For our story, my team defined *great* as everyone delivering on three common pillars: high tech, low cost, and a positive 'Total Customer Experience.'" The future story described the third pillar. "The merger gave us greater scale and ability to deliver a totally integrated solution set to all customer segments. This meant shifting from long-standing product silos to more integrated sets of solutions across divisions in response to customer needs."

The future story was shared with all employees through corporate global communications and "coffee talks"—small departmental meetings where leaders clarified the merger's purpose and direction. "[We] then focused on the twenty-three merger planning teams who developed the story into specific strategies, policies, and processes. Telling and enacting our new story wasn't a single event—the merger spanned four years. We gained confidence as each step was successfully accomplished. The possibility of realizing a great future story brought the vision alive for individuals in far reaches of the company," Arena says.

With radical change, leaders can leverage stories to engage employees in meaningful ways. Those stories that recognize employees' cares and concerns, while acknowledging the past and building positive anticipation about the future, can become a continual self-guided change tool. They can shore up employee commitment, freeing leaders to focus on delivering results.

CO-CREATING A VISION AND ROAD MAP FOR CHANGE

Enlisting employees to co-create change can be as effective as leaders providing the impetus. By 1999, within Hewlett-Packard's IPG Business Unit, monochrome and color laser printer firmware had developed autonomously—resulting in high operating costs, inconsistent customer experiences, and no common base code between product lines. "A strategic product decision to create a common base code put representatives from four autonomous lab sections into a single solution team. The project was called, 'OZ,'" says Sandy Lieske, director of engineering, the program's manager.

History is hard to forget. "The 130 engineers on the team remembered a similar initiative failing years ago. They were skeptical about success," Lieske recalls. There were more challenges. "Engineers were going to lose their autonomy. And there were over one million lines of code to rewrite. Product sales teams were applying pressure, afraid they wouldn't get promised printer features. A cultural assessment of the OZ project team reflected what I was feeling—we'd become a passive-aggressive, noncooperative group," she explains.

Lieske asked for Pat Duran's internal consulting assistance. Duran recalls, "After initial discussions with the team, I recognized a shared vision was missing." She told Lieske and her three project co-leaders, "Since you're responsible for fulfilling management's vision, you need to define a tangible vision for [everyone]."

Key project managers created this missing piece in a one-day visioning meeting. "Participants [described] the desired end state and challenges to overcome in getting there," Duran says. Simultaneously, a strategic illustrator translated ideas into simple metaphorical images on a wall-sized mural. "They could see their ideas become tangible and alive. That ignited a sense of excitement—something they could rally around," she recalls. While [they were] discussing challenges, *The Wizard of Oz* emerged as a metaphor. "It was perfect. We were enabling a monochrome code base to support color printers, just like film effects in the movie," Lieske recalls.

Duran adds, "Creating shared vision requires people to think beyond everyday experiences and embrace diverse ideas. With metaphors, brainstorming becomes self-perpetual. People accept individual viewpoints and move together with a common focus." The process she used with the team after engaging in this visioning exercise is on page 99.

"For me, the OZ project was proof positive of how metaphors can bring common focus to a diverse cross-functional team," Duran says.

A road map for change was also co-created at Endevco, a Meggitt Group company known for high technology. The division leadership team responsible for Endevco activities wanted employees to embrace its new high-growth and acquisition strategy. "We needed a more direct channel of open communication," remarks David Savage, president of Meggitt Electronics. What made this necessary? "We needed to honor the essence of what had sustained success to date, engage people's trust and passion, and turn their doubt into active participation. [Otherwise], future growth plans would've been at risk."

USING METAPHORS TO CRAFT A COMMON VISION

Contributed by Pat Duran

1. Brainstorm the issues and dynamics of the real situation.
2. Identify the elements that must change (or be added or removed) for a successful project.
3. Identify the metaphor. It can be a famous folk tale, a classic journey story, or a real-life story. What's important is that the selected metaphor [meet the following criteria]:
    a. Is something the entire team can relate to (for example: inventing or discovering something may be best for engineers).
    b. Isn't based on the real work setting (that is, it exists outside the organization as a fantasy or in a different industry).
    c. Is tried out by the group for synergistic fit, rather than imposing it without input from the group.
4. Study the metaphor and make a list of the key elements. For example, story elements in *The Wizard of Oz* movie that matched the project team's situation included the tornado (the business environment), witches (the competitors), and the yellow brick road (the journey).
5. Let the team discover and connect situational elements to the metaphor to identify, personalize, and really get engaged with the resulting vision and road map.
6. Put the discovery into a form (or container) so it can be shared. It may be a piece of art, a play, a skit, a large visual mural, or a new version of a familiar song. Match the metaphor to the situation and show how it is key to getting others involved.

Eric Ovlen, vice president of organizational effectiveness at Meggitt Electronics, adds, "Because the leadership team didn't want to imply this would be an overnight change . . . we portrayed the [strategy] time line as an illustrated story map . . . reflecting from the past the best of who we were and moving into the future with technology that isn't even invented yet. We depicted the past as an old castle of grandeur and the future as a space age metropolis."

To capture input, employee representatives throughout the organization attended one of ten discovery sessions. "We wanted answers to questions like 'What do we all share and care about the most?' 'What's the vital spark that's sustained us?' 'What do we all see as the best of Endevco,'" Savage recalls. Added to the map were stories from the past and present—company beach parties, past presidents working side by side with employees, and supporting missions to Mars—as well as perceptions of the ideal future. "These stories told [leadership] how employees see themselves when they're at their best—a group of people that are loyal, have great technological know-how, are innovative, and committed to solving customers' problems with pride," he notes. Employees also told stories about their concerns, including rumors of massive layoffs, which reflected anxiety, misunderstanding, and misconceptions.

Several poignant stories from discovery sessions were told in a company-wide town hall meeting. "We openly wanted to build on the positive and dispel the negative . . . in a way where we, as leaders, shared our views and answered questions about both good and difficult stories. We weren't happy that inaccurate stories were circulating, but we were proud employees spoke out. They simply wanted to know we really cared about their future and that their workplace wasn't in harm's way," Savage says.

Ovlen adds, "To memorialize the process, we [posted] story maps in the central employee break area. Plus, we hung a giant banner of the road map, complete with call-outs that reinforced our essential strengths, our mission, and guiding principles to realizing our shared vision."

Engaging employees and leaders in the creation of a common story and road map for change can catalyze solidarity. Using metaphors can enable the free flow of story expression. The key is allowing both positive and difficult stories to be told, heard, and discussed by everyone as a means to accomplish the vision for change.

OVERCOMING RESISTANCE TO CHANGE

Old ways of doing business are significant barriers to change. In 2004, the leadership team for what was to become Cerium Laboratories faced this issue as it undertook a strategic decision with a major impact on all thirty employees of its department at AMD. "We had to answer a fundamental question, 'Do we want to continue as an internal arm of a bigger entity or do we want to be the whole body?'" says Lynette Ballast. For her, the issue was, "Could we see ourselves as a stand-alone operation without the support of a parent organization, actually generating and managing our own cash flow?"

Clayton Fullwood says, "To make the change the entire team had to [embrace] a new vision and shift from a captive service division of a larger company to a commercial market-facing enterprise." Operationally, Ballast points out, "We had to figure out how to do everything from invoicing to managing expenses differently. Everyone had to rise to the occasion."

Pivotal to the decision process was a department-wide, two-day visioning session. First, the department's leadership team shared stories going back twenty-five years. "We realized we'd survived and thrived during lots of change," Ballast remembers. "It also became clear this workplace was a big piece of our lives. We recalled positives and negatives—parties, layoffs, and discoveries. Then we realized, '*Wow*. We want to stay together!'" A story map describing where the group had been, what it was envisioning, the new corporate entity's purpose, and how to make it happen was created simultaneously.

"Initially, people were reluctant to embrace the change," Fullwood notes. "We used storytelling to reframe perceptions. Hearing personal stories [about] past changes [helped us realize] we were capable of making the right decisions and influencing future success," he adds.

Soon after, the department spun off on its own. The story map hangs in the company's main lobby. Half was left blank. "We have to shift out of old behavior to complete our story," Fullwood says, adding, "We plan to reflect our desire to merge values we have at home and at work. When this happens our mission statement will become real." To reinforce this, a recognition program, "Our Future Is Bright," features stories of great behavior. "People are selected when they demonstrate a value we aspire to create. Their photo—with them wearing sunglasses—including a short story of what they did, is posted in the employee break area," Ballast says.

Like Cerium Laboratories, Hewlett-Packard encouraged story sharing when it hit resistance after the approval of its merger with Compaq. "The Executive Leadership Team decided a new customer-facing strategy was needed company-wide. The merger was the catalyst," says Jim Arena. Resistance was visible. "The environment was filled with cynicism. The field sales force at Hewlett-Packard and Compaq had been tinkered with many times over the years. [This] 'customer sales initiative' was seen as another program of the month. The feeling in the field was, 'If you risk championing a new initiative before the merger dust settled you were risking your career,'" he adds.

While the initiative affected sales offices everywhere, the biggest forecast growth opportunities existed in the BRIC countries: Brazil, Russia, India, and China. "In focusing on BRIC, we knew we had to break the mold. We had to neutralize the phrase, 'the way we do things around here.' [We needed] a new story that started with 'the way we will be doing things around here is—,' " says Leslie J. Berkes, Ph.D., director, Organizational Effectiveness Center of Expertise, Workforce Development and Organizational Effectiveness. This was not an easy task. "Breaking the mold required shifting to a focus on growth. *Shift* became the operative word, with metaphors, images, and stories of a race car competitor *shifting* into higher gear," he notes, adding, "We also stressed ownership for the change. This was an opportunity [for] BRIC leaders to behave as CEOs for their own business, while operating in unison with each other as one great company."

To facilitate this shift, a three-month planning process took place in each country, culminating in a two-day meeting for the region's senior teams. "Participants shared customer stories about difficulties and scenario stories about future possibilities. Then, each country leadership group submitted prepared business cases for change. The intent was for the country to drive HP, not HP corporate driving the country," Berkes recalls. "Personalized shared stories helped make the new customer-facing strategy more real. Rather than being a corporate edict, shared stories increased everyone's commitment and acceptance of a truly positive and global change," he adds.

Ultimately, each country created its own future story. "Clearly articulating what you're moving *from* and what you're moving *to* is the new form of storytelling during corporate change. Real change never occurs unless old habits are dropped and people are willing to invest their discretionary energy in the new direction," Arena points out.

When strategic meetings like these occur, varied stories get told. "We knew grapevine stories would circulate faster than an executive leader's future story," Berkes says. "The meeting had to yield positive stories—every time you fail during a change effort you make the future possibility for change less likely. By having each country plan in advance and create a future story of a positive end state, we offset the impact of negative grapevine stories."

Resistance takes many shapes. After creating a shared vision, the OZ project team within Hewlett-Packard's IPG Business Unit stalled, triggered by repercussions of a sudden change in product strategy. "My project leaders and I had to quickly convey the risk of delays and the pay-off of success to team members," says Sandy Lieske. They built on the *Wizard of Oz* metaphor using project vernacular. "Dorothy's ruby red slippers symbolized going home to the vision; the dog Toto became a change agent; and poppies, a metaphor for getting side-tracked from the project's purpose. In effect, imagery and words about the project were translated into a *living* vision," Duran says.

"One engineer rewrote the song *If I Only Had a Brain* to reflect real problems team members were facing," Lieske says. "Another engineer presented a short skit idea using the *Wizard of Oz* metaphor. [After] the project leadership team and I read [it], it became clear a novel presentation could engage [everyone]. We quickly turned the skit into a thirty-minute scripted play, cast leadership in key roles, and put on a performance in a large hotel ballroom that is still talked about today," she adds.

"The workforce was in awe. They watched leaders who'd upset the status quo now in a totally unexpected role," Duran recalls. "Everyone saw leadership having fun. They also saw how serious we were during the post-performance project presentation and question-and-answer session," adds Lieske. "Letting them see you as human is a way to gain respect and cooperation. Egos got put aside and the truth of what had to occur moved in. . . . The story metaphor made it easier for us to get along, for objections to be discussed, and for us to keep energy focused on real project issues," she notes. Afterwards, story metaphor language was integrated into project e-mail messages, presentations, and status reports.

The most difficult part of change is addressing the uncertainty and resistance that it brings forth. Purposefully sharing personal stories and those from customers, in addition to crafting and creatively visualizing stories about the future, can reframe people's perceptions, overcome grapevine stories, and provide the impetus for positive movement.

RESPECTING HERITAGE WHILE MOVING FORWARD

Change does not occur independent of an organization's history. As Lynette Ballast learned at Cerium Laboratories, "To get where we wanted to be, we had to keep recognizing we'd made it through change in the past. [Our past stories] reminded us we can get through anything."

FivePoint is also mindful of its history. After Erik Shaw's airplane story struck home, employees and Board members began to discuss altering the organization's name. "The management team and Board members shared stories of the past, explored why the credit union was in business, and who they were, individually and collectively," recalls Kristen Bellanger. She continues, "With outside help, we realized a new name that tied us to our history, values, and mission, including the Texaco colors and five-pointed star logo, could be a competitive advantage." The outcome? On September 7, 2004, Texaco Community Federal Credit Union became FivePoint Federal Credit Union.

"To announce the change internally, a five-week campaign was launched honoring the stories and values of the Texaco heritage, culminating with a premiere event in a local movie theater. All executives were dressed in formal attire. Erik gave a presentation that included his airplane story and the rationale for change. Employees watched a movie honoring the past and the future story complete with the new name; each received the movie, a *Reasons for Change* booklet, logo team shirt, and other items featuring the new name," says Bellanger, adding, "To stress our history, we placed a history wall in our stores, graphically telling the story of the credit union, its heritage, and its role as a community member since 1935."

Personal stories from the past and stories about an organization's history cannot be ignored. They provide the grounding people need to accept significant changes.

HAPPY ENDINGS (SERIOUSLY)

Stories can confirm the need for change and bring the future alive. "[At Cerium Laboratories], storytelling helped [us] get clear about how to move forward together," concludes Lynette Ballast. Clayton Fullwood says, "We were driven by a need to communicate about our past and our future—to get everyone to understand why we had to change. The communication came out as stories, giving everybody the chance to create what we've become and be part of the organization's future." In its first quarter as an independent business entity, Cerium achieved profitability and anticipates additional head count while other AMD departments shrank in size or merged to foster organizational growth.

Communication and other cultural factors also improved at Endevco. "A culture assessment was conducted before and six months after announcing the organization's new strategy [for high growth and acquisition]. Communicating, understanding strategic plans, and trusting leadership scores shifted into the positive by double-digit measures. The story discovery process was very instrumental in engaging employees and addressing misconceptions that led to some low [scores]," Eric Ovlen reports. "Through [story sharing], we became an even more unified community, deeply committed to our customers and our future, while remaining proud of our heritage," he concludes. According to David Savage, "I was skeptical of the story map process at first, but it enabled us to have open conversations about the more difficult aspects of the road ahead."

Open communications, trust, and measurable project outcomes characterize results achieved through stories at Hewlett-Packard's IPG Business Unit. "With OZ, we've seen a 619 percent increase in delivery efficiency over five years [through summer 2005]. Eventually we were able to produce ten to twelve new products per year, far beyond initial projections of a new product every six months. By the third release, we'd surpassed our overall expectations for common base firmware—we delivered on this business strategy," Sandy Lieske says, adding, "The change levers for these results were the metaphor and skit. The whole staff engaged in telling a common story." Pat Duran comments, "Seeing conceptual ideas about change take tangible form [through story] makes a project vision come alive. It gave us something bigger to rally around and believe in." Lieske adds, "When people saw leaders vulnerable on stage, it made us approachable. They started to talk openly about how to create success and get [rid of] negative behavior. It shaped me as a leader."

Measurable bottom-line outcomes are also visible at FivePoint Federal Credit Union as it celebrates its seventieth year and builds its fifth retail outlet. "Our 5 percent growth in membership in 2005 exceeds the national average; we're the largest credit union in the area we serve. We made it clear through old and new stories we weren't abandoning our Texaco heritage—we're proud of it. What we got in return was a motivated family of employees that made these results possible," Erik Shaw says.

As at FivePoint, growth is evident at Hewlett-Packard. Jim Arena and Leslie J. Berkes note, "All countries made great strides with the merger and new customer-facing strategy. BRIC doubled and tripled growth and sales increases are greater than other markets." For Arena, "The story process became self-perpetuating and fueled the lift we needed for change. I don't know another technique that could've worked." Adds Berkes, "What was very noticeable was the energy created by stories. Their exchange conveyed a common shared fate. Stories made the BRIC leaders' plans real. What was more important, they helped personalize the need for change deep down into the company."

MAKING CHANGE WORK FOR YOU

Stories—whether provided orally, in illustrations, or acted out—make it easier to address significant change. They help leaders get input, obtain results, and minimize resistance. To achieve similar outcomes, consider these ideas:

- Create the vision. Craft future stories and use illustrated story maps to bring the change to life and to encourage others to join in. Employ stories as metaphors for challenges and benefits.
- Make a positive beginning. Share stories to uncover what the organization really is, what it specifically must become, and to affirm what will not change. Evoke stories to understand what people value.
- Step off the edge into the future. Use stories to communicate the need for change and let go of limiting identity perceptions. Tell past success stories as proof the organization is capable of changing.
- Shift resistance and accelerate change. Find stories that turn abstract conceptual ideas into images that clarify purpose, inspire shared meaning, and promote trust and engagement. Challenge grapevine stories with stories of current successes.
- Break through to new perceptions. Use stories to provoke a new paradigm, open up new perceptions about work, and sustain the change. The proverbial "We've tried that before and it doesn't work" can become "Once upon a time. . . ."
- Be willing to be human. Telling authentic stories or acting them out can strengthen respect and cooperation, inspire courage and fresh insights, and affirm employees' emotional connections to the organization.

If you use stories in these ways, you, too, can help your organization successfully navigate any change journey.

Special Thanks

I appreciate the referrals, insights, and pearls of wisdom provided by Kevin M. Dulle, director of special projects at NewGround, and Cynthia Scott, founder of Changeworks Global, LLC. I am also grateful to Janet Schatzman, strategic illustrator and co-founder of Parnassus Consulting, LLC, for her inspiring ability to translate everyday organizational stories into visual maps for change as demonstrated in the examples outlined in this chapter.

PART TWO

How Organizations Are Using Stories Strategically

To survive in the long term and deal effectively with the uncertainty of a changing world and marketplace, organizations need to focus on strategic matters in addition to day-to-day operations. Sometimes, significant challenges occur despite the best efforts of leaders. How to address these challenges through stories and storytelling is the subject of Chapter Eight, "The Sky Is Falling: When Difficult Times Call for a New Story," by Michael J. Margolis. It covers leading through new stories, understanding what matters most, finding the stories to stand on, shifting public opinion, and forging a new culture.

Staying grounded in what matters—in good times and in bad—is the focus of Chapter Nine, "Why Are We Here? Stories That Define Us," by Evelyn Clark. Topics include the way founding stories set the stage for an organization, plus leaving a lasting legacy, capturing history and bringing it alive, and embodying stories. While an organization's values and history communicated through stories can inform present-day decisions and future actions, Madelyn Blair, Ph.D., brings forward the need to use stories to focus and align everyone around the organization's core strategy in Chapter Ten, "I Can See Clearly Now:

Bringing Strategy Alive Through Stories." It demonstrates how stories give birth to strategy, how to search for stories to inform strategy, and how stories can translate strategy into reality.

Rounding out the strategic discussion on story use is its application to marketing-related subjects. Chapter Eleven, "The Fog Is Lifting: Seeing Connections to Marketing and Marketing Research Through Stories," by Steven N. Silverman, Ph.D., and Susan J. Moore, reviews how organizations are grounding marketing and market research in time-honored stories, how observation spurs stories, the use of stories to communicate market research, and how stories are changing how marketing researchers report findings. Themes raised in this chapter are reinforced in Chapter Twelve: "What's in a Name? How Stories Power Enduring Brands," by Ashraf Ramzy, M.A., and Alicia Korten. This chapter covers what brings organizations to story, the positioning challenges that story can address, and three key branding questions: Where do we find our story? What is our story? And how do we tell our story?

CHAPTER EIGHT

The Sky Is Falling
When Difficult Times Call for
a New Story

Michael J. Margolis

—⁓— " Statements from management are, by definition, viewed with suspicion. To get past clichés and dig out the real stuff, you need to find the right stories," reports Chris Quin, general manager of Gen-i (a subsidiary of Telecom New Zealand), who reached this insight while overseeing a company-wide merger. "By deliberately seeking and uncovering [stories] you discover the best of who you've been. With this knowledge [you] can more confidently build the future," he notes.

The ability to craft purposeful stories can lead people out of difficult times. For the global creative firm Saatchi & Saatchi, storytelling became the engine of change after several business missteps in the early 1990s. Missteps also challenged the National Aeronautics and Space Administration (NASA). Following the *Columbia* Space Shuttle disaster and introduction of new mission priorities, NASA is embracing stories. City Year, Inc., a citizen service corps, welcomed stories shortly after its inception and again years later to help inspire the reversal of drastic federal budget cuts. Similar in motivation, oneVillage Foundation uses stories to inform its global economic development and technology efforts.

LEADING THROUGH NEW STORIES

Stories help leaders address tough issues. In the 1990s, Saatchi & Saatchi fell on hard times. "Unfortunate events led to removing the founding brothers, Maurice and Charles Saatchi. [The organization] was essentially orphaned by [them]. [They left] behind seven thousand employees. Several mergers and downsizings followed. The company was bruised, battered, and close to demoralized," says Bob Isherwood, worldwide creative director.

Kevin Roberts, CEO worldwide, inherited this situation in 1997. "Less than a week in, I [met] with two hundred top leaders. For three hours, I shared a handful of heroic stories about my twenty-five years' experience as a customer of the company. Then I [talked about] ten important things for me and the company in the coming year. None of it was about 'the numbers.' It was all about ourselves—what we had to do," he says. The presentation was successful. Roberts's stories shone a light forward for a company that had lost its way.

"We will not re-engineer ourselves to glory," Roberts assured battle-weary colleagues. Isherwood adds, "Roberts returned responsibility to each [Saatchi office]. He allowed senior partners to become shareholders over a multi-year period." To accomplish this, Roberts visited Saatchi's top forty offices within six months. Roberts notes, "There was lots of sharing—me talking and listening—and letting people ask me questions. No PowerPoint decks. No budget meetings. No [re-structuring] plans. I focused on three 'I' words—Imagination, Inspiration, Intuition—to inspire great people to do great work."

Why behave this way? "Change requires an instigator," explains Roberts. "You need a charismatic leader who believes in telling [and] sharing stories. This needs to come from the very top down, or it won't fly." He adds, "Effective communication is not one-dimensional but driven by dialogue. We didn't go into 'broadcast the message' mode. [We] chose to be inclusive—encouraging sustained conversations across the company." This distinction reinforces why a shift in leadership thinking is required before leaders can change the conversation.

A similar shift is under way at NASA's Goddard Space Flight Center through its Leadership Alchemy Program for midcareer employees. "We started the [program to] create 'ambassadors of positive change' who could respond to dynamic times and what's happening in the larger environment. We consciously designed storytelling into the program [through] conversations, learning experiences, and tools to deal with challenges that manifest in the workplace," explains Gail Williams, program manager.

Both storytelling—and story-listening—skills were reinforced. Kim Toufectis, program supervisor and mentor and a supervisor in the Facilities Planning Office, shares a story he tells to justify replacing outdated buildings built in the 1960s; one complex is valued at $850 million. "It's hard to carve away funding since it's cheaper to fix than to replace. I ask people whether they still drive the car they bought [when] they began their first permanent job . . . [because] we have to make a choice: Do we maintain [it]? You can put a new engine in, put a new bumper on, but eventually it makes sense to make a big change," he points out.

Rich Rogers, program graduate and mentor, uses story listening to surface key points during safety training. "Don't be afraid to mine people's wisdom—the stories are there," explains Rogers, a pilot and aviation safety officer. "I divide the class into [small] groups and ask people to tell each other a story about a time they saw exceptional examples of aviation safety in action. Not only do participants learn faster, but the stories create a level of trust that connects people."

In times of flux, organizations depend on leaders to bring forth the right stories to orient and guide people. Whether these stories are personal in nature, evoked from others, or about an organization's past, present, or future, what matters is the care and deliberation given to their selection and the time devoted to eliciting them.

UNDERSTANDING WHAT MATTERS MOST

Imagine the employee concerns when two companies merge. "We're going to be slower. We're going to lose customers. Bureaucracy is going to grow. We'll lose our identity. The bigger company is going to squash us," says Brian Smith, Gen-i's operations manager of field force. He adds, "We discovered that staff from Advanced Telecom Solutions, the acquiring agent, equally held its share of reservations. It was a fast and entrepreneurial culture that feared loss of status as it assumed the Gen-i brand name."

Unaddressed concerns can slow change and make it less effective. "People's stories define their truth. To understand culture, you must listen to the stories being told," explains Chris Quin. So what did the organizations do? "With twenty years' combined history, the new Gen-i needed to preserve institutional memory while forging a new path. To ensure continued performance we crafted a formal process to retain best practices of both companies and overcome negative merger tendencies."

"[Our] assignment was to create a 'best-of-the-best' merger," reports Smith, one of twenty-six people on the "Fusion" advisory team, which was composed of sales, operations, and engineering staff from both organizations. And Quin explains, "We didn't have all the answers so we went looking for them. The 'Fusion' team conducted many interviews, asking lots of descriptive questions about what people liked and cherished: 'Recount your best sales experience.' 'Describe the time you worked hardest.' 'What is your favorite part of your job?' And they listened." By inviting stories, Gen-i uncovered vital human elements that shaped its new culture.

Gen-i connected to stories that defined the context within which it operates. So has oneVillage Foundation. Founded by Joy Tang in 2003, this international nonprofit organization promotes a holistic community-development model for using information and communication technology (ICT) for economic advancement. "Technology development can take many forms, from computer skills training to sustainable farming and waste management. Gathering and sharing stories helps us understand the unique context of people's lives and how to introduce technology that will most benefit a community's evolution and its members' expressed desires," she explains.

Storytelling is core to oneVillage's model. "Many communities in Africa and Asia face great adversity and crisis—a complex story to unpack. Severe economic pressures and the ravages of AIDS increasingly threaten local cultures. Traditional modes of knowledge transfer and decision making between generations are breaking down. [Given] these sensitivities, oneVillage uses community-driven storytelling as a means of inclusion, inviting all community members to engage in defining their future," Tang notes.

However, story*telling* is only half of what unites people around a common goal. "Imagine the benefit to stories if we revitalized our ability to listen," says Tang, adding, "We embrace 'Radiant Listening' as taught by Dr. Katy Ha, California Hawaii Institute. Much of digging out important stories is making people feel at ease. Radiant Listening fully supports and acknowledges another's existence. When people feel this, they're willing to share stories from the deepest level." How does the process work? "It's facilitated in a circle, which strengthens the intent for listening. You ask for permission to talk. For listeners, no response is required and interruption or suggestive body language is discouraged."

When faced with unfamiliar circumstances, leaders deepen their understanding by listening to stories from multiple stakeholders. Inside these stories lives a wealth of data regarding people's motivations, fears, and hopes. Anytime worlds collide, stories can provide building blocks for strengthening trust and connectivity that collaboration demands.

FINDING THE STORIES TO STAND ON

Stories can strengthen an organization's purpose, thus guiding individual behavior when circumstances challenge it. "We stumbled across the power of stories while hosting our first training programs [in 1988]," says Alan Khazei, City Year co-founder and CEO. "We introduced two concepts—one through the Native American parable 'moccasins' ('One does not *know* unless one has walked in the shoes of another'); the second through Robert Kennedy's 'ripples' quote—an inspirational statement about how one person's actions can create a ripple that travels far," he explains.

"These concepts quickly appeared in conversations, as in 'This is a moccasins moment.' They're an effective tool for defusing conflict," says Stephanie Wu, senior vice president of people and programs. For example, "Two City Year corps members, with different life experiences, were in a heated argument. I separated them [and] asked each to reflect on the moccasin quote and what upset them. They each articulated back to the other what they'd heard. Sharing their views—and feeling recognized—went a long way toward resolving the situation," she notes.

As City Year's program expanded, new challenges emerged, necessitating a coherent set of organizational values that included both concepts. "We knew what we stood for—people of all backgrounds uniting on the common ground of service—but we hadn't formalized it. Stories became a tool for bringing everyone together," Michael Brown, City Year co-founder and president, notes.

For its fifteenth anniversary and its international expansion, City Year published a booklet called *Founding Stories*—twenty-one universal stories and quotations from around the world. "These stories found us; we didn't find them. If you're receptive to ideas that are right for you, they'll come," says Khazei. "We call [them] *Founding Stories* because they link to [our] origins and serve as a foundation for our work forward, representing our collective civic values [and civic engagement strategy]," Brown adds.

One parable, "The Traveler," on page 117, delivers the message that if you expect the best from people, you will tend to find the best in people. Similarly, it's disastrous to allow negative experiences to taint future expectations, especially in relation to people you have never met.

How are founding stories used? "We train on [them], largely through skits. We ask corps members and staff to act out stories and tell them through their own voice. We also expect people to reference and apply [them] in their daily efforts," Khazei says.

Founding stories are also integral to addressing organizational purpose at Saatchi & Saatchi. "Corporate stories have to center around the spirit of the company, not people and personalities. The dream and the spirit are what count. That's why people come to work. Stories need to connect the past, present, and future and link to a shared dream. Storytelling is about creating dreams, giving people what they never dreamt possible," Kevin Roberts explains.

The Saatchi dream is based on "nothing is impossible"—a motto coined in 1976 by the founding Saatchi brothers. "In that statement lies the immutable spirit of the company," explains Bob Isherwood. "You'll find those three words written in concrete on the front doorstep [of] our Charlotte Street office in London, once our world headquarters. In every office, the motto's prominently displayed," he notes. The motto, which aided the company's turnaround, does not stand alone. "Saatchi has dozens of achievement stories backing [it] up. Saatchi was the first creative agency in East Berlin after the fall of the wall. Saatchi put Margaret Thatcher and the Conservative Party on the map. An extreme example is when a Saatchi account director once drank his own urine to win a client," Roberts recalls. And Isherwood adds, "We've [made the transition] from a traditional ad agency to an ideas company. We believe ideas are the currency of the future. This attitude helps generate inspirational stories that feed our spirit."

Along with founding stories, Saatchi reinforces its purpose through employees' personal identity stories. "Every three months, [we] gather twenty employees from around the globe, who've never met or worked together. The full-day gathering begins with a session focused on inspiration. Ten people share a story about how they were inspired by

THE TRAVELER: A WEST AFRICAN FOLK TALE
Contributed by City Year

There was once an elderly and wise gentleman who lived in a village. He would often spend his days sitting in the shade of a big tree in the center of the village, reading books and talking to passers-by. One day, a traveler came upon his village and stopped and said, "Old man, I have been traveling across the countryside, and I have seen many things and met many people. Can you tell me what kind of people I will find in your village?"

The elderly gentleman looked up at him and replied, "Certainly I can, but first tell me what kind of people you have found on your travels."

The traveler scowled and said, "Old man, I have met people who cheat, steal, and aren't kind to strangers, and people who don't look out for one another."

The elderly gentleman looked up, and, with a faint look of sadness in his eyes, said, "Oh my friend, those are the people you will find in my village." The traveler kicked the dirt under his feet, scoffed, and marched off. . . .

By and by, as the elderly gentleman continued to enjoy his day, another traveler came walking through the village. Once again, the traveler stopped and asked, "Please, kind sir, I have been traveling across the countryside, and I have seen many things and met many people. Can you tell me what kind of people I will find in your village?" The elderly gentleman said, "Certainly I can, but first tell me what kind of people you have found in your travels."

The traveler replied, "I have found people who are kind and welcoming of strangers, people who care for one another, and people who love. These are the people I have met in my travels."

The elderly gentlemen looked up, and, with the faintest smile in his eyes, said, "My friend, those are the people you will find in my village."

Adapted from M. Brown and A. Khazei, "The Traveler," in *Founding Stories*. Boston: City Year, July 2004, pp. 47–49.

a colleague or work event. The [other] ten share a story about when they inspired somebody at work, and what that entailed," Roberts says. These framing questions evoke people's personal purpose, the topic of the afternoon session, thus ensuring Saatchi's core story remains relevant.

> ### FRAMING QUESTIONS TO EVOKE
> ### STORIES ABOUT PERSONAL PURPOSE
> *Contributed by Kevin Roberts*
>
> - When are you at your best?
> - What do you stand for?
> - Tell us about a song that describes your energizing principle and spirit.
> - Tell us a story about your life theme.
> - Tell us a story about where you want to be in five years.
> - Tell us a story about [something] you will never do.

People's story responses also strengthen relationships. "*Storyteller* is the wrong vocabulary—telling isn't sharing. We need a story-sharing approach. The reason we share stories is [that] individuals immediately put themselves in the story. If you choose the right story, they see in a nonthreatening, nonpolitical, nonhierarchical way how their roles relate to those of others, so you get integration inside the business. [Sharing] stories is a good way to make relationships work without being prescriptive," Roberts emphasizes.

Like Saatchi & Saatchi, City Year links to corps members' personal stories. "We ask our people to tell their story: 'Tell us about yourself and where you came from. Tell us your favorite day and why.' People have powerful stories in them," Brown notes. "From this, we find common bonds within the shared narrative arc and shared themes within the life stories. The arcs of personal transformation and civic transformation are intertwined," he adds.

Every organization needs to know where it came from to know where it is going. Founding stories continuously celebrate an organization's driving ethos and character. Along with personal identity stories from staff, they serve as a wellspring of both meaning and purpose, ultimately propelling the organization forward.

SHIFTING PUBLIC OPINION

When forging into new geographic regions, oneVillage often faces suspicion. "People feel dependent on development agencies for health, education, and economic funding that local government may not provide. [At the same time] trust is low because of the impact previous 'development strategies' have had on the community's way of life," Joy Tang says. How does oneVillage approach this situation? Jeffrey Buderer, program development manager, explains, "We're trying to frame a new story and model of *development* that doesn't impose Western views and biases. Storytelling's an important factor in restoring trust. By encouraging story exchanges between individuals and community stakeholders, people find creativity within themselves, which allows practical applications to emerge. It's best captured by the expression, 'Don't come help us, come to create something with us.'"

How do these stories arise? Tang says, "[In] Ghana, we were invited to participate in a town hall meeting that included tribal elders, teachers, students, farmers, technologists, and other village representatives. We asked, 'What are your aspirations for life?' Stories were shared— by a seamstress, then a blacksmith, an elder, several others, and finally me—as a means to understanding the conditions, concerns, and desires we respectively face in our living environment." These stories brought forward possibility. "Our stories reiterated converging interests and reaffirmed our desire to work together. Simply with the intent to find 'core issues,' we translated our initial intuitions into a methodology for economic development. [While] no promises were made, a technology skills training approach was organically defined by the words, agreements, acceptance, and shared experience identified in the stories," she explains.

Like oneVillage, City Year also needed to shift public opinion. "On June 6, 2003, we awoke to shocking news. The federal funding allocation for AmeriCorps, which contributes 30 percent to City Year's annual budget, was going to be cut significantly, resulting in an 80 percent decrease in AmeriCorps members nationwide. Without warning, we faced a fiscal crisis," Michael Brown reports. "Our reaction was shock, dismay, and deep concern, quickly followed by resolve and determination. The situation emerged because of bureaucratic delays and poor financial forecasts. No one said, 'AmeriCorps is bad. We have to eliminate the program.' In fact, following September 11, 2001, there was a huge surge in the desire to serve," he recalls. The implications?

Alan Khazei says, "Fifteen years of work [was] at stake. City Year served as a model for AmeriCorps, which has involved more than 400,000 Americans. The entire infrastructure that was built would collapse. National service would become a footnote of history, something America tried in the 1990s but died away."

"When the crisis hit, we realized people didn't know the story of AmeriCorps. We had faith that if people knew what was happening, they'd respond. Our goal was to tell the story about the value of AmeriCorps, the difference it was making, and what would happen if [federal] funding wasn't restored," explains AnnMaura Connolly, senior vice president for public policy and special initiatives. The action had to be dramatic. "We worked with other AmeriCorps programs to develop a strategy built around 'one hundred hours' of 'round-the-clock citizen testimony.' We quickly got a message out: Come and tell your story: How is AmeriCorps affecting your life and community and what would happen if it went away?" she adds.

"It turned into a scene out of the movie *Mr. Smith Goes to Washington.* [In four days], 650 citizens from 48 states—corps members, corporate CEOs, community leaders, mayors, and more than fifty congressional members—testified," Khazei recalls. Connolly explains, "Letters to Capitol Hill wouldn't have penetrated like this. These compelling stories helped decision makers understand what was at stake and inspired bipartisan support." While full funding was not replaced immediately, a hundred newspaper editorials were published and a thousand nonprofit organizations, two hundred college presidents, and forty-four governors signed a collective statement of support.

Every story has many public sides. Leaders must learn to uncover the untold story at the heart of their work and frame messages into appropriate forms that resonate with diverse audiences.

FORGING A NEW CULTURE

Significant unexpected events often provide impetus for major cultural shifts. "We [at NASA] were shocked when it happened again," admits Gail Williams, recounting the February 2003 *Columbia* Space Shuttle tragedy that followed the January 1986 *Challenger* Space Shuttle disaster. "The second accident was a wake-up call. Key studies underscored our culture had as much to do with the accident as the engineering. The need for effective upward communication and 'naming the elephant in the room' were emphasized in [post-disaster assessments]," she adds.

To create a culture focused on open and responsive communication, NASA has people tie personal stories to key business issues in its Leadership Alchemy Program. "[The program] was designed to match competencies of a NASA report stating, 'We need forward-thinking leaders,'" comments Kanu Kogod, program designer and facilitator. "[We] believe that everyone can and should be a leader. Leadership is more than 'what you need to know' and 'what you need to do.' We use stories to help people [connect] with who they really are and how they value their role at NASA Goddard," she notes. Williams adds, "Most powerful leaders are authentic. They aren't afraid of [demonstrating] vulnerability. Being able to present a collection of distinctive experiences speaks to depth of character. You can only really do this by sharing your stories. The program designs conversations that bring key issues to the surface, teaching participants greater awareness of how the stories they tell affect communications, decision making, and their relations to others."

Recognizing that everyone is a leader during its merger, Gen-i involved all 1,400 employees in crafting its new culture after articulating a vision statement. "We defined *irresistible leadership, passionate people,* and *raving fans* as the organizing principles that defined the new Gen-i," Brian Smith says. These principles grounded a story-based visioning process where staff across the merged organizations interviewed each other using structured questions.

Selecting story prompts is critically important. "We paid attention to what questions we asked," Chris Quin notes. "Posing a question to a system in turn influences the system to respond. We realized the questions are therefore a fateful choice," he explains. What did Gen-i learn from stories that were told? "We discovered that 'hero stories' in the culture were about sacrifice—not surprising for the information technology industry. These [stories] consciously helped the merged company evolve from the hero culture of firefighter to a hero culture of firelighter. In Gen-i's case, finding the right stories made all the difference."

Inside organizations, culture serves as the invisible fabric that informs visible artifacts and unspoken thoughts. Culture change can be motivated by having people tell stories attached to the essence of their being and from their life and work experiences that symbolize how business is done.

USING STORIES TO DEFINE CULTURE
Contributed by Gen-i

1. Tell me about your beginnings with the company. When did you join the organization and in what capacity? What were your most positive impressions when you first joined the organization? What initially attracted you to the company?
2. Tell me about a peak experience or high point in your professional life with the company—a time when you felt most alive, most engaged, and really proud of yourself and your work. What was happening? What made it a high point for you?
3. Tell me about a time when you experienced an individual who demonstrated leadership you felt was irresistible, whether it was a manager, a colleague, a friend, or someone else. Describe the situation: What made it irresistible? Who was involved? What did you learn from this situation about leadership? How did that experience change your own leadership style?
4. Describe to me the most passionate person you've ever worked with in the company—someone who was fun to work with, who encouraged and inspired others to contribute in similar ways. What made working with this person so engaging? How did this person work with those around them, including team, customers, and peers? How would you describe this person's approach to working with others? To what do you attribute this person's attitude? How did this person affect you and your contribution to the project?
5. There are times when customers, suppliers, and partners have been "raving fans" of the company. Write a testimonial as if you were one of these people, on the heels of one of their most ecstatic experiences. What did they say? To whom? What did the company do to make them talk like this? What triggered the switch from customer to fan? What did we do to keep them a "raving fan"?

THE RESULTS

Stories play a role in helping organizations navigate and overcome difficult times. But do they provide business results?

"Story [is] the conscious way we run our business," Kevin Roberts says. "We believe in mankind and try to put people first. We may not have the highest performing margins, nor be the most effective in managing headcount. We make people decisions first because it's a people business and we tell people that," he adds. "We moved from a company run by accountants into a company driven by the work," echoes Bob Isherwood. "Success for Saatchi & Saatchi is measured by sustained sales growth and by the top honors our creative campaigns receive from the advertising industry," says Roberts.

For Gen-i, story use helped build the bottom line. "The merger translated into a 10 percent increase in revenues and 30 percent growth in profits. This is unheard of in the typical corporate merger. We only lost one major account during the transition; we gained two new [accounts]. Staff turnover remained stable during our realignment and remains below the annual industry average of 15 to 18 percent. Our story-driven 'Fusion' process was the key to success," Chris Quin reports.

For oneVillage Foundation, story helped secure new funds in places like Nigeria and Ghana. "After several years of effort in Ghana, we raised money for AIDS treatment and education programs [through] Accenture UK, United Through Sport, ProLink, the Ghana Football Association, and two leading football teams in Ghana. Additional funding has been secured for the Jukwa community to purchase a new palm oil processing plant and technology. None of these results would've happened if we hadn't had tools of storytelling to engage in the dialogue and planning process," says Joy Tang.

Continued funding for AmeriCorps and City Year was also assisted by stories. "The personal dramatic stories [that were] told didn't immediately reverse the cuts but emergency legislation reduced proposed cuts from 80 percent fewer AmeriCorps members down to 55 percent," AnnMaura Connolly explains. "The real impact of citizens' testimonies were felt the following budget cycle, when AmeriCorps received its largest appropriation on record: a 60 percent increase of $166 million," Alan Khazei recalls. "Citizens telling their stories can lead to policy change. Decision makers understand and connect to their [organization's] message in a more powerful way," Connolly points out. The citizen testimony continues as an annual ritual on

Capitol Hill, bringing together a diverse group of champions to share their stories and reinforce a growing culture of civic engagement. For Michael Brown, "[The] testimony reinforced my belief in the power of storytelling to bring people together."

Codifying founding stories allows City Year to define and measure its social impact. "Almost every meeting begins with an open call asking for a 'ripple': a courageous act or statement. Participants share stories of how they or someone they witnessed embodied this value through their actions," Khazei says. Stephanie Wu provides another example: "The 'starfish' story helps us gather data for research and evaluation. Corps members report daily on a 'starfish moment'—the difference they've made in the life of a child or community member. These daily rituals, called 'civic power tools,' are a means for personal and civic transformation."

At NASA, stories continue their cultural influence. "Participants must design and implement a capstone action-learning project related to teaching and using storytelling tools. For example, one team facilitated conversations between two [internal] organizations with a contentious relationship. Using stories led to renewed partnership: The service-providing organization better understood its customer's needs and the customer felt heard," explains Gail Williams. Adds Rich Rogers, "Two-thirds into my career, the program regenerated my juices. It gave me hope and encouragement, motivating me to work better as painful reductions in staff and resources occur."

The Leadership Alchemy Program, in its fifth year, "is so successful [it's now] an inherent part of Goddard's leadership development opportunities. At graduation, we encourage a 'rite of passage' where participants share lessons-learned stories. They're awe-inspiring. Some audience members are so moved they decide right there to apply for the program," says Williams.

CONSIDER THESE APPROACHES

What can you do when faced with major challenge? How might you reframe the conversation? Consider some of the following story approaches:

- As a leader, share stories that invite people to personally connect with you. Also tell stories that help people locate themselves in transitional times.

- Listen for and acknowledge employee stories that speak to the emotions of fear, loss, and pain associated with change.

- Allow staff to explore and contribute their personal stories as part of addressing the difficult issue or afterwards to reinforce their link to the organization.

- Showcase stories that remind people of what matters most. Determine which are worth preserving and celebrating. These may be personal in nature or founding stories.

- Identify those stories that can inspire and guide the organization forward and strengthen the bonds between memory, dreams, and reality.

- Define core values, guiding principles, and related behaviors. Then promote stories showing these ideals in action.

- Determine how to institutionalize stories as part of the organization's culture.

Experiment with these approaches and you will discover that stories are living organisms worthy of respect, sensitivity, and careful attention. Embrace storytelling authentically and you will unleash an unbridled creative spirit that can face down many intractable challenges.

Special Thanks

Many thanks to Stephanie Jowers for her patient and unflinching support; to Nusa Maal, president of SenseSmart, for helping me to visualize this complex chapter; to Millie Jackson, Ph.D., of Grand Valley State University for her referral to oneVillage; and to story consultants Seth Kahan, principal, Performance Development Group, Inc., and Mary-Alice Arthur, principal, SOAR, for graciously sharing their respective story success with NASA and Gen-i.

CHAPTER NINE

Why Are We Here?

Stories That Define Us

Evelyn Clark

"As new people enter an organization, it's important to ground them in its mission and values. Sharing organizational history is the way to do that," says Mike Lassiter, vice president of media & external relations at Kaiser Permanente. "You also need to share history in a way that resonates with current employees. Stories are the most effective tool for connecting the present with the past to lead people into the future."

Organizations like Kaiser Permanente use stories to share their founding, history, core values, purpose, and enduring practices. Since its inception, World Vision U.S. has attracted supporters with the story of a little girl abused and disowned for accepting an unacceptable belief. The Society for the Protection and Care of Children (SPCC) of Rochester, New York, sustains its mission through the story of another abused little girl who inspired its formation. The 3,600-member National Speakers Association (NSA) cherishes stories about its founder, the late Cavett Robert. And retiring executives are the force behind the Leadership Legacy initiative at the U.S. Environmental Protection Agency (EPA), which is documenting their stories.

FOUNDING STORIES SET THE STAGE

"Started in 1950 by Dr. Bob Pierce, World Vision's 22,000 employees focus on disaster relief and long-term community development in over one hundred countries," notes Marilee Pierce Dunker, Dr. Pierce's daughter and child sponsorship advocate for the organization. "We're the 'first in and last out' when disasters occur," says Karen Kartes, communications manager. "Because of an interaction Dr. Pierce had in 1948 in China with a young girl named White Jade, the organization was founded on child sponsorship and supporting those living in extreme poverty," notes Dunker. A synopsis of Dr. Pierce's encounter as communicated by his daughter is on page 128.

"We have every letter Dad wrote during his mission trips. He never mentions this experience," says Dunker. "However, he often shared the story in public presentations along with the films he produced to challenge people to respond to the plight of orphans and refugees during the Korean War. It became part of World Vision's oral history. The earliest written reference we have is in a 1964 book, *Orphans of the Orient,*" she notes. "We share the story in new employee orientation and it's on our intranet and extranet sites. The story is also referenced in child sponsorship presentations at churches and Christian concerts," Kartes adds.

The tale of another little girl, Mary Ellen, on page 129, sparked the creation of SPCC, an agency focused on child abuse, neglect, and domestic violence. "SPCC was the first child protective services organization in New York state, and the first foster care agency, too," says Kelly Reed, president and CEO of SPCC of Rochester, New York.

"We tell Mary Ellen's story in all our presentations. New employees, volunteers, student interns, and Board members hear it in their orientation," Reed notes. "We reference it in annual reports, grant proposals, and funding requests. It's part of our heritage," adds Trina Laughlin, LCSW-R, a clinical supervisor in the family violence program. "We have Mary Ellen's picture from the day she was rescued—her dress is tattered and her legs are scarred by the scissors at her feet—and a photo the day she came to live in Rochester, wearing a beautiful dress and a smile. Reproductions hang in our boardroom to remind us of obstacles she overcame and the wonderful life she built for herself—her hopefulness runs deep in SPCC," Reed says.

SPCC's founding story kept it true to its mission. "Government agencies across the United States in the 1960s assumed responsibility

WHITE JADE

Contributed by Marilee Pierce Dunker

An American evangelist visiting China, Dr. Bob Pierce, delivered the gospel message at a school, after which a number of girls answered the altar call and accepted Christ. The following day, the mission school's director, Tena Hoelkeboer, introduced Dr. Pierce to a young girl named White Jade. Hoelkeboer explained that White Jade had been beaten after going home and telling her parents that she had been converted by Dr. Pierce's message. Her parents then disowned her. She had nothing and nowhere to go.

"You're going to take her in, aren't you?" Dr. Pierce asked. Hoelkeboer's answer was not what he expected to hear. "The school does not have the resources to help another child," she explained, adding a challenge, "What are *you* going to do about caring for her?"

Dr. Pierce himself had very little money. He was a missionary for Youth for Christ, whose own family at home depended partly on help from others. As he took White Jade in his arms, he felt her shivering and wondered, "What *is* my responsibility?" He was struck for the first time with the reality that people suffer consequences for embracing his message and accepting Christ.

He took $5 from his pocket—all that he had—and gave it to Hoelkeboer, promising to send more when he got home if she would take care of White Jade. It was a moment that literally changed Dr. Pierce's life and eventually led to the birth of World Vision.

Adapted from M. P. Dunker, *Man of Vision.* Waynesboro, Georgia: Authentic, 2005, pp. 82–84. All rights reserved. Used with permission.

for removing children from abusive homes. SPCC Rochester faced redefining itself or closing down in 1966. United Way suggested providing in-home health care for children," Reed explains. "But we started getting adult care referrals. Based on Mary Ellen's story, a wise person on our Board pointed out we'd moved away from our mission. So we sold our in-home health care program to a

TAKING CARE OF MARY ELLEN

Contributed by SPCC of Rochester, NY

A small child who lived in a New York City row house, Mary Ellen was being abused by her caretakers. Neighbors who took notice searched for help, and they were shocked by what they discovered: There was an agency in the community that rescued mistreated animals—but there was none dedicated to protecting children. So the little girl's neighbors asked the New York Society for the Prevention of Cruelty to Animals (SPCA) to help them find a way to protect her.

Mary Ellen's case eventually made its way through the court system, and the judge ordered that she be removed from her caretaker's home. The court awarded custody to a family in Rochester, New York, "where she could . . . make mud pies, go to charming birthday parties and become a normal child."

That was in 1874. The next year the SPCC of New York City was established followed five months later by the Rochester chapter. More than a century later there are a number of independently run community SPCC chapters in the United States and Europe.

Adapted from K. Reed, *SPCC: A Long Proud History.* Rochester, New York: Society for Prevention of Cruelty to Children, 2001. All rights reserved. Used with permission.

local agency and recommitted to our original mission of serving children."

In 1988, SPCC began helping families with domestic violence. "Children who witness violence are seen as innocent, unaffected bystanders. Abuse often takes place in their kitchens—the very room they go for nourishment—they are affected deeply by it. Remembering Mary Ellen's story gives social workers, clinicians, and psychologists the strength to keep advocating for children who to this day remain disenfranchised," Laughlin says.

Founding stories are a critical communications and alignment tool. They can also illuminate and reinforce an organization's core purpose for its internal stakeholders and capture the hearts of financial supporters.

LEAVING A LASTING LEGACY

At NSA, stories of its founder, the late Cavett Robert, abound. After a successful career that included a law practice as well as insurance and real estate sales, at age fifty-five he became a platform speaker. "Dad was enamored with great speakers like Norman Vincent Peale and Bill Gove. But there wasn't much of a speaking industry in the 1960s so he drew his own road map," says his daughter, Lee Robert, president of Cavett Robert Communications, her father's business. "Driven by the desire to make the way easier for those who'd follow, Dad invited some speakers to Phoenix, Arizona, to swap stories and exchange best practices. Called the Phoenix Summer Sales Seminar, it continued annually for a few years before the group formed NSA in 1972," she notes.

Cavett Robert's influence is fondly called "The Spirit of Cavett." For his daughter, "It's the unselfish desire to make a difference in other people's lives." According to Stacy Tetschner, CAE, executive vice president, "Within NSA, it's practiced through sharing and encouragement: 'How do you build a bigger pie instead of fighting for your own slice?' The beauty is people can take these concepts and fit them to their own situation." He adds, "Cavett was alive the first twenty-five years of NSA; many members knew him. Me included. He'd help anyone. If you sent him an audiocassette, he'd send back a note or audiocassette with feedback."

Whenever members gather, this spirit is palpable. "It's how we keep our heart," Tetschner says. "For first-timers at the annual conference, there's a session about Cavett—stories about what he brought to NSA, why he did what he did and why we continue his practices. I also provide a handout about him at board member orientation. And at the annual Cavett Award dinner, we show a four-minute video of him telling stories," he notes. Marsha Mardock, director of communications, adds, "We share his stories on our Web site, in our *Annual Member Handbook,* and at chapter leadership training." Recent new members have received a book he and his daughter wrote called *Cavett Robert: Leaving a Lasting Legacy,* Tetschner reports.

"Our challenge is to find the story of our own life. If we tap our passion, we tap into something divine—something greater than ourselves," Lee Robert says. This was true of Bob Pierce at World Vision. In 1980, Marilee Pierce Dunker wrote the first edition of *Man of Vision,* a candid perspective on her father's triumphs, flaws, and personal struggles. "Now that I have grandchildren, I realize it's important to pass on these stories of God's power and grace; this is their spiritual heritage. It also is for those who are carrying on our ministry. [World Vision] staff need to hear the stories about God's faithfulness . . . how he honored one man's faith and made a huge difference," says Dunker. "The latest book edition is given to our international directors, offered to employees at cost, and is sold on our Web site." For Dunker, "The power of Dad's story is the impossibility of this huge organization coming out of one moment [when he met White Jade]. Every one of us is challenged daily to make decisions that make an eternal difference in our lives and the lives of others."

"Dr. Pierce's quote, 'Let my heart be broken by the things that break the heart of God,' is well-known by employees and is displayed in our building," says Kartes. "It points to events in his life that grew from the White Jade story," Dunker notes, adding, "The quote's often referenced in our Wednesday weekly chapel." Kartes says, "Marilee spoke about her father at chapel. She talked about keeping a balanced life, a key value for us. Because we're dedicated and our work can be addictive, it's easy to misplace family priorities." And Dunker reports, "By demonstrating how a belief affected my dad's life, his story offers both positive and negative role models, illustrating what works—and what doesn't."

Like Cavett Robert and Bob Pierce, Henry J. Kaiser and Sidney Garfield, M.D., held strong values that ground Kaiser Permanente. "They were partners in advancing prepaid health care based on industrial health care programs for construction, shipyard, and steel mill workers during World War II," says Tom Debley, director of heritage resources. "Kaiser, an industrialist, was a man of tremendous lore. Dr. Garfield was a pioneer in medical care delivery and a medical computing visionary. Together they forwarded five values: prepayment for medical care, a focus on preventive medicine, group medical practice, all health care facilities under one roof, and innovation."

Mike Lassiter says, "We connect stories to these values in two ways. We start with our values and search for stories from our founders that support them. Or we start with a founder's story and find ways to link it to our values—or practices related to them. . . . For example, we're interested in promoting the concept of a 'total health organization'—helping individuals manage their own health given they have little interaction with physicians." Debley adds, "I discovered the last research project Dr. Garfield worked on as principal researcher in the 1980s was called 'total health.'" As Lassiter observes, "People find it reassuring to hear these stories. Instead of thinking a new term is the flavor of the month, they realize it isn't different [from] what we've previously done—that they're carrying on traditions."

Stories of passionate individuals dedicated to a greater purpose inspire people to embrace these individuals' values, dreams, and innovative ideas. Stories about their determination, courage, and experiences provide an enduring legacy and foundation for organizations to build upon.

CAPTURING HISTORY AND BRINGING IT ALIVE

How can organizations purposefully capture their history and build on it? "Within two months of joining Kaiser Permanente as northern California's media relations director, I pulled together historical information for our fiftieth anniversary. After [I became] statewide director, my boss and I wrote a proposal for a regional department to collect and use historical documents in an organized way," Tom Debley notes. "Then I was invited to a Heritage Advisory Committee meeting the [former] CEO convened to advise us on developing Rosie the Riveter/WWII Home Front National Historic Park, which includes the Henry J. Kaiser Shipyards. At the end, one physician from the founding generation said, 'We have some advice you didn't ask for. We're getting too old for this work; you should think about institutionalizing it,'" he recalls. "We immediately recast the proposal to be national in scope." The Heritage Resources department was created in 2003, he adds.

"Until recently, we've relied on verbal histories from our founding 'fathers and mothers.' Now we're formalizing their stories," Mike Lassiter explains. According to Debley, "We're documenting them in print, on videotape and CD, and electronically through our corporate intranet. We're also digitizing and transcribing oral histories of seminal organizational leaders to preserve them and make them searchable, including three hours of Dr. Garfield." Lassiter adds, "We're also capturing contemporary history real-time in print and electronically."

"I constantly look for stories," says Debley. A story he crafted is on page 133.

"Stories like this are shared at new employee and leader orientations, staff meetings, and professional development workshops," Debley explains. "My goal is to deliver Kaiser Permanente history to 140,000 employees and more than 12,000 physicians—the largest nonprofit

DIVERSITY AS A KAISER PERMANENTE VALUE BORN ON THE HOME FRONT OF WORLD WAR II

Contributed by Tom Debley

They were ordinary men and women—some barely teenagers—from all walks of American life. When Pearl Harbor was attacked in 1941, they rose to defend their country not with guns but hammers, welding torches, and garden hoes on the Home Front of World War II.

Thousands poured into Henry J. Kaiser's shipyards in Vancouver, Washington, and Portland, Oregon, in the Pacific Northwest, as well as those along San Francisco Bay in Richmond, California. Thousands more gave blood, rolled bandages, or tended Victory Gardens.

Kaiser Permanente, founded to serve health needs of men and women in the shipyards and their families along with their children, honored those civilians by sponsoring Home Front events at America's Celebrate Freedom Salute in Vancouver, August 26 to 28, 2005—culminating a nationwide series of events commemorating the sixtieth anniversary of the end of World War II. Kaiser Permanente's partner in Home Front activities was the National Park Service, with programs and displays about both the new Rosie the Riveter/World War II Home Front National Historical Park in Richmond, Washington, and the Northwest Kaiser shipyards. Among the activities were multiple reunions honoring World War II–era workers and volunteers, including Kaiser shipyard workers, nurses, and wartime volunteers as well as service organizations like the American Red Cross, [along with]Boeing aircraft plant workers and women who served on the Home Front.

Many who attended told stories of life in the Kaiser Vancouver shipyards run by Henry Kaiser's son, Edgar. Many proudly announced they received their medical care from Kaiser Permanente for the past six decades.

No story was more touching than that of Robert Monroe, a hearing-impaired student at the Washington School for the

(Continued)

Deaf during World War II. The school, serving Washington State since 1886, is located a short distance from the wartime home of Edgar Kaiser. Monroe and other students were employed by Edgar Kaiser—doing yard work at his home. When they heard that several young deaf men had been turned down for jobs at the shipyard, some of them went to Kaiser's home to ask him why.

Monroe says, "When Kaiser heard about the problem, he picked up the telephone and ordered a limousine to be brought to the house. He then took us with him down to the shipyard, bawled out the hiring manager, and ordered him to hire deaf workers because he knew firsthand that 'they were excellent workers.'"

Monroe himself was hired as a machinist's helper and then trained as a welder. He expressed his enduring thanks for the skills he learned on the Home Front in the Kaiser shipyards.

From this [situation] came Kaiser Permanente's first documented community benefit program. Permanente physician Clifford Kuh studied men and women with disabilities in the Richmond Shipyards for the government's War Manpower Commission. His focus was on what they could do, not what they couldn't do. His findings were distributed nationwide to help communities place disabled war veterans in jobs after the war.

[This] spirit of diversity was infused into the medical care program from the outset, described by founding physician Sidney R. Garfield in discussing his first meeting with Edgar Kaiser, who was responsible for bringing [him] into partnership with the Kaiser industrial organization. "Edgar," he said, "had strong feelings about how workers should be treated and about the need for a single class of medical care for everybody. . . . His principles seemed so high to me that I was impressed."

health care organization in the United States. People want to know they're doing something at work that's contributing to society."

At EPA, the challenge is to capture its history before the 10 percent of its executives who have been with the organization throughout its thirty-five year history retire. "A wealth of institutional knowledge was about to leave EPA. How do you capture lessons learned and best practices in various environmental program areas?" asks Susan Smith, senior program analyst for executive resources, Office of Human Resources. "We decided to tape one-on-one, professionally facilitated interviews with thirty executives on executive core qualification topics: leading change, leading people, communicating, driving results, developing business acumen, and building coalitions. From them we created transcripts and an eighteen-minute video featuring ten diverse stories. We presented the video at a senior executive meeting with an outline of next steps. And we showed it to various program groups."

From this was birthed the Leadership Legacy initiative. "While we obtained general leadership stories, we needed to refine interview questions to obtain scientific knowledge. In focus groups with scientific organizations inside EPA we asked, 'What would you appreciate in terms of knowledge from people who are leaving?'" says Smith. "People said, 'Wouldn't it be great to have some sort of collection of mistakes so we don't repeat them?' A light bulb went on. The initiative fit well with our new knowledge management program so we incorporated it into the program."

"The Agency was also working on a branding initiative to capture its essence, values, and esprit de corps and communicate them to employees and prospective recruits. Themes like balancing work and personal life, protecting the environment, and its role as a regulatory agency. We also meshed with this work," comments Jamie Langlie, program analyst, Office of Human Resources/Office of Administration & Resources Management, and current project manager for the initiative.

"Executives interviewed and videotaped in round two were asked, 'What are the most valuable resources when you have a problem to solve?' and 'How do you evaluate a valuable resource?' Stories surfaced about key values: building collaboration, earning trust with communities and community officials, and contributing effectively within a bureaucratic environment," Langlie explains. "We're incorporating these stories into new-hire orientation and leadership development training modules," she notes, adding, "Ultimately, we'd like to catalogue the digital video stories and house them on our intranet for ease of access by senior executives and those working on training and marketing programs Agency-wide.

"It's a privilege to learn Agency history from people who helped start it," says Langlie. "This is a values-driven agency. People here believe in the mission. It's inspiring."

Stories of history can ground an organization's values and current practices as well as provide impetus for innovation. Being attentive to them is key. So is capturing them in multiple, easily accessible media for transmission to stakeholders.

EMBODYING STORIES

While founding stories can benefit organizations, so too can their current-day embodiment. "We're story listeners and we intrinsically become storytellers. At SPCC, sharing client stories while respecting client confidentiality humanizes us as mental health professionals," Trina Laughlin says. "Hearing current accounts of tragedy as well as stories with happy endings rejuvenates us because we know we're making a difference."

World Vision donors are encouraged to talk about children they support through the organization's Web-based "A Child Is Waiting" program. "We encourage sponsors to write stories about the child, how they came to sponsor him or her, what sponsorship means to them, and how they've grown as a result," says Karen Kartes.

Tom Costanza, a photojournalist and senior video producer in Creative Solutions, and his wife, Kari Costanza, communications manager in Information Resources, also document modern-day versions of the White Jade story to support fundraising. Each periodically goes into the field, identifying children who personify urgent community needs. "We sit in a hut and listen to what's happening in people's lives. Some parts of the stories are similar to ours, such as parents' concerns for their children," Tom Costanza says. Kari Costanza adds, "Parts of the stories are different, such as the ravages of AIDS and other diseases."

What considerations play out in these situations? "We don't bestow resources and take charge of others' stories," says World Vision's president, Richard E. Stearns. "We walk alongside them with assistance as they work to lift themselves from poverty. We're contributors to the stories of those we serve as well as those of our caring donors, but *they* are the authors."

Stearns has met children forced to eat rats to survive, encouraged traumatized survivors of natural disasters, and comforted mothers whose children are dying of preventable diseases. "World Vision is willing to enter into some of the most tragic stories imaginable. Through powerful storytelling, we help change hearts and lives by serving as a bridge between nations and cultures," he says. Marilee Pierce Dunker adds, "It's my privilege and joy to tell the stories, show the videos, and acquaint people with the names and faces of children in desperate need, much as my dad did."

Bob Pierce's beliefs are personified in World Vision staff members. "Paco Peña, Mexico City's program director, introduced me to Jesus, a fifteen-year-old boy, and Monserrat, a thirteen-year-old girl," Kari Costanza recalls. "Peña suggested I get acquainted with the children by having lunch with them [since] lunch is a way of helping. Sharing a meal helps build trust. What struck me was how Paco placed the order. He specifically asked the counter person to hold the lettuce and pickles for Monserrat's burger. Out of hundreds of kids, he'd gotten to know and care about those two so much he ordered their food exactly as they like it," she says. "This experience backed up everything children say about our staff—that they're angels from God. Because I see small acts of kindness every day, I'm a believer in our program and the people who serve those street kids."

At NSA, Cavett Robert's beliefs continue in symbolic ways. "At the annual conference, we used to keep an empty chair in the front row designated as Cavett's chair. He was always at conferences and meetings, the first to shake a speaker's hand and give encouragement," Stacy Tetschner recalls, adding, "Because Cavett's compassion and heart encouraged us to act like family, I tell conference hotel management that if there's a piano anywhere, expect NSA members to gather and sing."

"At committee meetings, people invoke Cavett's spirit to get things done or challenge ideas. An example is a community task force created in 2005. The group wrote a statement of community behaviors where sharing was the underlying intent," Marsha Mardock says. "NSA also embodies his ideals in *Professional Speaker* magazine articles and through the Cavett Institute for Aspiring Speakers, where members share hard-earned lessons through stories, revealing embarrassing missteps for others to avoid. Informally, members form mastermind groups with like-minded people to share business information and discuss issues," Tetschner adds. According to Lee Robert, "My dad was so passionate about helping audiences that it fed his energy. We all have that capacity."

It is one thing to share founding stories or stories about people making a significant difference. It is another for organizations and their people or members to find ways to capture the essence within those stories and bring them forward to continually reinforce important messages. Both are critical to success.

MEASURING RESULTS

How do these organizations assess whether their story efforts are successful? Their measures vary.

"New members are surprised by the information and time people give at conferences and meetings. They're also touched to be told Cavett's story—they feel more a part of what's happening at NSA," Marsha Mardock says. "He helped us develop almost everything the profession has today, including our code of ethics," Stacy Tetschner adds. "NSA had a big hand in starting and funding the International Federation for Professional Speakers (IFFPS). There are eight groups worldwide that belong—we individually gave them lots of guidance on starting a freestanding organization like NSA. IFFPS held its first global summit in Singapore in 2005; we also had a hand in it. All of this flows from Cavett's practices."

Capturing practices from retiring executives made a difference at EPA. "We realized this is a really valuable organization and that people are doing good work we didn't know about," Susan Smith says. Notes Jamie Langlie, "The big bang for the buck is practical problem solving applied to uniquely EPA situations. We're also providing leaders with good examples of how to trust employees, manage them, and broaden their horizons. The initiative is integral to our workforce development strategy in human capital management."

Promoting history at Kaiser Permanente makes a difference to its employees. "Keeping our history alive is integral to our brand strategy. When employees see what we're doing today is right in step with where we've come from and when leaders remain dedicated to the values and confirm for employees those values are intact, people are more motivated," Mike Lassiter says. "The organization's heritage builds awareness and knowledge of our core values that gives credibility to other messages, including advertising," notes Debley. "We have no trouble recruiting employees. Our reputation and tradition resonates with people. Our history is always the most highly rated part of employee presentations. We get comments like, 'There's a heart and soul to Kaiser Permanente and I saw it today,' and 'This presentation should be shared with every employee for us to better appreciate where we work.'"

A founding story can provide stability. "Mary Ellen's story gives SPCC pride and purpose. It's sustained and kept us going when we might not have—at least three times in our history. We thrive because we remember why we started," Kelly Reed comments. "In turbulent financial times, there's a tendency to chase dollars. When a funder says, 'We've got a pot of money to create a new service,' organizations often say, 'OK, we can create a program to work with that.' Unless you remember your story—who you really are," says Reed, "you become victim to those dollars as opposed to remaining committed to constancy of purpose."

"When there's funding we need and we know it's being slashed," notes Laughlin, "once we start talking about our history and continued alignment with Mary Ellen's story, we tend to receive it." Reed adds, "We included Mary Ellen's two photos with her story in a recent annual report. We received great feedback from fundraising donors who didn't know much about us before."

"When you combine a good story with an action plan, that one-two punch creates results," points out Kari Costanza of World Vision. "Numbers don't move people. . . . People's stories move people. There's no greater way to advocate for people than to tell their story and offer solutions that honor and create a better way of life for them. [For example], in our World Vision chapel I heard about a pastor who'd been dragged, kicking and screaming, to a luncheon about AIDS in Africa. After listening to statistics and how his church could help, he was ready to return to the office. Then he saw a video about Africa called *The Hidden Faces of AIDS*. [Afterwards, the pastor] went to his car and wept. Then, with help from World Vision, his church took action. Today, it's combined efforts with other churches to sponsor thousands of African children," she explains.

Emphasizes Kartes, "A vast majority of employees also sponsor children. They often do so to see how the program works, like I did. But, as communications get going, you see the real impact of your efforts."

BUILDING MEANING

How can organizations capitalize on stories reflecting their founding, history, core values, purpose, and enduring practices? Here are several ideas:

- Preserve the history of the organization. Archive stories. Establish a system for preserving historical documents and key records. Assign responsibility for maintaining and sharing history.
- Find ways to link historical stories to proposed innovations and changes.
- Identify the organization's core values. Collect engaging personal stories from founders and current leaders that enliven the organization's values, and look for ways to link existing stories to specific values. Tell these stories to all stakeholders.
- Listen to stories people want to share about the organization. Also create time and space for employees to share their experiences and lessons learned. Be prepared to capture stories whenever and wherever they are told.
- Encourage leaders to relate personal experiences, share feelings, and explain lessons learned from both their successes and their failures.
- Continually retell favorite stories that keep legacy alive and reinforce the organization's core purpose.

Stories that define an organization engage employees, keep them focused on what matters, build strong relationships, nurture trust, and generate support. They get results.

Special Thanks

Special thanks to Joan Mussa, division director of branding and communications at World Vision; Michael Kull of Amplifi for recommending EPA; and Stacie Keller of the EPA Press Office and Linda Ernst, president of Training Resource, for suggesting Kaiser Permanente.

CHAPTER TEN

I Can See Clearly Now

Bringing Strategy Alive
Through Stories

Madelyn Blair, Ph.D.

Organizations need to go beyond written plans to inspire, develop, and communicate strategies at an initiative or enterprise level. "Story is the genesis of strategy. How do you articulate a visionary future in bullet points and spreadsheet entries alone?" asks Robert Allen, founder and CEO of i.d.e.a.s. (which stands for innovation, design, entertainment, art, and storytelling).

Why are organizations using stories in this way? "People are saturated by media messages, advertisements, and calls to action. We need communication techniques that take us back to our primal roots . . . to cut through the daily cloud of messages," notes Mike Lee, director of client services in Web Strategy and Operations, AARP Services, Inc. According to Melinda J. Bickerstaff, vice president of knowledge management and chief knowledge officer (CKO) for Bristol-Myers Squibb, "Stories tap into many senses. They're effective in communicating complex ideas." For Cele Peterson, founder and president of Cele Peterson's Fashions, "Stories communicate caring." Adds Nancy Shendell-Falik, RN, MA, vice president of patient care services, Newark Beth Israel Medical Center, "Stories are more powerful at connecting people and providing a rich communication process."

Lynne Wiklander, live learning and interactive media instructional designer for Groh Productions and Groh Records, links these ideas through an example: "If I [were] to say, 'Hello. I am name, age, birth, degree,' I've told you nothing that's interesting. But if I start wrapping that with a story . . . you can apply experience or imagined experience [to it]. Story invites us to participate emotionally, empathically. It breaks through boundaries in ways that pure objective communication cannot." These are all key factors in making strategy work.

STORIES GIVE BIRTH TO STRATEGY

Robert Allen created i.d.e.a.s., a former Disney operation that has been an independent creative content studio company since 2001, by crafting a story during the buyout process. "I wrote a future story about what an enterprise looks like when it's working the way I envisioned it," he says. "I told that story to *me* and then I extracted from it the parts of a business plan. Without this story I wouldn't have been able to write the plan. It became the structure and architecture for the business."

The first chapter of the story that he wrote is on pages 143–144.

"I initially used the story as a vision for the company," Allen says. Today he uses it with staff, prospects, and existing customers. "It keeps us focused on where we're going and . . . from getting distracted . . . [and] just doing things to make money. It gives the company a heart and soul," he reflects. Allen offers this advice when crafting a future story: "Don't confuse story-making with strategic planning or analytics. Working with stories is a fearless act of creation. Once the story is compelling, you can bring the analytics and information to the passionate framework of the story and give it life."

As at i.d.e.a.s., story gives birth to strategy at Groh Productions, a film production, publishing, and distribution company. "We've always used storytelling with our customers and employees. Because of this, our customers' stories have influenced our business strategy," says Katalina Groh, founder and president of this company and Groh Records. "When someone calls, we elicit stories that answer the question, 'What are you trying to do?' This information and their company's profile are put into a customer inquiry database. My employees and I share these stories with each other. I also relate stories I hear from distributors who sell our products," Groh adds. Here is one result: "We learned that diversity and conflict resolution are the biggest priorities for these organizations and there

I.D.E.A.S.: THE STORY— CHAPTER ONE—BIRTH

Contributed by Robert Allen

Out of the chaos of the "dot bomb bust," a chilling economy and the double punches of 9/11 and the Iraq war, large corporations contracted, revamped, and retreated to the perceived safety of their "core." This retrenchment spawned a massive unemployment rise on the downside and an unprecedented profusion of new, entrepreneurial energy. Not only were new businesses created, new forms for businesses were hybridized, synthesized eclectically from the tried-and-true. The "virtual company model" and the organic try-it-on-the-fly—that is the province of entrepreneurs.

i.d.e.a.s. is a child of this moment. Like all children, it has its parents' genes. They are the best DNA of the tradition of Walt Disney and the entertainment giant that bears his name. There's no "corporate genome," but it's reasonable that both useful and destructive genes were passed on. i.d.e.a.s., looks, thinks, and acts in many ways like its parent. That's the nature part. Then, there's the nurture part.

In 1968, I received two gifts for my fourteenth birthday. A well-preserved late 1940s vintage Argus C3 35mm view camera with a simple viewfinder, one fixed 50mm lens, a full set of glass filters, a light meter, and an on-board flashgun (for flash *bulbs*). I converted a bedroom closet into a darkroom, adding trays, safelights, tanks, and hangers for negative processing, and a used contact printer. The other gift was a Fender Newporter, which blended the slim truss-rod neck of the Stratocaster electric guitar with a modified dreadnought acoustic body. Between the mad scientist working in the acetic fumes of stop-bath and the mind-altering experience of imitating music from *Big Pink* by The Band, I began an eclectic passion for combining imagery and music. It was the age of Marshall McLuhen and psychedelics, the Beatles, Jefferson Airplane, and what was exotically called "multimedia."

(Continued)

The clumsy experiments with slides, home-recorded music, and "special effects" (using a slot-car motor on a rheostat with a cardboard shutter wheel attached to make a *strobe!*) were the original works of what later became i.d.e.a.s. These early starts were refined over the next thirty years through college, rock and roll, underground radio, theater, advertising agencies, Disneyland, Imagineering, and Walt Disney World marketing and operations. In the late 1990s when all that experience coalesced, it resulted in a buyout of a Walt Disney World–based production and post operation. What never changed over time was the fervent belief something fundamental lay beneath and was common to television commercials, live rock shows, the creation of a ride, new hire orientation and training, and the making of television programs.

That essential discipline always felt good. *It* was grounded in the anticipatory stage of every project and when done well, *it* always created the greatest sense of unlimited possibility and genuineness. After three decades of bathing in *it*, *it* turned out to be nameable. *It* was storytelling. The same act that bonds parents to their children, shamans to their disciples, and audiences to their favorite sitcoms. The same act that's recounted in the opening lines of Genesis—"In the beginning was the Word"—and the third component of reality as defined by M-Theory physicists—matter, energy, and information. Storytelling was the take-off point when birthing i.d.e.a.s. It forms the foundation and the roof-beams of the enterprise. It's sacred, nonnegotiable, and not to be trifled with or labeled as a "hook." i.d.e.a.s., after its long dormancy in the DNA of its predecessors, has been born as a storytelling organism. Creating new realities out of stories is what it does.

isn't an exceptional product out there in the market. It's now our foremost new initiative."

Once a year, customer and distributor stories are shared with the firm's Advisory Board. "They spark ideas about where to take the company long term," Groh says. For example, "One night at dinner I was sharing stories with John Seely Brown, a board member. He immediately saw an opportunity we weren't aware of based on a Web site he'd seen: how to expand the role of storytelling on the Web by having customers—and anyone else—create their own little stories on all different subjects using digital film and the tools and formats we'd provide via the Web. Then we'd give them a place to post their stories on our Web site and the opportunity to share their reactions about others' stories," she explains. "At the next board meeting, we shared the idea with everyone. They were all very excited," she recalls.

"The new strategy, however, didn't happen right away. About six weeks after that meeting, I had an epiphany and called together all the creative staff, our CPA, and our attorneys. I finally saw clearly what John meant. By radically innovating, we could create global conversations that others could learn from," she explains. "We are now designing and providing a platform for organizations and individuals to tell their stories in order to start building communities," notes Cynthia Stewart, director of global customer community development. Stewart describes the power behind this strategy: "Storytelling is like lighting a candle. When the wick is lit, the true essence of the candle is revealed. When people begin to tell their story, they disclose the hidden treasures of who and what they are."

What are the implications of this strategy to Groh Productions? For Lynne Wiklander, "It's about inviting people to participate and become part of [our] story." Adds Groh, "Long term, we're defining our brand by who our customers are and what they're doing with our work." She explains, "It's human nature to focus inward to define a company. But [when] you're mature, secure, and confident, you [realize], 'Maybe it's not all about me.' Only then can you genuinely begin to respect what comes in as you're listening to a customer, an interviewee, or an employee."

Compelling stories from company founders or from customers and other key stakeholders have the ability to give rise to strategy—at both an initiative and a firmwide level. They also have the power to shape business plans and an organization's branding because what is embedded in these stories is what is most important to those who tell them and can provide a treasure chest of ideas to those who use them.

SEARCHING FOR STORIES TO INFORM STRATEGY

AARP Services creates stories describing multiple futures to inform long-term technology strategy. "We were awash in year-to-year Web trends. When a few of us discovered scenario planning, which has a story component to it, we knew it would help us decide which trends were relevant to informing future planning," says Mike Lee. "We're most interested in how boomers and seniors will use the Web five to ten years out. So we contracted with a firm to help us. After attending a one-day workshop where luminaries gathered to [discuss] the future role of the Internet, and reviewing interview feedback from high-level AARP executives as well as literature in the field, we held a two-day working session with internal Internet-savvy directors and external thought leaders who study the future of technology. The session focused on, 'What will the role of the Internet be in people's lives in 2011?' Twenty-five of us crafted four scenarios, boiled down from imagined headlines of the future. These initial story narratives were each two pages long.

"After chewing on these for several weeks, we held another meeting to create emblematic characters—people who'd live in these four scenarios—and narrative around what their lives would be like," Lee continues. "We wrote one page per scenario on each emblematic scenario character. Then we aligned the scenarios to our internal organizational strategies to yield some next steps. Future work includes identifying key indicators and how to monitor them based on the scenarios and taking the process into AARP's strategic groups and then laterally and downward into product units and state offices."

While stories that describe the future can help shape strategy, so can strength-based stories about the past. At Newark Beth Israel Medical Center (NBIMC), hundreds of patients are transferred, or "handed off" from shift to shift, unit to unit, and nurse to nurse every month. "Based on information from the Institute of Medicine, about 80 percent of medical safety errors are communication-related. Thus, improved hand-offs are significant in lowering the incidence of error, therefore improving patient safety and nurse satisfaction," Nancy Shendell-Falik says.

How did the strategy to improve hand-offs originate? "I was selected for a Robert Wood Johnson Executive Nurse Fellowship, which provides $30,000 in matching funds for improvement projects led by fellowship recipients. I proposed improving patient care safety [because] I wanted a project I could pilot and then move into other areas in the medical center," she explains.

After creating a workable project scope, Shendell-Falik and others approached the project by "applying Appreciative Inquiry (AI) philosophy—asking questions, being open to and seeing new potentials and possibilities, recognizing the best in people and the world around us, and affirming past and present strengths, successes, and potentials," she says. Here is why: "In medical centers we often don't use a strength-based approach. We're always trying to 'fix' things. I didn't want to lead a project that reports the million reasons why it didn't work to avoid blame."

Shendell-Falik was purposeful in collecting stories to inform the strategy for improving hand-offs. "I wanted stories containing positive examples from the past—stories about patients being welcomed, of managing patient belongings, and about how things went when they worked well. I wanted to build a vision for the future using these positive stories," she says. Shendell-Falik made time for staff to share stories across units and participate in shadow days with their hand-off counterparts.

A committee identified insights from these positive stories. "It developed five new initiatives to specifically enhance the hand-off process," Shendell-Falik highlights. This included a welcome script for patients in narrative form. According to Marcia McGregor, RN, BSN, nursing director of the Telemetry Unit, "It's really different when you say [to the unit], 'I'm bringing Mrs. Smith up. She's a mother of three and this is what happened with her in the Emergency Room.' [And then], once Mrs. Smith arrives, the unit says to her, 'Mrs. Smith, you are going to be well taken care of here, we have been expecting you.'"

"Implementation of the project wasn't without issues. At first, staff thought it was just another NBIMC flavor-of-the-month program," says Shendell-Falik. Based on a suggestion, she made time available for staff to continue sharing stories across units. Soon she heard comments like, "'We owe this to the rest of our patients and staff' and 'What do you mean *my project*? This is *our* project.'" Shendell-Falik adds, "We now have very few barriers."

Like NBIMC, i.d.e.a.s. also searches for stories before defining a project's strategy. "We begin by asking the client to tell us the story," says Robert Allen. "At meetings, we habitually let staff and clients take the extra time to tell their whole story. Providing the space for stories to emerge is just as important as storytelling; you have to be able to listen in order to tell," explains Duncan Kennedy, vice president of innovation.

"The Tulip Photographer" on page 148 describes how story factors into the front-end development of a client-requested project.

THE TULIP PHOTOGRAPHER
Contributed by Duncan Kennedy

We were helping a client launch a suite of patient communication tools to introduce a breast cancer risk-assessment test. The first thing we did was listen to the stories among our team about surviving cancer, so we could get a feeling of how we'd been touched by the specter of cancer. Then we had to deal with identifying "What is risk?" We spoke with members [of] breast cancer survival groups to get a sense of the issue.

From all these examples, we developed our own stories about the experiences of different "meta-characters"—for example, a woman at risk who doesn't want to know or a younger woman with a high family risk level who wants to take the test now rather than wait for her doctor to recommend it. These "back stories" might not be something the client will ever see, but it ensures that we are coming from an authentic awareness of the real issues facing women, instead of the faux image of a woman-riding-a-horse-on-the-beach presented by American advertising.

One option we gave the client for the visual aspect of the project was a luminous, delicate image of tulips. The photographer spent all day setting up the lighting and waiting for the right moment to capture their exquisite fragility. There was a very moving background to his art. The photographer had lost his daughter to breast cancer at age forty-two. He poured all the love he felt for his daughter and all his desire to prevent breast cancer for other fathers and daughters into the making of these dazzling photos. This became a quiet source of poignant motivation for us.

The other ideas we'd come up with seemed to be more about marketing savvy when compared to this approach.

As it turns out, the client chose the tulips to serve as the front for their publicity, without ever hearing the "back stories" (which we shared with them later). The back stories ended up making it into the education media so women could hear these stories as part of their decision process whether or not to take the test.

"This is the depth at which we use story to get past mental clutter, right down into the soul, to make that searing imprint of 'we get it,'" Kennedy says. He describes why story is the key to strategizing around client needs. "When you use story effectively, you're able to achieve a level of communication, comprehension, and recall that you can't with any other means. Whether in the way we interact with clients to understand their needs or in the way we make product for them . . . story is much more powerful than barraging people with content. We see the actual medium of story as the vehicle in which we can best communicate ideas," he explains.

Stories can inform strategy in a variety of ways. Stories can be created to depict various future scenarios and characterizations of those who may live within them. Gathering strength-based stories about the past can provide insights into how to structure a project or initiative strategy for maximum impact. And stories from clients or customers, staff, and others related to a need or issue can provoke innovative approaches.

STORIES TRANSLATE STRATEGY INTO REALITY

While Robert Allen based his firm's business plan *on* a future story, soon after arriving at Bristol-Myers Squibb (BMS), a global pharmaceutical company, Melinda J. Bickerstaff and her team crafted a future story *about* a strategy, namely knowledge management. She told the group, "The president isn't going to read our fifty-page strategic plan. We're going to write a story in the future that assumes all that we want to accomplish in our strategic plan was successfully accomplished." How did the team respond? "They looked at me like I was from Mars."

But she did not give up. She mentioned this idea at her leadership team's next meeting. "We have to tell a story, from a future vantage point, of how this knowledge management strategy is actually going to work, how it'll improve the performance of BMS, and more importantly solve some problems we know the president is worried about," she says. They answered with, "We don't know how to do that." To which she responded, "If you can't explain or operationalize your own strategy, then who can?"

Bickerstaff persevered, recalling, "The third time I mentioned it, a creative member of the team said, 'Hey, I think I know what she's getting at. The president is from the U.K. I bet he reads the *Financial*

Times. What if we wrote our story and put it in the *Financial Times* [format]?'" That seemed to be the key. "We wrote a story three years out as though the strategy were done so people could see what the end would look like. It took seven weeks to put it together. Then we handed it to a really excellent journalistic writer for refinement. . . . After that there was no resistance from team members. This story was theirs. More importantly, they could actually [envision how to] implement their own strategy."

The story, "Bristol-Myers Squibb Named Top-Ranked Global Pharmaceutical Company: Managing Intellectual Assets Attracts Top BMS Alliances—Blockbuster Drugs Follow," was crafted using the steps on page 151.

Prior to a scheduled meeting, Bickerstaff provided the president with the completed story and another actual article published by IBM. She describes what happened next. "The president went to a board meeting . . . and took reading materials with him. As he read the future story in reprint form and noticed his photo and the date, it dawned on him that it wasn't an *actual* reprint. He told me, 'I thought to myself, I don't remember this interview or photo shoot. Did I miss something?' Then he realized this was a story about the future," she says. What happened when Bickerstaff met with him? "He said, 'I finally understand what your group is trying to do and what knowledge management can do for BMS. I'll send this to all to my direct reports and ask them to meet with you.'"

After receiving the president's approval, Bickerstaff's leadership team members needed to get their respective employees to actually implement the strategy. "The team wrote a second future story that painted a picture of their future jobs and roles for implementation and put it in the *Knowledge Management Review.* It worked, too," she remarks. Why does this type of future story work? "People get it more quickly. If you've never seen something before, you can't imagine it. I tell the story and they can see the picture without [my] having to explain it over and over," Bickerstaff says.

At Bristol-Myers Squibb, a future story was used to actualize this new strategy. But how can organizations use stories to translate timeless business strategies into daily behaviors? Having owned Cele Peterson's Fashions for seventy-four years, Cele Peterson has a business strategy that goes beyond a desire to sell. "I want people to feel they rate, that they are something special," she says. "Each customer has her own story. Is she someone that likes traveling? Or a homemaker? When you work

STEPS FOR CREATING A FUTURE STORY
Based on the work of Melinda J. Bickerstaff

Create the Vision: Define What Needs to Happen
- Involve the team that knows what the vision means to the work.
- Outline the issue that requires a strategic decision.
- Formulate the vision of what the future would look like if everything you wanted to accomplish were actually accomplished. Answer the question, "How will it work?" Also identify how the vision will solve known business problems. Be specific.

Identify the Decision Maker: Find the Best Vehicle
- Be clear about who needs to make the decision.
- Identify the publication (periodical or newspaper) the decision maker typically reads.
- Determine the kind of story that would be published in this publication.

Get It Done: Make It Seem Real
- Write the vision of the future as a story in the style of the selected publication.
- When the story is finished, put it into a format that is akin to the format of the publication.

Get the Decision
- Deliver the future story.
- Stand ready for more than you asked for!

with people they'll tell you a thousand things about themselves. [By listening to their stories], you make them feel they're cared for and that you're interested in doing what's best for them," she explains.

In addition to teaching employees to listen closely to customer stories, Peterson also shares customer stories that exemplify a strategy of caring with staff. According to Susanna Moon, sales associate, "Cele often talks about a woman who came in looking really awful. Her skirt was held together with safety pins. No one wanted to help her. But she turned out to be a millionaire. Later, I remembered that story when a woman came in who looked really poor. I waited on her and was friendly. She has since become a regular customer and a great friend."

Key to customer care is outfitting a customer with clothing that is uniquely hers. "If you're going to do something, you need to dress—and look—the part," Peterson says. To personify this, she relays this story to staff. "A lady had a presentation in Colorado. She came in looking for a suit. I told her, 'With a suit, you look like anyone; you want to make a *statement.*' She wanted color, but we found her a gorgeous black dress with silver circles on the trim and a necklace that was a silver circle too. She looked like *today's woman!* And she left the store high as a kite," Peterson explains.

This storytelling has a customer relationship-building aspect that reinforces the store's strategy. "Not a day goes by," says Moon, "that Cele doesn't share a story with a customer." These stories are based on Peterson's life experiences. Her employees model this same style. Says Peterson, "With stories, people understand and believe what you're trying to tell them because they're your true experience. Stories create comfort. The relationship is instantaneous."

Similar to Cele Peterson's Fashions' customer care strategy, Groh Productions' and Groh Records' employees are coached to share and listen to stories during communications with customers and distributors. "The values are ingrained: storytelling, listening, validating other people. We all live in the same world, we all matter. . . . [We] make everybody feel like what they have to say is equal to anybody else," says Stefani Piermattei, production coordinator. "Every time we have a new customer it's important that we know where they're coming from as individuals, not just as a person in a company that's buying our product," she adds. According to Katalina Groh, "Because we encourage customers to tell their stories, they become loyal and interested in us because we're interested in them. They call regularly with unsolicited feedback—how they're using our product, what's working, how successful it is." Piermattei remarks, "Listening to customers helps our company to be human. I think that's why our products have done so well."

Stories can aid in taking a strategy from concept to reality. Future stories can translate what appear to be remote goals into doable activities and desirable outcomes. And stories from staff and customers, or clients, can be used to convert timeless business strategies into routine daily behaviors.

SIGNIFICANT OUTCOMES

Both i.d.e.a.s. and Groh Productions and Groh Records attribute their financial growth to the strategic use of story. "In five years, i.d.e.a.s. has grown to $5 million in revenue and thirty staff members," says Robert Allen. "Since 1997, Groh Productions has experienced 15 to 20 percent quarterly growth. Our products are being distributed in eighty-eight countries," reports Katalina Groh.

"Employee stories are also integral to our future growth," Groh notes. "Everyone here . . . gets asked to share their stories. The benefit of having people feel they're part of the company and that their story is interesting is that customers can immediately tell what we're about. Word-of-mouth growth comes from that," she adds. At Cele Peterson's Fashions, a similar outcome has been achieved through stories. "They've been a significant contributing factor in repeat business," remarks Cele Peterson, adding, "Just this morning I had women come up from Mexico because their mothers bought from me thirty-two years ago."

At Newark Beth Israel Medical Center, improved hand-offs resulted in strengthened relationships based on collaboration and pride. Says Nancy Shendall-Falik, "[Staff] told me things like 'Now I know that so-and-so will do everything possible to help me.'" Marcia McGregor concurs. "If we were at a four [rating] in terms of positive [staff] feeling, on my unit [when we started], we're now at a nine or ten [rating]."

McGregor has numerous anecdotes about improved patient care based on collaboration and the new welcome script. Here is one example: "When one man came [to our unit] he had numerous family members with him—eight to ten at least. We can't have too many people [in the room]. Because they were concerned, the nurse allowed them in and tried to reassure family and the patient. She did the welcome script with the nurse [who brought the patient to the room]. After the patient got better and was discharged, he came back. [The unit nurse] wasn't there, so he came back a second day to thank her. He also wrote her name on the [standard discharge survey]," McGregor explains. She notes, "Thank-yous like these from patients are on the rise." Consequently, other medical units want to use the work developed by the pilot group. "Three additional telemetry units and five medical surgical units have started using our hand-off process," Shendell-Falik remarks.

Storytelling has built more than staff relationships. "Staff turnover in the pilot area improved about 5 percent and satisfaction scores are up about 10 percent," reports Shendell-Falik. "Overall changes in patient care safety demonstrate that nutritional assessments are up 11 percent, skin assessments are up 70 percent, compliance on cardiac enzymes is up 9.2 percent, and medication administration record compliance is up 82 percent. We aren't saying our project is the only reason these scores are up, but it's a big part of it," she says.

At Bristol-Myers Squibb, the faux *Financial Times* article achieved its intended result. "I didn't have to spend a minute of our thirty-minute meeting convincing the president about the value of knowledge management. He wanted to go into action and tell me what he was going to do to make our programs work for him and BMS," Melinda J. Bickerstaff recalls.

"Other [departments] have adopted this method of 'future' story," she comments. Stephan Taylor, Ph.D., director of learning and informatics solutions in Process R&D, enlisted Bickerstaff's help to create a future story about an electronic notebook initiative that had been under discussion for years. It was titled "Bristol-Myers Squibb Process R&D Embraces the New World of Electronic Scientific Knowledge Management." Taylor says, "Since all our chemists read *Chemical Engineering News,* we put it in the format of this publication." And the results? "It sparked people's interest. They even asked, 'Can I get it?' It also helped us recognize those early adopters we might not have recognized," he notes. There was an unexpected outcome. "Next time I'd make it less realistic. I had to field all these calls about 'How could you go to press without telling anyone?' and 'How come I don't have an e-book yet?'" he says.

While the story scenario initiative at AARP Services is still under way, benefits to crafting scenarios as stories have already appeared. "They make scenarios more accessible to a wider number of stakeholders and easier to communicate. Looking at possible futures and presenting them through compelling stories is an attractive way to spark conversation and to bring together groups that normally wouldn't work together," Mike Lee says.

LESSONS TO TAKE FORWARD

How can you use story to further strategies within your organization? These pointers may help you:

- Story can be applied to both organizational and initiative-level strategies. Knowing what you are trying to achieve beforehand will help you determine which techniques to use.
- Create future stories to give rise to a strategy or to communicate a strategy to others. Familiar style and format and elements of today's reality make it more believable regardless of how far it stretches the imagination.
- Craft stories about the future that depict responses to critical scenario questions.
- Share strength-based stories and listen to those from others. Spend time developing prompts to elicit stories effectively.
- Seek out all kinds of stories that can inform a project's vision and strategy.
- Select stories that serve one or more business needs and align them with the organization's overall business strategy.

Once you employ these techniques, be prepared to watch your organization's strategies go from a plan on paper to a living, breathing process.

Special Thanks

This chapter would not have been possible without the contributions from those who helped me get to the examples in this chapter. Among them are Steve Denning, Bernard Mohr, and Susan M. Osborn, Ph.D., M.S.W. Special thanks to Atieno Fisher of Usoni Transformation Services, who brought energy, clear thinking, and brilliance to this endeavor, and to Chara Watson of the National Storytelling Network and to Marcy Fisher for their support and assistance.

CHAPTER ELEVEN

The Fog Is Lifting

Seeing Connections to Marketing and Marketing Research Through Stories

Steven N. Silverman, Ph.D.
Susan J. Moore

Have you ever sat through a marketing research presentation or read a report and wondered, "What does this mean?" You are not alone. "In a society of heavy data immersion, marketing researchers are not getting through to people," notes Hedy Lukas, senior director of marketing services for Kimberly-Clark Corporation, a consumer goods company.

Christopher J. Frank, director of corporate research at Microsoft, concurs. He presents an alternate approach: "Market researchers have to communicate information in a way that can help managers consume and recall it so they can take action. A story focuses attention on important issues and aligns with how the mind naturally works. Storytelling is a fundamentally different and better way to present results."

Kimberly-Clark and Microsoft, along with Fisher & Paykel, a durable goods manufacturer; Cheskin, an innovative consulting firm; and Tutta Bella Neapolitan Pizzeria are embracing stories and storytelling in marketing and market research. Frank explains how stories work: "If you're a captain and I'm your navigator, I could give you a long report before you sail indicating the longitude and latitude of where there may be rocks in the water. You may or may not remember or act on this information. On the other hand, if I told you that I have a light shining on three big rocks directly ahead, it's more likely you'll turn to avoid the problems." And Lukas adds, "Storytelling triggers the mind in a way that facts don't. It makes the data come alive."

GROUNDING MARKETING AND MARKET RESEARCH IN TIME-HONORED STORIES

Tutta Bella has built its marketing efforts around a single story, the one that inspired the restaurant. "It's very personal," says Joe Fugere, its owner. "I started Tutta Bella based on my upbringing and roots in the Italian community and food and beverage experience with Starbucks. I knew it had to be authentic. The best way to do that was to be trained in Italy. So in fall 2003 I traveled to Naples. There was no formal schooling; I was immersed in these methods simply by being around them. Every day late in the afternoon, activities shut down and all gathered to relax with friends and 'have espresso.' We would talk about pizza. I learned how important tradition is to the Neapolitans and how passionately they talk about simplicity in cooking. That is the experience I'm working to bring to Tutta Bella." His chef, Brian Goijdics, says, "The key is absolute simplicity. The ingredients, the process, the table experience all must be simple."

The story of Tutta Bella is prominently displayed on the company's Web site and is shown here on page 158.

"Once each server knows the menu and can tell the Tutta Bella story in their own words, they earn a cloisonné pin of a San Marzano tomato, the restaurant's logo," Fugere says. But he does not expect staff to merely retell the story. "I hire talent based on whether they can tell [our] story and about why they've joined Tutta Bella. I want everyone to have their own stories to tell guests—about the restaurant and the food," he says. Goijdics demonstrates this as he recounts the story of each ingredient: "Pure *fior di latte*—fresh mozzarella. The flavor is very clean and fresh and when it cools it is reminiscent of milk. San Marzano tomatoes from the valley around Mt. Vesuvius with low acidity and low sugar content have a bright, brilliant tomato flavor. . . . Locally harvested basil. . . ."

Discussions about "authentic and simple" are constant at Tutta Bella. "We started with pizza. While most restaurants try to do more,

THE TUTTA BELLA STORY

Contributed by Joe Fugere

The inspiration for Tutta Bella Neapolitan Pizzeria stems from a passion for the authentic, fire-roasted pizzas born in Naples and found throughout Italy. For a century and a half, the pizza makers (or "pizzaioli" as they are known in their home town) of Naples have been producing unique, mouth-watering pizzas using the freshest ingredients available. It is estimated that nearly seven million of these pizzas are produced in Italy every day.

In the mid-1990s, a group of pizzaioli decided to join together to create an organization, Associazione Vera Pizza Napoletana (VPN), to defend the integrity of their product. They sought to establish a DOC (denomination of control) for pizza, a designation that can be compared to winemaking DOC zones. For wines, the Denominazione di Origine Controllata outlines the permitted ingredients and defines the production process. For DOC Pizza Napoletana, the process encompasses everything from specifying the origin and freshness of the basic ingredients to the stone-cooking surface of the oven.

In June 1998, the good news arrived: authentic pizza napoletana, "Verace Pizza Napoletana," had become a protected legal entity. The regulations do not state that the pizza must be made in Naples, thus opening the opportunity for any restaurant in the world to make the DOC guarantee that the production of their pizzas meets the association's strict requirements. To date, only a handful of pizzerias in the United States have chosen to do so—Tutta Bella Neapolitan Pizzeria is the first restaurant in the Northwest to be DOC certified. The restaurant received its VPN certification on April 3, 2004. The owner, Joe Fugere, has been trained and certified as a pizzaiolo.

we ask how we can do *better* with a simple menu—ten pizzas and four salads. It's tempting to offer more but to be consistent and consistently good we focus," Fugere points out. "Our growth has led us to offer an espresso and cappuccino menu. It is entirely authentic, too. When we add something to our menu we ask, 'How simple can we make it?'"

Fugere adds, "To create a special place you have to be different. My interest was to create authenticity and goodness. We don't break the rules. We do the right thing. Nothing is added to our restaurant for its own sake—only for consistency with the Tutta Bella story and to reinforce a singular experience."

The same holds true for Fisher & Paykel, a New Zealand–based organization. "Storytelling is important. The term we use is *narratives.* They help us understand our business and our customers," says Malcolm Harris, chief operating officer, New Zealand. According to Craig Douglas, vice president of sales and marketing, Fisher & Paykel Appliances, Ltd., "We don't use storytelling consciously. It's a natural way of behaving for us. By telling stories, we preserve our culture and history." Harris agrees: "The stories told in the company start at the board level. One story that conveys our initiative and innovation is about one founder, Mr. Fisher. He was in the company café and wanted a meat pie. But he couldn't find one he liked. So he designed a new meat pie and bakery on-site [for us to] manufacture it. We use this story to remind ourselves we can create great solutions that no one else has yet found. It guides people to be creative."

The company's worldview and its storytelling history are grounded in four elements—style, integrity, care, and innovation—what it calls its DNA. The story (on page 160) from the company's Web site speaks to its commitment to creating innovative designs.

Storytelling has changed the way sales representatives talk about innovations. "We had to communicate about the world's first top-loading dryer in Chicago at a trade show," Douglas recalls. "Our U.S. sales rep was a fantastic storyteller. We videotaped his story about the benefits of the top-loading dryer and showed this video in Auckland. It gave them a lot of confidence about the market—not just feedback—but confidence. The sales rep could explain with clarity the unique differences and simplicity versus technology and graphically demonstrate the ease of loading wet clothes from the top-loading washer into the top-loading dryer."

About Us

Contributed by Fisher & Paykel

Our heritage dates to the 1930s with the manufacture of designs made under licence. The pioneering spirit established by the founders encouraged a culture that challenged conventional appliance design and production systems.

By making appliances under licence we determined that we were only destined to make a more expensive version of others' products. We couldn't generate economies of scale so we had to find other ways of creating a point of difference in our markets.

The answer lay in technology. By developing plastic liners and insulation using polyurethane foam we were the first in the world to commercialise this technology.

Another major breakthrough came in the late 1960s when the company saw the need to find a way of producing short runs of various models through common manufacturing machinery.

The idea of being able to make every model every day, just in time, had become reality and export opportunities opened up.

Learning to control flexible machinery lines during this phase had started to create another major advantage that was to come in the future.

Flexible machinery brought with it the notion of manufacturing cabinets using pre-painted steel. In tandem with the Japanese steel mills, appliance grade pre-painted steel was developed that enabled coiled steel to be processed through lines of machinery that could notch and pierce various sizes and shapes. The first product to incorporate this technology was the compact dryer—a ground-up design conceived by our own engineers.

This technology carried over into refrigerators and washing machines and is now standard across all of our appliance range.

Time-honored stories about an organization's founding, inspiration, or experiences from key executives can frame an organization's marketing and marketing research efforts. To have impact, these stories need to be embedded into the daily practices of employees and be consistently communicated throughout its marketplace.

OBSERVATION SPURS STORIES

"Fisher & Paykel is looking to differentiate itself from competitors to give it the opportunity to be the world's best. Given our position, we can't afford to create 'me too' products," Malcolm Harris says. Internal processes are important here. "The link at the creative stage between marketing and engineering is a tenuous link. The initial seed comes from people studying, sleeping, eating, and breathing in the customer's world. But then, engineers have to understand. That's where we use stories to tell what we've seen. These stories drive our designs," he explains.

According to Craig Douglas, "Storytelling is part of our culture and communication style. Some story from a customer will be shared over coffee or lunch. We share them constantly." How is this possible? "Our open offices let us sit in a common space. Our approach is 'immersion' with each other—with our teams and our customers. We don't work in isolation."

Observing consumer behaviors and telling stories about them has led to two appliance innovations. "Our engineers looked at every dryer on the market and found they all were front-loading. This meant customers had to take clothes from the top-loading washing machine and move them to a front-loading dryer. The ergonomics are terrible. Our engineers wondered whether that could change. That led to the top-loading dryer, which took a lot of engineering innovation to develop," Harris says.

An even more powerful innovation came in dishwashing. "We looked at people's kitchens and found they were filled with drawers. We wondered why drawers were so plentiful and realized they're convenient to wherever you are and have certain ergonomic characteristics that people value. This led to the creation of the DishDrawer®," Harris notes. Here is the company's DishDrawer® story, as told on its Web site: "[The] DishDrawer® [can be] by your side wherever you are working in the kitchen, like a single drawer in the island to handle preparation dishes. Imagine a single drawer on either side of the sink, eliminat[ing] all bending required to use your dishwasher. You can even have the panels match your cabinetry for a completely integrated look in your kitchen."

Cheskin also creates stories from consumer observations to facilitate new product development for clients. "In working with a cell phone carrier, we used diagrams to create a phone for children that graphically showed what children were telling us in their interviews. These diagrams told a compelling story that was very powerful for the client. The diagrams showed what was learned from the interviews, the features that the data suggested, and finally the forms of a product. In fact, the manufacturer has not planned to develop the product but the story showed the logic between the research and the product idea . . . and it came directly from real people," explains Terri Ducay, vice president of design strategy.

Additionally, Cheskin uses employee stories to inform its marketing strategies and positioning. "We aim to take each client on a 'learning journey' that provides new *learning,* deep *collaboration,* and *inspiration,* leading to a *transformation* of the way that clients approach marketing to their customers," adds Lee Shupp, vice president of business strategy. "These four principles embody the experience we want clients to have when they engage with Cheskin. To provide this experience, we strongly believe we need to live it ourselves [so] we conducted an off-site where Cheskineros brought in personal stories around these themes. We had an internal owner for each, who created a shrine with photos, audio, other visual imagery, and text that described the experience. Because we combined personal experiences [involving] these 'design principles' with the idea they're important both to personal and company success, they were adopted enthusiastically. People connected on an emotional level and at a deeper, visceral level. This approach is transforming us as a company."

Observing consumer behaviors and translating them into oral or pictorial stories can shift people's perspective. This can lead to innovations and a deeper appreciation of what consumers need. The same processes can be applied internally to shift and frame thinking around the organization's marketing strategy.

COMMUNICATING MARKETING RESEARCH TO OTHERS

"It's not enough to give a research study with facts. . . . We need to convey what people can do with the data. Storytelling does that by giving meaning," notes Hedy Lukas. According to Jeff Drake, director of marketing research at Kimberly-Clark, "Massive PowerPoint [presentations] numb the brain. How do we break through [and] personalize this information? Stories are critical to creating the context that makes it is easier for people to remember research results."

General Manager R. Jeff Hansen experienced these challenges in his previous role at Microsoft, where he and a hundred-person research organization led one of the company's largest efforts to understand its market. "When we presented the research to executives, the deeper meaning of what customers were experiencing wasn't getting through. We decided we needed more than just analytical facts. We needed to help executives view things from a different mind-set—to help them go beyond the paradigm they were thinking in," he says.

Hansen and his team took the research and focused on "the heart and mind of the story" underlying the data. "We used a story to put executives in the mind-set of a customer and guided them to think about questions that customers had about Microsoft. We put things more personally. We explained who customers are, what they do, and what they think and feel about Microsoft. We took both a customer and an internal view. We used no data and focused entirely on meaning. After several months of work they understood customers in a very different way," he reports.

What did Hansen learn from this experience? "[You can't] think just about the data or just about the story. You have to think about your audience. What do they need to hear to understand data and relate to the story? That's key to presenting a nonanalytical and meaningful experience to change how people think and act."

Terri Ducay from Cheskin agrees. "People do not need more data. They need better ways to access it. You can tell the story of how it was gathered so it becomes alive and more human," she says, adding, "We can [present] bar charts to illustrate the size of market segments, but coupling that with video of people from each segment provides the glue that puts the facts in a human form. Video tells a story that people can see and understand in ways that words cannot."

At Kimberly-Clark, Drake also sees the enhanced power of stories when video is used to tell the tale. "We bring data to life [through] a database of video clips. At any time we can search video of our customers telling stories about their experiences or new features they want. For example, we video people changing diapers and giving babies baths to improve our products and packaging. Customers also tell stories about why we should carry or not carry something on a [store] shelf," he says. Additionally, the organization captures verbatim responses to products from consumers over the Internet. "We find we get more content and that people are more truthful than if we interview them in person or talk to them on the phone," Drake notes. How does this help the organization? "First, we recall the exact language used or not used. Secondly, we recall not just the facts, but also the flavor of the learning. [This allows us to] focus on the motivations and emotions behind the facts . . . and lets consumer actions speak for themselves."

Ducay uses another technique to convey meaning and insight from Cheskin's marketing research. "I use storyboards to tell a story. Storyboards condense a lot of data into a small footprint [and] clients do not have to connect data to implications themselves, making it user friendly. This worked very well with one technology client because the client could identify what the data meant. One [of the client's] senior vice presidents used it in a kick-off meeting with several hundred engineers. They liked the storyboard. It really resonated. It was a source of entertainment and spoke to them in a manner that allowed substance to come through," she explains.

"When others retell a story, it's powerful," says Christopher J. Frank. "Important ideas have always been handed from one person to another through fables and oral history. Putting research data in story form enables other people to share that data by telling the same story. If you give them a table of data, they won't talk about it. But people can go into a meeting and tell a story. The story is retold by the business manager, not the researcher, which increases its distribution and helps it gain credibility. The more the story is told, the more likely it is that there'll be action taken on the data."

Stories can make market research data more meaningful and drive people's understanding and action. Techniques such as videos, pictures, and storyboards can tell a story or add to the one being told. The true power of story is when it moves from the purview of market researchers into the hands of business leaders and is continually shared with critical stakeholder groups.

CHANGING HOW MARKETING RESEARCHERS REPORT FINDINGS

Getting researchers to embrace storytelling is not easy. "Researchers feel uncomfortable doing it. Some think storytelling waters down results and doesn't fulfill the role of the researcher. They may have tried to tell a story but fell into the trap of discipline expertise and then said, 'Oh, you see, that storytelling didn't resonate.' Sometimes they don't believe their own stories. If you don't believe the story you're telling, your audience isn't going to believe it either," Christopher J. Frank says. "Telling a story is taking something very complicated and making it simple. It's very hard to make the complex simple. It's also a new way of presenting information."

How can researchers create believable stories? "Researchers can look at themselves to find ideas for how to frame a story. They can find analogies from their day-to-day experience in their own lives," Frank says. An example is on page 166.

The need for people who can transform research into stories is changing how companies hire and train marketers and researchers. At Kimberly-Clark, Jeff Drake has committed to training his employees. "We've held two one-day seminars on a thirteen-step program for crafting a story and structuring presentations using them. They've been well-received because attendees see how they can influence business action," he says. He also offers some advice: "It's important to prep people before training so they can better appreciate it when they walk into the room. [In addition], be aware there are various formats for stories to address specific situations. Stories need suspense and they need to be embedded in the truth."

Hedy Lukas identifies broader implications from the training: "We used to think it was sufficient to present managers and executives with information and it was up to them to use the facts. We're learning that through a good presentation you can convey the story by illustrating an application. Now it's incumbent on us [as researchers] to extend our capability to a more consultative role." She explains, "Demand for these skills is going to change things. We expect people to be more consultative. Academically, business school marketing and market research programs will have to find a broader crossover between standard MBA skills and research skills so they are locked in step."

Terri Ducay echoes the need to transform marketing and marketing research practices. "We're going to have to learn how to tell stories. Some people can learn a lot from a film course. You have to develop a plot and know how to arrive at the final result. It's like that in our research and consulting work. We have to know the data but if it's not internalized it'll go nowhere. You have to give people the means to absorb and embrace it and be able to tell the customers' story to others. Movies do that. That's what we need to learn to do."

HOW TO MAKE STORIES REAL

Contributed by Christopher J. Frank

When I study customer satisfaction, I may learn there are three important factors we have to watch. I can explain this with a bunch of tables or I can tell a story. For instance, most people can relate to a car dashboard. So I might decide to describe customer satisfaction using this analogy.

I can explain that I have three dials that matter at Microsoft. Now I can use this metaphor to convey research findings using a car dashboard analogy to indicate how well we're doing on those satisfaction indicators. For instance, I might point to the dashboard and ask if things are getting near the danger point by saying, "Am I redlining on any of the important dials?" Now "redlining" becomes a term from the dashboard analogy that we can use to assess how well we're doing on our satisfaction metrics.

To build on this, I can ask my audience to consider what to do if I'm redlining or if the check-engine light comes on. Should I start banging on the dial and asking for more information about the situation? Do I think the dial is garbage because it isn't telling me how to fix whatever is wrong? No. I know enough to bring it to a mechanic—a researcher—who can run additional diagnostics. Managers need a way to know when they need more information and where to turn to get it. But it needs to be simple enough for them to know what they need and when to act.

Analogies are all around us—a lighthouse, a ship, a car. Figure out what works for you and use it. Think about where people go every day and put the research in a context they can understand. But do this relatively quickly. If you have to spend a lot of time thinking about a story, it's probably artificial. It should be intuitive or you'll have a hard time telling it. When you use everyday analogies you'll become more comfortable telling stories and you'll have break-through communications.

Training in how to craft and tell believable stories can aid researchers in overcoming their hesitancy in using stories. So can use of commonly known analogies and the study of movie production.

AND THE RESULTS . . .

Stories can translate data into action that can make a difference in an organization. Here are some tangible results.

"Tutta Bella started in January 2004 with seven employees. In less than a year, we grew to seventy employees and seating expanded from 35 to 160 seats. Sales have grown by 300 percent and a second location is now delivering similar performance," Joe Fugere says. Doing the right thing has paid off. Even Seattle's mayor, Greg Nickels, recognizes Tutta Bella's success. "Tutta Bella has helped put Seattle's Columbia City neighborhood on the map. Tutta Bella has used story, authenticity, and great food to establish its unique niche. Tutta Bella is a true Seattle gem," he notes.

How has the story that R. Jeff Hansen and his team put together affected Microsoft in the long term? "That story changed executives' views of relationships with customers, and that has driven behavior in the company, in the field, and around the world. They created a new language centered on customers and customer experiences and committed to significant investment in developing a new direction for Microsoft, which ultimately led to a new corporate message: 'Your potential. Our passion.'" According to Christopher J. Frank, "The use of stories to convey research insights has been formally built into the training curriculum for researchers at Microsoft. This has led teams to create summaries of several projects entirely around a story format. Additionally, they're used with internal business partners to increase data consumption. In one story we presented data around climbing the mountain of satisfaction, with the goal to reach the apex. This story took root across business units, resulting in common nomenclature when discussing satisfaction research. Storytelling has proven a powerful tool. It's removed the language barrier between the science of research and the language of business."

Story factors into marketing and marketing research at Fisher & Paykel through its history, its creation of stories based on customer observations, and in product marketing. How has this benefited the organization? "Speed to market [when developing new products] is critical for us. The customer story is an important part of making that happen," Malcolm Harris says. Craig Douglas adds, "We are actively marketing [through] product platform stories. This gives us a conscious brand." What about the story the sales representative told about the top-loading dryer? "We had two wins. It was a win for engineering and a win for marketing. Years of work on a unique feature paid off. This is an example of how we were able to tell our story in a mature market," Douglas notes. This product is now available in many international markets and is generating growth for the company.

What results have occurred from Kimberly-Clark's training? "Six weeks after the first course, a key customer came to visit. We asked, 'What can we tell as a story with what we have?' We told a story about what the data meant to the retailer's business that gave advice on how to increase sales. It was very well-received," Jeff Drake says. "Several folks have crafted stories for one-page talking sheets for use with internal customers. These customers tell us they understand the total business situation better. And they still recite the information a week or two down the road," he says. Hedy Lukas adds, "Before we started training, I'd have said I'm not sure storytelling has a role in marketing or research. I now see it as an opportunity to more meaningfully convey factual information to people throughout KC."

Cheskin sees results both internally and externally. "The impact of storytelling and related methods with clients has been significant. It's led many to comment on how these methods have clarified the marketplace and customer views in ways they hadn't previously understood. Companies are now seeking out Cheskin to apply our methods to bring insights across a wide range of marketing issues," Lee Shupp notes. According to Terri Ducay, "Storytelling inspires our staff to take action. It brings people to life—research becomes more dynamic [and] is more entertaining so you naturally do a better job at the task at hand. Our teams discuss stories passionately just standing in the hallway. These stories ground us so that everyone can look at the research and react to it [and] be involved in stimulating the creative process. Once you get a taste of storytelling, how it becomes fun, and the rewards it provides, naturally why would you want to go back?"

THOUGHTS FOR USING STORIES
IN MARKETING AND RESEARCH

Research in the form of numbers, tables, graphs, and charts is not enough. Creating stories from research is a much more effective marketing strategy. How can you bring these thoughts into your organization?

- Consciously use stories to drive internal actions and communications with customers. Make them a part of how you do business.
- Commit to employing stories more centrally in research and marketing efforts. They can drive innovation, new product development, employee behavior, and management decisions. Use them to build shared meaning inside and outside the organization.
- Get everyone involved. Stories have the most impact when people make them their own and retell them to others.
- Make stories real. Telling a story will seem artificial if the storyteller is not authentic. Stories can be created from personal experience based on the data. The more we believe our own stories, the better we are able to persuade others to remember and act on them.
- Fight the urge to resist stories. Training people and continuously encouraging story use helps ensure employees engage in the practice.

While market research cannot exist without its core emphasis on scientific and statistical rigor to establish the validity of the work, research cannot successfully drive managerial behavior without a story that is used to convey meaning about the data. It is like a lighthouse: cutting through the fog of market and organizational behavior may well depend on being able to clearly and brightly point out the path with stories that light the way.

Special Thanks

Thank you to Andrew Abela, Ph.D., Catholic University of America, for his referral to Kimberly-Clark Corporation. From Steven: Thank you, Dana, for loving and supporting me in so many ways and allowing me to have the time to do the work that brings me joy. From Susan: For John—the hero of my story.

CHAPTER TWELVE

What's in a Name?

How Stories Power Enduring Brands

Ashraf Ramzy, M.A.
Alicia Korten

Ⅰn the play *Romeo and Juliet,* Shakespeare asks, "What's in a name? That which we call a rose by any other name would smell as sweet." What is in a name is everything that defines a company's unique worth to its employees and customers as well as what differentiates it from its competitors. A name embodies a company's story about itself, its consumers, and its product. That is why Michael Perman, senior director of consumer insight for Levi Strauss & Company, says, "Stories become the legacy of a company."

People do not buy products; they buy the stories these products represent. Nor do they buy brands; they buy into the myths and archetypes these brands symbolize. Levi Strauss, the inventor of blue jeans, knows this. So do premium whisky producer Chivas Brothers Ltd. (a business unit of Pernod Ricard SA), which makes Chivas Regal; VSM Geneesmiddelen bv (VSM Pharmaceuticals), a company that manufactures and markets homeopathic medicines; Kimpton Hotel and Restaurant Group, LLC, a collection of forty independent boutique hotels with adjoining fine dining restaurants located throughout the United States; and Erbert & Gerbert's Subs & Clubs, a gourmet sandwich chain with forty-two franchised shops in Wisconsin, Minnesota, and North Dakota.

While spanning the corporate landscape, these organizations have one thing in common: to address their unique brand positioning challenges, they reached not for more facts and figures but for a vehicle to convey deeper meaning and higher vision. They reached for a story.

WHAT BRINGS ORGANIZATIONS TO STORY

What propelled these companies to use story? Han Zantingh, international marketing manager for Chivas Regal, explains, "In 2002, Pernod Ricard acquired the brand Chivas Regal. In times like that you go through a big rethink: about your positioning, who you are, what you are, what you are not. We realized we had wonderful stories to answer these questions. We saw how valuable these stories were and started a project to document them." This level of reflection is also what inspired VSM Pharmaceuticals (VSM). Although its market had grown, its market share had not. CEO Jan Zwoferink sums up the problem, "VSM turned to story because we realized we had lost the plot. We needed our story to create our future."

When creating the brand for his chain of restaurants, Erbert & Gerbert's Subs & Clubs founder Kevin Schipper was reminded of stories from his childhood. Michelle Ranum, director of marketing and brand development, describes what happened. "In 1987, [Kevin] was thinking, 'What am I going to name this place?' He didn't want it to just be Kevin's Subs. The idea came out in a brainstorming session with his brothers and sisters. Someone said, 'What about Erbert and Gerbert's?'" Ranum notes that Erbert and Gerbert "are [the main] characters from bedtime stories that the founder's father invented. [They are] "Two young boys who traveled through time and space to learn a little bit about history, science, and nature and a whole lot about being a friend." These bedtime stories were a critical organizing tool for a large family. Adds Ranum, "As you can imagine, the house was a bit chaotic. But the stories were enough to quickly gather round ten small children before bedtime."

For many organizations, the drive to use story in branding emerges at a critical moment—a time of endings and beginnings. A time of renewal.

THE POSITIONING CHALLENGES
THAT STORY CAN ADDRESS

Sometimes, traditional marketing techniques are unable to resolve brand positioning problems such as gaining consumer relevance or achieving competitive differentiation. What role can a storytelling strategy play in addressing these issues?

In the case of consumer relevance, Chivas, VSM, and Levi Strauss all faced the same question: How do you reconnect with an estranged consumer base in an emotionally compelling and relevant way while remaining true to your own identity? Reflecting on Chivas Regal, Han Zantingh notes, "The brand had lost relevance with its consumer base. To reconnect, we needed to revitalize [it]. Chivas was a whisky your father drank, something you gave as a gift but wouldn't drink yourself. The brand was known but completely not relevant." He adds, "We needed to educate our public and nothing educates as powerfully as a good story. That's why we developed *The Chivas Legend*, a larger story that connects the many stories we already had within us."

Like Chivas Regal, VSM had also grown distant from its consumers. "Our consumer research told us our brand image—which had always been gentle—had become timid," says Jan Zwoferink. "The brand had lost its passion. People viewed [us] as clinical and distant. We needed a way to convey strength without sacrificing gentleness and to recapture the pioneering spirit and market leadership we once had. These problems led us to rediscover our story."

Recapturing its past also became a factor for Levi Strauss as it addressed consumer relevance. The company specifically faced the challenge of not selling "in the value channel—in discount stores such as Wal-Mart and Target—where more and more consumers are shopping," explains Michael Perman. Stories from working-class individuals who shopped at these stores helped the company to launch Levi Strauss Signature®, a brand sold exclusively in this value channel. The president of Levi Strauss Signature®, Scott LaPorta, notes these stories helped staff members not only to understand but to embrace the "working class hero" that had been the company's original customer. "We developed a successful brand strategy to give the company and the name back to this consumer."

In addition to consumer relevance, stories can address positioning issues related to competitive differentiation. Here, the key question for Erbert & Gerbert's and Kimpton Hotels was, How do you gain competitive advantage within a saturated market and a highly competitive market while remaining true to your own identity?

"How do we stand out from other sub shops?" asks Erbert & Gerbert's director of training, Tammy Berend. "There are a million sandwich shops out there. Even 7-Eleven [the world's largest convenience retailer] sells sandwiches." The answer was to use the myriad characters involved in the dozens of Erbert and Gerbert bedtime stories told over the years—characters like Comet Morehouse, Jacob Bluefinger, Girf, and Shortcake.

How to leverage differentiation was the challenge for Kimpton Hotel and Restaurant Group, LLC. As Chief Operating Officer Niki Leondakis explains, "We have forty hotels from coast to coast. We had a huge opportunity to send a Denver guest to a San Francisco hotel that we weren't capitalizing on. But how do you create a brand that has a common promise when they are all different? We had to figure out, 'What is a Kimpton Hotel? What does it mean to each guest?'"

How did the organization answer this question? The Kimpton tagline says it all: "Every hotel tells a story." This tagline reinforces that each hotel has its own personality and embodies its own adventurous tale while, at the same time, providing a sense of continuity between them. Emphasizes Leondakis, "Essentially, each hotel has a brand of one." Adds Steve Pinetti, senior vice president of sales and marketing, "Traditional brand strategies followed by the large companies focus on sameness. Our edge is that we focus on what is different. We highlight the unique personality of each hotel. It's the opposite of what traditional hotel quality control and branding is about."

Whether the positioning challenge is one of gaining consumer relevance or achieving competitive differentiation, organizations can use a story-based strategy to address it. Doing so will help them stand out in a crowded marketplace and connect more closely and deeply with their consumers while remaining true to their identity.

WHERE DO WE FIND OUR STORY?

To create their brand stories, organizations first need to identify the raw material for them. For Erbert & Gerbert's this task was straightforward. Michelle Ranum explains, "Kevin brought family [members] together to choose their favorite stories. His father then wrote these down and Kevin commissioned an artist to do drawings." While Schipper drew his organization's brand stories from his childhood past, Chivas Brothers looked to the company's history. "First we did research to unearth stories that had been around for a long time," notes Han Zantingh. "Based on that material we created *The Chivas Legend.*" He adds, "Then we commissioned a whisky journalist to write a book about Chivas Regal. It is a very factual book, for the aficionados and connoisseurs. We know our story is rooted in our history and our legend in truth."

For inspiration, VSM also pulled from its history as well as its future dreams. "We identified our finest moments. The stories we uncovered had one theme in common: We were at our best when championing a vital cause in health care. That's how we started," states senior product manager Johan van der Molen. He continues by describing the company's history. "In the nineteenth century Dr. Samuel Hahneman, the founder of homeopathy, was horrified to see that the remedy was often worse than the disease. So he set out to introduce a different, more natural kind of health care." But history was not sufficient to create a brand story. Adds program manager Maarten van Walsem, "We also had to ask the big questions: 'Who do we want to be and where we do want to go?' We needed to benchmark the memory of who we were with the vision of what we could become."

Like VSM, Levi Strauss explored a future possibility as it searched for a brand story for a new venture. However, it looked outside the company for answers. Michael Perman explains how his team uncovered a story that helped it launch the Levi Strauss Signature® brand. "We spent time with people that shop in the value channel [we wanted to enter]. We came across a woman named Heidi—a young woman living in a tract house in the small mainstream town of Pueblo, Colorado. We got to know her, saw her kids, went shopping with her. She kept saying brands were really important to her. But she wasn't wearing any brands. Yet she said she would travel sixty miles to stores to get a brand-name product."

He continues, "At the end of the day we were in her driveway saying good-bye. We asked again, 'Why was it important for you to have those brand names?' Finally, she told us. They weren't for her; they were for her kids. She said the stuff at Wal-Mart 'was for those other people.' We asked, 'What do you mean 'those other people? Who are they?' [She responded,] 'They were the people on welfare.'" Says Perman, "What a profound moment for us. She wanted a brand that respected her. This had value. She was willing to go sixty miles for this. She thought the retail presentation [in the value channel] was disrespectful and messy. What a profound opportunity if we could provide her with something that would bring her respect."

Similar to Levi's, Kimpton Hotel and Restaurant Group often looks outside the company for inspiration. Steve Pinetti says, "When developing a hotel story, the first thing we do is look at the roots of our hotels—the history of the building, the bones of the initial architecture, the town it's situated in—to find where we can have some fun," As an example, the Hotel Monaco in San Francisco "is in the theater district," notes Niki Leondakis. "So founder Bill Kimpton wanted it to be theatrical." To capture drama, Kimpton placed life-size sculptures of frogs in ballerina skirts and monkeys drinking from wine bottles throughout the hotel's lobby and adjoining restaurant.

To uncover brand stories, organizations may draw from within themselves—the company and its founders, leaders, and employees—or from others—customers and factors in the external environment. This information can come from their past—the world of history, origins, and early beginnings—and from their future—the realm of dreams, ambition, and vision. Independent of the source, the story needs to be credible. To be credible, it needs to be imbued with authenticity. Thus, the process ultimately begins with discovering a truth about the organization—a truth that has either been forgotten or has not yet been uncovered.

WHAT IS OUR STORY?

"How do you create a story from historical facts?" asks Han Zantingh of Chivas Brothers. "We wanted to support and nourish our brand essence: rich and generous. The original Chivas Brothers ultimately made a rich and generous blend because they themselves had a rich and generous attitude [toward] life. This insight, these two words, helped us select the material." He explains how the organization proceeded from here: "We decided that we would find twelve core themes because Chivas Regal is a twelve-year-old whisky. These themes are actually our milestones, our finest hours. . . . The royal warrant we received from the Queen when she came to Balmoral in the nineteenth century. When Chivas Brothers became royal suppliers to the throne. That Strathisla, the signature malt of our blend, comes from the oldest operating distillery in the Highlands, built in 1786. Our success in the 1950s in the United States, resonating with the spirit of the times, also perfectly embodied by the Rat Pack—Dean Martin, Sammy Davis

Jr., and Frank Sinatra. We took all those themes and integrated them into one story: *The Chivas Legend*."

The Chivas Legend is roughly seven thousand words in length and reads like a novel. Its opening lines are shown below.

Just because a brand story has been crafted does not mean it is immutable over time. "A brand story is more than words on paper," explains Zantingh. "It is a living thing that evolves constantly."

Not unlike Chivas Regal's, VSM's brand story emerged as the management team processed insights from the past and determined their effect on its future. "Suddenly," says Jan Zwoferink, "the storyline was born. 'VSM is a guide [that] shows people the way to natural healing

---

THE CHIVAS LEGEND

Contributed by Han Zantingh

The Scottish chieftains eye each other warily across the peat-smoke laden air. You could cut the atmosphere with one of the razor-sharp dirks, flashing silver in their belts, poised ready for action. The host tosses back his long knotted hair, leans forward and splashes a generous portion of pale liquid into a large wooden quaich; a traditional Scottish cup of friendship, hewn from some great ancient oak tree, long since felled.

As he hands the wooden vessel to each of the chieftains in turn, he cries, "I give you the water of life."

Weather-beaten faces, streaked with blue dye, slowly nod in appreciation. As if by a secret signal, they all toast the host in unison. "Life!" they roar. "Life!" replies the host softly.

Hard stares soften. Frowns gradually fade. Lights dance in tired, ice-blue eyes. Outside, a brutal wind still pummels the walls but in here the moment has triumphed. Clenched muscles relax. Down-turned mouths break into broad smiles. Laughter cuts through the tension and fills the room, like the sweet smell of heather.

This is the role that whisky traditionally played in medieval Scotland, the Scotland of the clans.

and wellness.' The story had a hero: It was about our company being the best it could be. The story had a plot: It was about our company doing what we passionately believe in. It had an audience: mature people who realize how fragile they are, how precious their health is to them, and how much they need to be responsible for their own well-being. These three building blocks helped us define our internal and external communication and our business development." Maarten van Walsem recalls, "As we developed our story, we realized we had become strangers to ourselves. When we realized this, people literally had tears in their eyes."

Developing a brand story can be a powerful experience. It is like alchemy—part science and part art, part logic and part intuition, part reason and part emotion. The challenge inherent in this development is identifying themes and patterns from myriad sources, and then transforming the most vital facts and truths into narratives and visuals and the resulting information into inspiration.

HOW DO WE TELL OUR STORY?

Once an organization discovers and develops its brand story, it needs to tell it. This work includes embodying the story within the organization and sending consistent messages to consumers about both the function and the spirit of the story. As VSM's Jan Zwoferink points out, "The only credible story is the story you tell with actions and behaviors."

To prepare employees to tell the organization's brand story, VSM commissioned the development of a cartoon book featuring a young Adonis, a composite character who embodies the journey and concerns of the story's audience. An excerpt from it is on page 178.

The Adonis portrayal of the brand story, along with the brand story itself, has rekindled a sense of purpose for the staff. Comments Zwoferink, "All downsizing does is feed fear within a company. Our brand story offers people a new perspective, a sense of hope, a focus for further growth. [It] fuels ambition [and] unleashed inspiration and energy in the company . . . reminding employees why they first started working here."

Brand stories can also change the environment within which people work. Levi Strauss is creatively aligning its internal culture with its Signature brand story. "Our conference room used to be sterile," offers Thom Masat, vice president of design for Levi Strauss Signature®.

CARTOON STORY

Contributed by VSM Geneesmiddelen bv
(VSM Pharmaceuticals)

There once was an Adonis who, in his youth, thought himself immortal, invincible, and invulnerable. And he lived exactly the life that goes with such youthful beliefs. Then slowly but surely age took its toll. Adonis' body began to give, until finally he hit rock bottom. At this dark place, he realized something fundamental. "We should never forget how fragile we are and how precious good health is." And in this moment, the Adonis began to let his body guide him back to health.

"Now the decor tells a piece of the brand story—with jeans, old crates, and even a moose head gazing down at the conference table."

Staff also find ways to portray consumer stories, which form the foundation for the overall brand story. Masat says, "I don't want to read about our consumer on paper. The Consumer Insight Department has started getting me pictures and videos." To inspire his design team, Masat has created a "family album" complete with photographs and profiles of real people—consumers—inside it. This strategy has been instrumental. "The stories create empathy within the company toward [our consumers], which then leads to insights about branding and strategy," says Michael Perman. He adds, "The success of [the Signature] brand is that [staff] knows their consumers better than anyone."

In addition to influencing employees and the company's culture, organizations have to deliver their brand story effectively to targeted consumers. However, this delivery may not be obvious at first blush. Inside Kimpton's flagship hotel, the Hotel Monaco in San Francisco, is a symbol of the company's deeper story: an upside-down book resting on a branch of the life-size bronze tree in the hotel lobby. Notes chairman and CEO Tom LaTour, "This is because the company's founder, Bill Kimpton, was dyslexic. Bill believed that travel is lonely, and that everyone is fundamentally insecure. Bill's own insecurity was a result of his learning disorder." Kimpton's personal belief that travel is lonely has shaped the signature elements infused into each hotel—values of care, comfort, flavor, fun, and style.

To bring these elements to life, Kimpton Hotels creates situations in which guests become characters within a story. Here is an example: "At the Hotel Monaco we give guests a goldfish," explains LaTour. "It's your pal. You get to name it. After you leave, your goldfish 'Joe' will write you a letter: 'Haven't seen you in a while. I'm lonely here in [San Francisco].'" Chief concierge Angela Prager explains how effective this technique has been. "People get very attached to their fish. One woman put hers in a jar and tried to take it back to Japan." Pinetti notes, "This is a great example of how [two] Kimpton brand signature elements—care and comfort—come alive in a genuine way." This consumer involvement strategy has helped fuel the organization's growth. "We attract the kind of guest who likes to tell a story—and especially a story about 'a great boutique hotel' they just found. Kimpton guests seek out unique experience and enjoy a sense of discovery," explains Pinetti.

Similar to Kimpton Hotels, Erbert & Gerbert's has used its physical environment to tell its story to its customers. "The walls of [the] sub shops are filled with paintings of characters and written stories that explain the strange names of the sandwiches. These stories help build customers' connection to our company," says Tammy Berend. The story and graphic depicting the character "Boney Billy," who provides the name of the company's best-selling sandwich, are on pages 180–181.

Embodying these stories does not end with wall paintings and sandwich names. When a new franchise was opening in Minnesota, Erbert & Gerbert's advertised for employees with an "Opening Soon: Storytellers Wanted" sign above the shop. "People were intrigued. It was a great way to get attention. It created a buzz [among potential customers]," says Michelle Ranum.

Chivas Regal also has its storytellers—employees it calls "brand ambassadors." Han Zantingh explains, "These are people that are

BONEY BILLY

Contributed by Erbert & Gerbert's Subs & Clubs

One day, Erbert & Gerbert took refuge in a strange and myste-
rious house while trying to escape from Comet Morehouse.
Unfortunately, it was filled with evil ghosts. The boys lit several
candles to brighten up the room. However, the candles began
to flicker and go out one by one. No matter how quickly the
boys ran around relighting the candles, they soon found themselves in total darkness. Soon they heard footsteps approaching
and a low evil chuckle emanating from inside the room. They

backed to the wall and waited, a panel in the wall opened and a boney hand pulled both of them out of danger.

ERBERT SAID TO GERBERT, SAID ERBERT TO GERBERT "GERBERT . . . I hope that is a friendly skeleton!"

Boney Billy was not only a friendly skeleton but one with a creative parttime [sic] job. To support himself, he hired himself out to new rich families. By having Boney Billy on the parttime pay role [sic], these families felt that they had arrived socially as they could proclaim to the world that they had a "skeleton in their closet."

E & G Franchise Systems, Inc., "Boney Billy poster," 2002. Used in all Erbert & Gerbert Subs & Clubs locations since 1988. All rights reserved. Used with permission.

passionate and knowledgeable about the brand. They visit bars and tell stories about whisky. They're our storytellers."

Where can employers find potential staff with the creative skills needed to successfully implement a story approach to branding? "[For Kimpton Hotels,] it's better to go to Carnegie Hall than the Cornell Hotel School for recruiting," notes Steve Pinetti. However, this poses a hidden recruitment challenge: "You have to make sure that [people] can run a business as well as provide the creativity and inspiration to bring their hotel story alive."

There are myriad ways to embody a full, rich brand story that is aligned both inside and outside an organization. Whether it is presented through oral telling, symbolic depiction, or environmental design, a story can shape internal organizational culture, consumer dialogue and experiences, and the presentation of products and services.

HERE ARE THE RESULTS

These organizations have achieved impressive results—growth and financial success, increased visibility, differentiation, brand equity, and reduction in turnover.

"By creating *The Chivas Legend*, we reconnected our heritage and our audience," says Han Zantingh. "[It] not only stopped the decline of our market share in a brutally competitive arena, it reversed the trend. Our sales volume is now growing at double-digit rates." Growth has also resulted for Kimpton Hotel and Restaurant Group. "We are on the cusp of something big, akin to the dot-com boom," says Jimmy Hord, general manager of Kimpton's Hotel Monaco San Francisco. "We've doubled the number of our hotels to forty in the last five years, and we're poised to double again." Steve Pinetti echoes this sentiment: "It's incredible! Fifty-five percent of our customers are repeat guests! The average rate of repeat customers in the service industry is 20 to 25 percent."

Levi Strauss has had similar financial success. "We were a company that sold riveted jeans to gold miners. Yet our company was no longer targeting working-class heroes," explains Scott LaPorta. The story of a working-class woman named Heidi brought the company back to its roots and inspired the creation and launch of the Levi Strauss Signature® brand. Michael Perman says, "The brand has grabbed 12 percent of the value channel in our category. In the first full year of business [2003] the brand generated more than $300 million in sales!"

Increased visibility has also been a key outcome for two companies. Erbert & Gerbert's Subs & Clubs "is getting a lot of press coverage for our focus on story," notes Michelle Ranum. "We're getting noticed in places like *Nation's Restaurant News* and *Franchise Times*. These are big magazines for restaurateurs and franchisers. The story is hitting a nerve with people wanting to invest for the long haul." Kimpton Hotels has been noticed too—a boon for attracting new customers and interested investors. Hord says, "Early [in 2005] the *Wall Street Journal* featured us on its front page."

In addition to increased visibility, brand stories are having an impact on consumer perceptions. For VSM, CEO Jan Zwoferink notes, "Our brand story is shifting how consumers view us, and is guiding our efforts to start a flagship store." The Chivas Regal brand reports a similar change. "We know from brand tracking that brand equity is improving dramatically in our key markets and the brand is becoming more relevant and engaging to our consumers," reports Zantingh. What does this mean for their future strategy? "Going forward we are creating new brand stories to strengthen ourselves further."

Finally, Kimpton Hotels notes one more outcome from its brand story strategy. "When compared to industry standards, independent survey results show turnover at Kimpton Hotels is lower than any other major hotel company in the United States," Pinetti says.

TIPS FOR THE JOURNEY

These companies chose a story-based brand strategy to connect more deeply with their consumers and to differentiate themselves from their competitors more effectively without sacrificing their uniqueness and authenticity. This approach enabled them to create value and meaning because their brand was grounded in their identity and stories that captured who they were and what they wanted to be. This move has allowed them to reap substantial rewards.

How can your organization benefit in similar ways?

- Capitalize on critical moments—endings, beginnings, times of renewal—to create or revitalize a brand story.

- Embark on a journey of discovery. Reflect on the organization's history, listen to what consumers are saying—or not saying—and reach for its dreams and aspirations. Begin to uncover truths that have been forgotten or that have not yet surfaced.

- Look for the patterns and themes in the information you collect. Weave the most vital elements into integrated stories, with characters and plots—stories that capture and convey what the organization stands for or wants to be, stories that showcase the heart and soul of consumers, or stories that capture the essence represented by specific brands.

- Live the story. Internally align employees and the culture of the organization with the brand story through various media and visible environmental changes. Incorporate the story into the design of products and services.

- Find creative ways to deliver the story to consumers. Consider including them in how the story plays out over time.

With these steps, when your organization is confronted with the question "What's in a name?" it will be able to discover, develop, and deliver a story that conveys true meaning and authenticity. In this way, it will be able to communicate the unique and distinctive worth of the organization, its brands, and its products and services to employees and customers.

Special Thanks

Thank you to Gerry Lantz of StoriesThatWork™ for his valuable insights into where marketing ends and storytelling starts, and to Amman Werner for his enduring friendship, inspiration, and encouragement. Thanks to David Polinchok of Brand Experience Lab and Steve Denning for identifying possible companies. Our heartfelt thanks to Jeff Saperstein of Jeff Saperstein and Associates and to Margaret Chambers for bringing Levi Strauss & Company to our attention and making the appropriate connections.

Levi Strauss Signature is a registered trademark of Levi Strauss & Company.

PART THREE

Moving Stories into and Across the Organization

How can a single person spearhead the use of stories and bring storytelling into an organization? What types of approaches work best? These questions guide Chapter Thirteen, "It Pays to Be a Pioneer: Blazing a Trail for Stories," by Lori L. Silverman. Topics covered include three ways to introduce stories—through strategy, special projects, and daily work—as well as using stories to instill new ways of thinking and behaving and tips on institutionalizing story use. Pointers from researchers in the field of storytelling are added to this conversation in Chapter Fourteen, "What Do You Suggest We Do? Finding Answers and Ideas in Research," by Jo Tyler, Ed.D. The chapter starts out by explaining how story research occurs inside organizations and then moves to subjects such as re-storying to counter organizational attacks, stories leaders tell—and hear, story and knowledge management, the possibility and desirability of teaching storytelling, and thoughts on getting started.

Throughout this book you have heard from 160 people representing seventy-two organizations. They have provided specific examples of story use or advice on bringing story work into organizations. In the aggregate, what are they telling us? Chapter Fifteen, "There Are Five Sides to Every Story: Which Are You Missing?" by Lori L. Silverman synthesizes these examples and suggestions with additional insights and practices from eleven additional people representing nine organizations.

CHAPTER THIRTEEN

It Pays to Be a Pioneer
Blazing a Trail for Stories

Lori L. Silverman

"In the mid-1980s, I noticed that executives who told stories were the most influential. People followed them. I decided to model what I saw," says Mark Steiman, first vice president and senior human resources manager in Washington Mutual's Home Loans Division. According to Nancy Driver, leadership program manager in the Office of Employee Development, U.S. Geological Survey (USGS), "Twenty years ago as a scientist attending conferences, I noticed stories made science more exciting. I encouraged other scientists at work to use story in presentations and began using it myself." And Mary Grace Ketner, education specialist in the Programs Management Department with the Institute of Texan Cultures at the University of Texas at San Antonio, says, "In the 1970s and '80s, I used stories as the director of religious education for a church to provide meaning and value to teachers."

Story pioneers are everywhere. Dorothea Brennan, director of process improvement at The United Illuminating Company; Lynne Feingold, one founder of Golden Fleece (an international community of story practitioners) and a program analyst in the U.S. Department of the Treasury; Larry Forster, staff engineer for technology planning & implementation, Shell Exploration & Production Company; Arlene

Jorgenson, BScN, RN, COHN-C, CEO, and president of HEALTHSERV; and Tom Mosgaller, adjunct faculty at The Asset-Based Community Development Institute, all have experienced the power of story first-hand and found opportunities to bring the approach into myriad organizations.

STRATEGY GUIDES APPLICATION

Strategic changes are an effective conduit for story use. "I led the mortgage business for the largest bank in Connecticut. At the time, the industry was paper-based, but technology was emerging to streamline this challenge. As we changed processes and technology, I wrote a story about a customer and her experience to give staff a vision about life if we capitalized on emerging technology and gave customers what they wanted. The story's vision was ahead of the industry's technology capability," Dorothea Brennan explains. "The staff embraced the story. They added richer details about technology features, how their work was changing and how life would be better. By the time I left three years later, we had made enormous progress in making the story real."

Nancy Driver also brought in story to achieve a vision at USGS, a scientific organization with ten thousand staff in four hundred offices who assess the earth's natural resources. "Part of our organization's strategic plan is to develop innovative leaders. Our vision is to create a leadership-centered culture throughout the organization," she says. "We established our leadership program in 1999 and purposefully integrated story into it. We now have two 1-week leadership courses, 101 and 201, taught by senior managers. They share USGS stories to instill pride. Years later you hear participants retelling stories told in 101," she adds, continuing, "201 is for returning graduates. They share their leadership experiences through stories—what they learned in 101 that worked and didn't—and an outside consultant teaches a full day on storytelling," she notes. Storytelling continues past the classroom. "When both courses end, we give participants a coin to reward someone for exceptional acts of leadership. The objective is to pass on the coin. Leaders present it publicly and share a story of what they observed. They also write it up and put it on a Web site."

According to Driver, "Because storytelling falls under the umbrella of leadership, it works. Today we offer all employees a two-day leadership intensive course where we influence, share, and educate through story, in addition to providing four hours on storytelling. Graduates of 201 teach the story module. To be effective, storytelling has to be modeled."

Both organizational and initiative-level strategies can give rise to story work. Stories that encapsulate a vision and the behaviors needed to realize it motivate people to action. They also spur ongoing story use.

SPECIAL PROJECTS ARE
THE ENTRY POINT

Special projects can provide conduits for introducing stories even if organizational strategy does not. "In 1991, I was a docent at a museum that was looking for a scriptwriter to write anecdotal stories for radio about diverse ethnic and cultural groups that colonized Texas. The museum contracted with me to write them," Mary Grace Ketner recalls. "These daily radio spots were ninety seconds long. They were used as public service announcements." Here is one of them.

AMEN!

Contributed by Mary Grace Ketner

Fireman R. S. Hutcheson was an "extra" for the Southern Pacific Railroad who was sent to Miller Yard in Dallas to work a temporary vacancy in the switch engine on a graveyard shift. He had noticed that "Mr. Beckman" was in town, so he and the other workers were very careful to do everything exactly by the book. Beckman was a humorless man, one of Southern Pacific's "Traveling Engineers," whose job it was to check up on fellow workers and issue demerits to anyone caught violating the rules.

At about 3:00 A.M., the crew of the yard engine went to a nearby beanery to eat, as scheduled, all except Hutcheson who had brown-bagged it that night, so he had his sandwich and coffee in the cab of his engine. He had just finished when he saw Mr. Beckman walk by. He sat real still in the cab with his head down, hoping to go unnoticed.

But Beckman noticed him.

(Continued)

"Aha!" he thought. "I've caught someone sleeping on the job!"

He slipped up to the engine, eased open the door of the cab, and grasped his flashlight, relishing that moment of victory when he might shoot the beam into the violator's face.

But the satisfaction was not to be his. Just as Beckman's thumb felt for the switch, he heard Hutcheson murmuring devoutly, " . . . and God bless Mr. Beckman. Amen."

Radio script from M. G. Ketner, *LIFETIMES: The Texas Experience.* San Antonio, TX: UTSA's Institute of Texan Cultures, 2001. All rights reserved. Used with permission.

"These stories were offered to radio stations in Texas. More than fifty stations played a story daily. The biggest country and western station played one twice a day," Ketner says. "By the time I was eventually hired, the organization knew my storytelling skills. I'd also written a children's book and co-founded the San Antonio Storytelling Association.

"The staff never had someone who only used story. Story was always paired with pictures, artifacts, and drawings," she explains. "When I asked a question, the business director would say teasingly, 'You are the storyteller. Why don't you tell us?' He kept using the word so they gave me the title. That's how storytelling gently worked its way into the organization."

As Ketner demonstrates, stories often creep into organizations through special projects, sometimes in surprising ways. Such is Larry Forster's experience at Shell. "In 2001, I had an assignment to get our organization to do projects faster, using a standardized approach. I had difficulty getting the approach accepted, but I finally did. [Once] things got rolling I became involved in a task force to communicate what had been learned in 2001 to the rest of the organization and how we could improve as a result. Like others on the task force, I was frustrated, thinking all the analyses of the data we'd collected—the categorization, prioritization, and reasons why we *should* do something different—would likely fall flat [in a presentation]. They'd been tried many times before," he recalls.

Then something happened. "The facilitator for the task force said, 'Listen to this story and then let's discuss it.' It illustrated how mental models might impact choices and behaviors. The group was in a different space after that story. Our thinking was different. At that point, I remembered I'd [heard] a presentation by Steve Denning a few months earlier and [thought] at the time, 'Yeah, one day when I get around to it, I might think about applying storytelling.' It occurred to me this was the time. Story was the only thing that could clearly and meaningfully communicate a need for change," Forster says. "I [had] to convince the rest of the task force this was a good approach. So I called an ad hoc meeting and took the task force through a narrative of where we had been and what our thought process had been. At the end, I suggested we tell the senior leadership team a success story about how we'd done things differently."

How did the group respond? "The story method worked. People got on board. It generated enthusiasm. We put together a special hour program for the senior leadership team [that included] the success story. [It resulted in] higher-quality discussions with our senior leaders than in the past. The session was well-received."

Forster replicated this work. "[A year later] plans were being discussed for a series of Leadership Engagement Forums to be held in the next year to share learnings and promote dialogue. I volunteered for the steering team, thinking the introduction of stories would be beneficial, since what I'd been hearing up to that point was a lot of intellectual debate. As the [team] got rolling, I introduced using stories and helped put together part of the early forum sessions. At one session, participants got in small groups and came up with stories about their work that impressed them positively or negatively. They dialogued about them," he says. What happened when people started talking about the experience? "Stories changed the demeanor in the room [and] people's level of interest—they felt [the strategy communicated in the forum] was worth doing. We collectively, as an organization, got to what was really important. There was an urge to move away from the abstract to concrete actions."

Moving people to action motivated Lynne Feingold to introduce stories in her work. "In 1998, I was assigned to the U.S. General Services Administration (GSA) to determine best practices and lessons learned from the initial government-wide implementation of smart card technology. The public sector was waiting for the private sector to do it and vice versa," she recalls. "I interviewed public and private sector leaders and heard stories around nine government-wide smart card pilot [projects]. This gave me thirty pages of findings. I was scared my report would sit on a bookshelf. Presenting them through PowerPoint didn't feel right. So I asked my boss, 'Can I present lessons learned around smart card technology and the killer app as a dramatization?' He gave me the go-ahead."

Feingold had stories about the past, the present, and what needed to be done in the future to share. "I created a fortune-teller called Madame Lynne. I dressed and acted as an archetypal sage. In my presentation, I [synthesized] all the interview stories and shared our collective story. People heard their passions and frustrations. They saw a need to collaborate. It motivated them to action," she explains. "Afterwards, I was asked to make a video of my dramatization. It was taken to IT conferences around the world, including a G7 meeting. Even foreign delegates requested it."

Stories can bring special projects to fruition more effectively by serving as a helpful communication vehicle. Modeling stories or dramatizing them can help others warm to their application and to the messages they deliver.

MAKING AN ENTRANCE THROUGH DAILY WORK

"How can you get a higher-performing team and generate growth?" asks Arlene Jorgenson. "Life is too short to have all possible experiences, even through training. I transmit stories about difficult clients, noncompliance issues, and tough situations through e-mail to my five employees and contractors at HEALTHSERV to ensure learning points are preserved. If someone says, 'Did I tell you what happened on the weekend when I was called out to this company?' I say, 'Write it up and e-mail it to everyone. Make a point about what you'd do differently.' "

Jorgenson elicits stories every day. "When staff return from two days of hearing testing, I'll say, 'Give me two of your best stories' while we're having coffee. Tell me how things went," she says. "In a department meeting I'll ask, 'What is the story of the week?' Or I'll assign someone to bring a story to discuss. Then they're put on the coffee room bulletin board. I also share stories orally in meetings: 'You wouldn't believe what happened today. A client came in and said this.' "

Jorgenson helps staff members use stories. "If it's your turn to do an in-service, you're asked to pick a few significant stories to share with everyone in a meeting. I coach the person beforehand. This type of story sharing teaches critical thinking skills," she remarks. "The staff love it. Stories are integral to our business."

Coaching people on story use works. Mark Steiman has introduced story in this manner at Washington Mutual. "I engage with executives to address challenging situations or develop presentations. For example, I coached a leader who was going to use over fifty PowerPoint slides within a fifteen-minute talk. I told him, 'Let the story tell the story. Tell me the movie in your mind,'" he says. Do executives listen? "Sometimes they're reluctant until I provide a story example."

Steiman also coaches new executives on how to tell stories to build engagement and credibility. "I tell them, 'People want to understand who you are. Put away the PowerPoint!' To get at values I ask, 'Tell me what you've learned growing up that is important to you today.' To get over skepticism from high-performing teams, I say, 'Tell me something about your last group that moved it to the next level of success even though others thought things couldn't get better.' To help people get to know them better and identify where they can help, I ask, 'What keeps you up at night?'"

Steiman also finds ways for leaders to use stories with other leaders. "I coach leaders on getting a subordinate leader who is resistant to take a lateral move or promotion. The subordinate might be thinking, 'I'm a big fish in a small pond. I might not be as visible.' To address this, I'll ask the person I'm coaching, 'Recall a time in your career where you took a career risk and it turned out good for you.' Then I'll have the person share the story with the subordinate leader by saying 'I want to share something with you' or 'I remember when....'"

When stories are barely visible in an organization, making them part of a leader's daily work can take time. "More than a year after starting with United Illuminating, an electric utility serving south central Connecticut, I started using storytelling ideas with my boss and colleagues. Our group includes strategy, project management, facilities management, business continuity, and process improvement," Dorothea Brennan says. "We then held a four-hour event for those working on process[es] to share their stories. Since my boss was supportive of my developing a course in storytelling for the whole department, I had an outside consultant do a one-day event for us. I also incorporated story into process overview training." This work occurred over eighteen months.

At the same time, Brennan coached staff and leaders on story use. "I helped people develop presentations. I noticed the president sharing his own organizational experiences so I encouraged expanded use of company-based stories," she recalls. "Then I worked with process managers to create a story to integrate into a presentation the president gave on our strategy and goals that included a new rate case. Seventy-five leaders heard it. At leadership meetings that followed, we tied back to this story to update people on our execution of the rate case."

Sometimes, integrating stories into the way an organization approaches its work can be done fairly quickly. "At The Asset-Based Community Development Institute, our work revolves around five community assets—associations, institutions, individuals, physical attributes like parks and lakes, and the local economic situation," Tom Mosgaller says. "A few years ago at a faculty meeting I suggested through a story that we add a sixth asset—the ability to understand story and culture—since communities are built on strengths, not deficiencies. Everyone quickly agreed. They saw that storytelling and the creation of story are to communities [what] policies and procedures are to institutions—they're the bedrock of getting people to share in a community."

Community members are very receptive to stories. "In community meetings, faculty ask, 'What are the powerful stories that hold communities together?' People share a story about why they appreciate this community or chose to live in it. Some share immediately; others jump in afterwards with, 'I've got another story that connects to that,'" Mosgaller says. "After we've identified the community's assets, we close the gathering by going back to the opening stories and asking, 'Have other stories evolved during the course of the day? Or are there embellishments to the stories we heard earlier?' In the report that's sent back to the community are key points from these stories and those that are in the process of being collectively created."

Infusing stories into daily work through coaching is a subtle way of increasing employee and leader effectiveness and productivity without distracting people from what they are doing. Well-planned prompts can elicit powerful stories in the moment. When leaders provide storytelling examples and training, they inspire others to model the skills.

INSTILLING NEW WAYS OF THINKING AND BEHAVING

Once story work makes its way into an organization, it often shifts people's thinking and behavior. This is true for HEALTHSERV. "We save certain stories for client training to teach supervisors how to handle reasonable suspicions around substance abuse in the workplace," Arlene Jorgenson says. "Without breaking confidentiality, with client contacts we also share stories—collective stories—that we hear from their employees during hearing and drug tests and medical exams. We'll say, 'Here's what we believe are the needs of your employees. We heard this over and over again and we need to make it a priority.'" She adds, "Through theses stories we open our clients' eyes."

Opening employees' eyes to new ways of working has moved Dorothea Brennan to insert stories into training at United Illuminating. "Everyone takes a two-hour course called Process Overview Training. In it, we tell a story about restoring power. When customers lose electric power, they don't care that several departments work on an outage. Because we're focused on the process, call center reps, dispatchers, and power delivery crews must look across functional boundaries to meet about customers' needs," she explains. But there is more that employees need to know: "To improve our restore process, we measure the accuracy of our estimates using a ninety-minute window. By analyzing what drives results, [we show employees] we can develop ways to make our next estimate better."

Brennan adds, "When I started training, a crewmember said, 'Why not use an eight-hour estimate so we don't disappoint customers?' After showing a photo of a restaurant owner, we use this story to put employees in the customers' shoes, to help them think cross-functionally and recognize that 'when the lights go out' the customer cares about electricity *and* accurate information." The story she uses is on page 196.

"After telling the story, I ask the class, 'How does the chef feel about us? After all, we restored his power in two hours.' The good news is they all recognize that the customer is unhappy and that his business would be harmed by an inaccurate estimate of restoration."

Tom Mosgaller also knows how stories can improve thinking relative to process improvement efforts. "As director of quality for the city of Madison, Wisconsin, I saw the need for problem-solving teams to move beyond quantitative data and empirical information," he says. "We had a situation with refuse collectors who were to line up at the refuse plant to unload their trucks. Many of them waited for hours. The data suggested a problem with the refuse collectors. The real issue was they were all scheduled to unload at the same time. The team got the story. They learned to balance stories with facts and a systematic problem-solving approach and to turn a situation into a story so others can appreciate needed changes."

Creative story techniques can help people attach to personal stories and alter their behavior. "Ballroom dancing is effective in revealing

WHEN THE LIGHTS GO OUT, IT'S OUR TIME TO SHINE!

Contributed by Dorothea Brennan

Imagine you are the chef or restaurant owner whose picture we just saw. It is Saturday afternoon at 3 P.M.; due to the holidays, reservations are completely booked. Suddenly, your building loses electricity. You call the electric company's customer service line. You are pleased because you don't have to sit on the dreaded "hold." But then, the news is bad. Really bad! You hear, "Due to an equipment failure, we expect to restore your electricity by 11 P.M." You have to close! You just lost what would have been one of the most profitable nights of the year.

You send your staff home. You start calling your customers to cancel. It's now 5 P.M. If the electricity were on, you'd be serving the early bird specials. Instead you just reached the last customers and gave them the bad news. As you are walking out the door and locking up at 5:05 P.M., the restaurant lights flicker back on. Your electricity is restored! You could have stayed and taken walk-ins, but you sent your staff home earlier—the night is lost.

great leadership stories. The activity I've developed uses experiential right-brain, body-based learning followed with left-brained expressions of what transpired to make it work. Through dancing, people step into different stories of leadership and experience the stories they've habitually heard and told," Lynne Feingold says. "I used this approach in a seminar with successful IT professionals. It facilitated the participants' gaining better understanding of how gender differences in communication and leadership styles impact business results.

"Both participants and the organization benefit by the new stories co-created in the room. Participants share stories that evoke new understandings such as, 'When my organization goes through a challenging time, ballroom dance will give me a framework on how to *get*

SWEPT OFF YOUR FEET

Contributed by Lynne Feingold

1. Introduce ballroom dance as a way to reveal stories of successful leadership. Say to participants, "Ballroom dancing is a metaphor for leadership because it shows people experientially their stories about leading, collaborating, responding to change, and being in the flow of a great organization. The dance floor is a metaphor for the organization and the dance steps symbolize communication—the core of outstanding leadership."

2. Use professional dancers to demonstrate the waltz as leadership: how communication flows in leading (initiating) and following (responding). For demonstration purposes, two professional dancers are sufficient for a group of twenty participants. For the actual learning of the dancing, have each participant work with a professional dancer.

3. Invite participants to be paired with a professional dancer. Keep traditional roles in ballroom dancing (that is, the man leads).

4. Debrief using the question, "What leadership stories were evoked?"

5. Switch roles. Have the women lead.

6. Debrief using the question, "What additional leadership stories were evoked?"

7. Have participants partner and waltz, dancing identical steps at the same time. This means both people move forward or backward on the same step. They will either step on each other's toes or move apart. Then, debrief results. Ballroom dancing requires reciprocal but different steps, showing the need for diversity and collaborative leadership through listening and talking. Without this dialogue, there's no movement and the dance doesn't go forward. It's like a story—the dance requires listening and talking.

8. Have participants share habitual and new leadership stories by recapping the entire dance experience. Each time a

(Continued)

dancer's learning is facilitated, there are new stories. What's important here is the awareness of how we hold stories about leading, initiating, responding, and following as they relate to leadership in the workplace.

Developed by Lynne Feingold, organizational consultant and storyteller, February 2002. All rights reserved. Used with permission.

back in step'; and 'It takes more than one person to create a successful organization. Diversity is critical,'" Feingold explains.

Getting people to shift their thinking and behavior is a challenging task. Telling people topic-appropriate stories and engaging them in activities that elicit specific types of stories can trigger changes in mind-set and performance.

INSTITUTIONALIZING STORY USE

When individuals pioneer the use of stories within organizations, attached to their efforts come many insights. "Link story work to the organization's strategic plan. Give it a business context," Lynne Feingold says. Nancy Driver notes, "It must serve the organization's mission and vision." Personal intent is also key. "Clearly understand why you want to do it," adds Mark Steiman.

Mary Grace Ketner advises, "Identify where there's a natural fit for stories, like the organization's history. It's your job to bring story out, not bring it in. You can't impose storytelling on organizations. Bide your time. See blessings each step of the way and be grateful for them. If it's true and good, it'll rise to the top." Tom Mosgaller adds, "As Parker Palmer says, 'You can't go crashing through the woods and see any animals.' Listen deeply. Stories are there. Draw them out respectfully."

Dorothea Brennan says, "Culture matters. Can you use the word *storytelling* or is it better to use story without naming it? To determine this, read storytelling literature and reach out to people who're doing it." But Feingold says, "I talk about it as *business narrative* because it sounds more businesslike." And Mark Steiman reports, "My credibility would be shot if I sent out an e-mail saying 'calling all storytellers.' I model the behavior and tell people what I'm doing so they use it as a communication vehicle." Larry Forster admits, "I get resistance when

I tell people *about* stories, but I don't get resistance when I *tell* them stories." For Driver, "Modeling is the best way to diffuse it through the organization."

Ketner recommends, "Say yes to story anytime anybody asks you." Jorgenson suggests, "Invite customer service stories at staff meetings. It's a safe route. They'll give you a report card on how well the organization is doing." Steiman adds, "Mine and collect stories that already exist and find purpose and meaning in them."

Feingold says, "Be an ambassador. Bring in storytelling articles to get top people to see its value. Invite people to Golden Fleece and Smithsonian Institution events." Steiman adds, "Identify individuals inside the organization, external consultants, and organizations like the National Storytelling Network that can help you. In my organization we have a secret club. We don't formally get together but we instant message to test ideas or plan a meeting strategy."

Feingold says, "[I encourage] creating formal opportunities for people to become storytellers. Make it conscious and deliberate." Driver recommends "teaching people some processes and having them practice with no criticism." She says, "Oral presentation of stories is very powerful." But there's a caveat: "People can feel intimidated when their stories are audio- and videotaped. Watch that you don't impede the incredible process of sharing stories." Mosgaller adds, "Remember to reinforce people when you hear them share a story."

Forster also offers a caution: "Once storytelling becomes formalized, once it becomes official, it risks losing its essence and what's really important. Stories are like the people they come from. They live and breathe. They need space. If you try to clamp down and micromanage and get predictable, they'll die."

It is important to be conscious and purposeful when bringing story work into an organization. Using a variety of resources can help. So can formal training. Always be on the lookout for applications and be mindful of the challenges associated with formalizing a story initiative.

THE RESULTS ARE IN

All of these story pioneers have found their work pays off. "At Washington Mutual I've seen managers who were unapproachable become engaging, approachable, and increase personal power," Mark Steiman observes. According to Larry Forster, "Within Shell Exploration &

Production Company, people involved in the Leadership Engagement Forums are using stories without my prompting. They're telling success stories that are generating additional success stories. Leaders are also using more stories in meetings and one-on-one conversations."

Tom Mosgaller says, "At The Asset-Based Community Development Institute we've helped community members notice stories and reaffirm their value. We're capturing and telling more stories within communities and helping people develop the eyes and ears to get stories." For Lynne Feingold, "The seeds for story use that were planted in GSA were used in other work I've done with the State Department. My GSA boss said, 'Your work really made a difference in the strategic rollout of smart cards in the military. It got people to understand complex information in an easy way.'" At HEALTHSERV, "We've gotten more funding clients. If they aren't already sold on regulated testing, stories help sell it. Internally, stories get people on the same page—good wages and fair benefits are not enough today," Arlene Jorgenson explains.

At The United Illuminating Company, Dorothea Brennan acknowledges, "We've had success with stories in process overview training. In our one-day storytelling training, we saw real skill and story content improvement and enhanced ability to deliver stories because we worked on one story throughout the training." For Nancy Driver, "We have long waiting lists to get into 101 and 201 classes at the U.S. Geological Survey. We're also seeing significant improvements in the 360-degree feedback on participants before and after 101 and 201 training. The story part of 201 is consistently the highest rated. . . . More stories are used in the communications department and by managers and scientists in presentations and conversations. The organization is more conscious in its strategic use of historical stories. Our anniversary publication, *Celebrating 125 Years of the U.S. Geological Survey*, contains fabulous historical and scientific stories."

Story is also permeating UTSA's Institute of Texan Cultures. "Over the years we've incorporated storytelling through our Mid-Winter Tales Program, various festivals, and the New Texan Program that brought photographs and stories of newly naturalized citizens into a teaching curriculum on immigration and citizenry," Mary Grace Ketner notes. "The organization sponsors the Texas Folk Life Festival—a stage is dedicated to storytelling—and there's training on storytelling for docents. Our executive director is a storyteller and a member of the National Storytelling Network."

BLAZING A TRAIL

Story pioneers are deliberate in their actions. Consider these pointers as you bring story into your organization:

- Stay abreast of your organization's vision and strategies. Find opportunities to attach story to them or to the initiatives and special projects they generate over time.
- Integrate stories and training on storytelling into required training or training that is highly visible in the organization.
- Take the initiative to bring stories into various aspects of special projects. Model their power for others.
- Elicit stories that focus on strengths and successes as a way of introducing the concept of story to others.
- Be creative in how stories are communicated to or brought forth from others.
- Use story prompts on a daily basis. Hone your skills in this area.
- Coach people to apply stories to presentations, to their feedback with others, and in overcoming challenges.
- Hand out books and articles to increase people's awareness of story use and its benefits.
- Find ways to formally teach storytelling skills.
- Be patient. Allow the process of story to unfold in your organization. If it is right, people will embrace it.

It pays to be a story pioneer. Employees, leaders, and organizations all benefit. So do you. Open your eyes to the opportunities around you and find ways to capitalize on them.

Special Thanks

Thank you to Jo Tyler, Ed.D., of Pennsylvania State University for connecting me to Dorothea Brennan, and to Lynne Feingold for suggesting this chapter.

CHAPTER FOURTEEN

What Do You Suggest We Do?

Finding Answers and Ideas

in Research

Jo Tyler, Ed.D.

◈ In the workplace, people are quick to gather data to address issues. They look where the light is good—in places that can be reached efficiently or appear to be the most obvious. Or they ask within their network of colleagues who may be able to help implement potential solutions and avoid pitfalls effectively. Even though research in the field yields solid and useful results, its findings tend to go unheeded. Why is this? Perhaps, like "Nasrudin's Key" on page 203, these results are located where the light is not as bright.

What results have been generated in the field of storytelling? All these researchers have much to say on the topic: David Boje, Ph.D., professor of management and the Arthur Owens Chair in Business Administration at New Mexico State University; Barbara Czarniawska, M.A., E.D., the Swedish Research Council & Malmsten Foundation chair of management studies at Göteborg University; Robert Dennehy, Ph.D., professor of management at Pace University; Simon Kelly, Ph.D., research associate at the Centre for Excellence in Leadership, Lancaster University Management School; Roger Schank,

Nasrudin's Key

Contributed by Gail Rosen

Nasrudin Hodja was on his hands and knees peering through the grass and sifting the dirt with his fingers. A neighbor arrived and saw him there.

"Hodja, teacher, why are you crawling about?"

"I have lost my key," replied Nasrudin.

"Let me help you, then," said the neighbor. He began to crawl and meticulously search in the dust.

Another neighbor came, and then another, and another. Each one asked and then offered to help look, all of them crawling about, all around the Hodja's house. The sun began to set and the streetlamps were lit. Still they had not found the key.

Finally, the first neighbor said, "Nasrudin Hodja, where was the key when you last saw it?"

"I dropped it when I was in my basement," said Nasrudin.

"Then why are we looking here, outside?!"

"Because, my friend," said Nasrudin, "it is dark in my basement, and I am alone. Out here, [it] is light and [I have] many friends to help me."

Adapted from a traditional tale.

Ph.D., founder of the Institute for the Learning Sciences at Northwestern University and CEO of SocraticArts; and David Snowden, founder of The Cynefin Centre, an organization that spun off from IBM in July 2004 and is currently based in a network of academic institutions.

STORY RESEARCH OCCURS INSIDE ORGANIZATIONS

Researchers who focus on story are not stereotypical scientists conducting tests, reading documents, and drawing abstract conclusions in laboratories far removed from the real world. They work in the field—within a variety of organizations. Why is this? "Storytelling is not something one person does alone, but is collective behavior," David Boje contends, adding, "I feel practitioners need a living story approach—one that's based on research instead of speculation." Instead of bringing people to him to tell their stories, or reading written accounts of their stories, Boje goes to the heart of the story: "I go into organizations and . . . I observe the storytelling system. I collect stories *in situ* with a tape recorder. I go through the archives and look at the stories that the organization is telling about itself on its Web pages, in its annual reports, and in its displays to customers. I go where the action is."

"[People inside organizations] know all the current technology, but they're still not actually solving problems. They've got structure, they've got hypotheses, and that's all. Our method gets them closer to what's really going on," says David Snowden. "Going in, [researchers] don't have any assumptions. We're not intrusive and we can capture narrative representations of what's really happening that are hard for executives to ignore."

Like Snowden, Simon Kelly, concludes, "Practitioners are interested in any analysis connected to their lived experience." Stories are the rich vessels for conveying that lived experience. "Stories explicate everyday practice," he explains. "Stories begin because somebody has an idea and they want to make it happen, or the other way around: because something has happened and people in an organization need a way to react to it," Barbara Czarniawska adds, "You cannot experience this interplay between the cause and effect of stories from outside of the context of the organization, separate from its processes."

Because of this, Boje steers people away from popular books on story not well grounded in field research. "Most practitioner books on storytelling," he says, "treat each story as a relic, a dead object to measure and dissect. What practitioners are led to believe about storytelling is a rather esoteric approach to stump speeches . . . or fairytale archetypes told by a CEO, coached by a consultant to think that a two-minute story grafted into a speech is what storytelling work is all about." Snowden and Boje agree that narrative material in organizations is rarely in fully formed stories, but comes as fragments (Boje) or anecdotes (Snowden), and that the packaging of stories into neatly produced sound bites is dangerous since, as Snowden suggests, "you end up with a form of propaganda."

By situating themselves as direct observers inside organizations, researchers can shine lights into shadowy corners that have been misunderstood or even ignored by organizational insiders. Shifting the research process into the workplace broadens the range of questions researchers can ask and the types of research methods they employ to find the answers people need to address critical issues.

RE-STORYING TO COUNTER ORGANIZATIONAL ATTACKS

Imagine your firm's reputation has been attacked. How do you shift the organization's story to handle this? David Boje researched how McDonald's rewrote its story to create a new image of its "fast food" as "healthy fast food." This occurred simultaneously with the release of a documentary film, *Super Size Me,* which graphically demonstrated the extreme effects of a steady diet from the chain's menu. "In response to the public attention, McDonald's launched a new story, a worldwide initiative promoting healthy living of nutrition and fitness as their global strategy," Boje comments.

McDonald's is one of many organizations over time that has found itself in a position of needing to shift its story. "The big point I want to make," Boje says, "is that storytelling organizations are spinning stories in reaction to other stories. So I focus on how people and organizations can re-story. Practitioners will find re-storying very beneficial." How does re-storying work? "We are captive in a dominant story told by ourselves and others. The problem is how to deconstruct . . . the dominant story so that we can re-story a new story from all the bits and fragments of stories that defy the logic of the dominant story," he explains, adding, "Part of the process of re-storying is to get a grip on the ongoing storytelling system—on the dominant story that has a grip—and loosen that grip so a new story can be told. One that is transformative."

Why is this important? "Dominant and marginal, official and unofficial stories all vie for attention of customers, employees, managers, vendors, and leaders. . . . If you want the story to be more than spin, you have to have something worthy of telling. When you make up a story about your stock performance or your assets, like Enron did, the sky does eventually fall," Boje explains.

Re-storying also has as impact at the level of the individual. Based on his research, Robert Dennehy notes, "How to re-story the organization is also [about] asking the question, 'How can you re-story yourself, re-story your role in the organization?' Jack Welch did it when he re-storied himself from engineer to leader, and then into a leader who listened. It's not easy and you can't do it alone. But you can do it."

When an organization is experiencing turmoil with its story, it may well be time to consider crafting a new *authentic* organizational story to reposition it in the hearts and minds of its internal and external stakeholders. On the other hand, the organization may only need to develop new credible stories around the personas of its leaders. And then there will be times when the stories at both levels need to shift.

STORIES LEADERS TELL . . . AND HEAR

Listening to stories can aid in developing an understanding of the effect of overall strategy changes on organizational leaders. As part of her "Managing Big Cities" research program, Barbara Czarniawska worked with a public utility in Warsaw, Poland. "The organization was facing significant change as its role shifted on the basis of the maturity of its underground transportation system. [It] was changing from being the constructors of underground transportation to operating and maintaining the transportation system."

Czarniawska shadowed managers in the utility company. "I had a chance to see what they were doing, and listen to them talk to each other about it . . . how they represented themselves and their actions in the stories they told to others about their work," she says. She outlines her rationale for shadowing them: "The managers told each other stories of their work that were filled with humor and plots and heroes. Pierre Bourdieu made a distinction between 'logic of practice' and a separate 'logic of representation.' [Because of my research], I was able to contrast these two forms of logic to better understand the effect of organizational change on those in leadership roles."

Simon Kelly's extensive field research in the United Kingdom with senior administrators in further (that is, higher) education has focused on the collecting and retelling of their stories. "These stories are accounts of work that usually wouldn't be documented and passed on, but which provide detailed descriptions of work that's done and suggestions of how such work can be supported by others," he says. "[By] observing [administrators], attending meetings, taping conversations, taking photographs, and making field notes, we don't just focus on the content of the stories; we look at the occasions in which stories are told. And not just inside the organization—outside it, too. Places outside of the formal structures of the organization, like a pub, for example, provide members with an informal and safe environment in which certain kinds of stories can be told."

In his work, Kelly distinguishes between "invited stories" resulting from interview questions and "naturally occurring stories" collected in observational work. "The invited stories said very little about what leadership actually looks like in practice [and] . . . were told with a purpose or a moral lesson that the manager wanted to convey. It was the naturally occurring stories, with their rich detail, conveyed without a persuasive agenda, which became a 'powerful tool for understanding leadership in action.' Since people make sense by telling story in conversation, and story is familiar to people, it is a useful way to explicate what goes into the everyday work of leadership."

Kelly echoes Boje's point about stories that run contrary to the dominant story. "[Any kind of] story often challenges the dominant story of the good, heroic leader and business excellence. This makes them controversial," he notes. So what can organizations do to honor these stories? "[Organizations can] create nonjudgmental spaces in which people can discuss how difficult [leadership] is. Where they can tell stories of failing and falling short." This kind of conversation is meaningful when people can "accurately reflect back" what is really happening. "It has a cathartic quality to it because it provides a message that you're not the only one doing your job a certain way," he contends. "While these spaces can be created in training classes and in the social time that follows them, they need to be *democratic and authentic* with no effort to try to replace practitioners' sense of the world they work in with a glossy version," Kelly adds.

"Try soliciting stories from your organization about your organization and really listen to them," Robert Dennehy suggests. Like Kelly, he is interested in the authenticity of stories and the dynamics of the spaces in which they are told. "I'm most interested in *two-way storytelling* and the social setting that allows it to take place. Jack Welch and Jeffrey Immelt [at GE] moved from making presentations to providing frameworks for people to talk and listen and gain information, to storytelling for everyone," he says. What helps make two-way storytelling effective? "The key is to get a handle on what outcome you want. Ask the questions and listen to the answers. Don't just use that traditional concept of the storyteller—a librarian with children at her feet. The listeners are interpreting the stories. It's those interpretations you want to know. How do you find that out? Get them to tell their stories, so you get the interpretations."

Getting leaders to tell stories has significant benefits. So does story retelling. By sharing the stories he has collected through his research, Kelly has helped others examine the true nature of leadership in action. "We've used stories from the research to start a dialogue in the leadership development programs offered at [Lancaster] University. The stories provided a common ground for further dialogue and provided participants and trainers with 'teachable moments' that might not have occurred without listening to the story first. [Through these stories] we draw attention to the skills and knowledge that leaders have and examine the dominant story. We can unpack the story of leadership and even celebrate its collaborative nature," he explains.

By helping leaders to listen to story narrative through a technique known as pre-hypothesis research, The Cynefin Centre assisted leaders of one organization in uncovering what causes people to shy away from new technology. "A South African Bank was convinced the reason for lack of penetration of its services to a township was the consequence of the residents of that township not understanding banking. The bank's hypothesis-based market research confirmed this hypothesis, but more education did not produce a result," David Snowden says. So what did the bank do? "By capturing a body of narrative and allowing the residents of the township to interpret their own material without the use of experts, it became evident that the issue was the new Automated Teller Machines (ATMs) being installed in their neighborhoods.

"Working with the customers of the bank who were unaccustomed to using the machines, the self-analysis of their stories revealed that customers saw the ATMs as 'a focus for crime.' They were putting their money in there. When you put money in the machine—it was *your* money in the machine. So if someone robbed the machine they were taking *your* money. However much you put in there, it would be gone," Snowden explains. What did this insight teach the bank's leaders who installed this equipment? "The management made all kinds of assumptions about the reasons behind residents' behavior. The bankers' hypothesis was based on their own perspective, as would have been that of the expert interpreter. They didn't listen to the narrative of the customer, so they got answers that supported their hypothesis."

In Snowden's view, narrative is becoming increasingly relevant, beyond the popular concept of storytelling. "Similar work in North America showed that an agrochemical company's hypothesis (supported by market research) that its competitor was more effective was not supported by narrative material from farmers, which made no mention of the competition. Stories revealed that today's farmers are highly educated in science and require seed representatives of agrochemical companies to be the same. As in South Africa, the hypothesis was blinding the organization to the authentic voice of the narrative," Snowden asserts.

Soliciting or inviting stories from leaders as well as listening to those that naturally occur can help in understanding the effects of strategic changes and everyday leadership behaviors. Finding or creating nonjudgmental spaces for leaders to tell their stories can ensure that difficult and authentic stories emerge. In addition, getting leaders to pay attention to the naturally occurring stories of others can aid them in taking appropriate business actions.

STORY AND KNOWLEDGE MANAGEMENT

The interest in using stories to manage knowledge is growing. "Narrative," David Snowden points out, "is the next big wave in knowledge management and strategy."

Roger Schank's interest is in developing video databases that are specially constructed and used for "collecting two-minute stories from the best people doing 'X.'" He adds, "The problem is one of indexing. How do you get the right story at the right time? You need to simulate it on a computer so that you can do an idea search. You need the search mechanism to be user friendly, intuitive, and detailed because 'you can't build a database with a point of view.'"

David Snowden has also recognized this problem of indexing. He describes what he's developed as "indexing that's more accurate than surveys, for example, linking stories to archetypes of self, or archetypes of leaders, or HR archetypes, such as 'miser, ghost, or eager beaver.'" He outlines the process: "Employees choose one or two or three archetypes and themes that connect to why the story was told, or they interpret their own stories in terms of the archetypes. In this way, the database becomes a monitoring device for trends about organizational archetypes—archetypes of self [or] archetypes of leaders, for example—that can be mapped and analyzed."

Snowden believes particular stories should not be privileged by managers or experts. This means they should not be given a higher priority or more visibility just on the basis of the story's form or content. "The stories that people tell when prompted by an indirect question about their experience and the way they index them all provide meaning, whether they are good or bad in terms of outcome or structure. People pay more attention to failure than success because they learn more from it," he says. As a result, his method captures and records all stories in their original format and allows serendipitous encounters with those stories based on an index query.

"We need to use computers to reflect naturalistic human processes rather than force humans to conform with taxonomic structures designed for the convenience of the computer," he maintains. Snowden provides a query example from an early project that demonstrates this: "We asked, 'Tell me all the stories told by a rational archetype around the theme that our product kills people, told with high emotional intensity from the perspective of a first witness.' That query threw nineteen anecdotes on the screen in their original form. The reader was then able to interpret those stories in the context of a current need. [This produced] an interaction between current need and historical raw stories, which reflects a modern version of the oral tradition."

Because David Boje views stories as living phenomena, he voices a concern about capturing them: "There are illusions about story knowledge management work. Practitioners have been led to believe . . . they can collect stories from workers, put that tacit knowledge [embedded in the story] into a story database, and with a wave of their magic wand successfully transfer workers' story knowledge into a management information system that allows knowledge retrieval once the workers have been laid off. Here is a big illusion: You cannot do it. All the computer storage in the entire world could not put in all the nuances of all the story knowledge of just a few workers. It's sheer fantasy!" With this said, Boje believes there are ways to pursue the connection between stories and knowledge management. "I've been working with Theodore Taptiklis, a former McKinsey consultant from New Zealand, [who has] developed a novel approach to story knowledge. He developed software that allows people to record living stories on any kind of digital recorder and then make that story part of an interactive database. The people who input the stories control who gets access; they retain their story rights," he notes.

In any knowledge management application, it is important to consider that not all stories may be created equally or with equal value. "There's good storytelling and there's bad storytelling. You should only tell stories that you want to hear," Barbara Czarniawska suggests. Roger Schank reinforces this observation: "The only thing that memory has is a collection of stories, but some are more interesting and important than others."

The role of story in knowledge management is an important one. Organizations will need to determine how to appropriately handle the collection and indexing of stories and their retrieval given the challenges that have been raised by researchers.

TEACHING STORYTELLING: CAN WE OR SHOULD WE?

Researchers debate whether or not story can—and should—be taught. "Storytelling isn't something that can be taught," Simon Kelly maintains. "It's a recognizable feature of everyday life. The focus should be on making experience *storyable,* rather than on making stories," he contends. Roger Schank provides a similar view: "It's not so much that storytelling needs to be taught, but that everyone should be debriefed at the end of their day or their assignment. Maybe it should be like they're at a bar, and someone asks them, 'What was your day like?' . . . Instead of teaching people to tell stories, we need to learn to create experiences for people that make them want to tell stories. Constructing the story is constructing the memory. After a while, you only remember what you said [about the story you have lived]."

Robert Dennehy, who has worked extensively with leaders at GE like former CEO Jack Welch, says, "Storytelling is real conversation about real work in real time." But at the same time, he is a proponent of teaching it. "Everyone in my classes at Pace University becomes a storyteller," he explains. "Good managers are storytellers and students can't get out of my class without being a storyteller. I saw it with Welch. He emerged from being an engineer to being a real storyteller. His engineering background was the starting point of good narrative, but he had to learn how to tell stories as well as lead."

Perhaps the issue of training people on how to tell stories is not an either-or proposition. It may be that creating experiences in which people want to tell stories and providing them the tools to do so in a meaningful way are both useful perspectives. The key is careful consideration of the nature of your goals and the organization in which you work.

THOUGHTS ON GETTING STARTED

People in the workplace frequently ask, "How do I get started with using stories and storytelling in my organization?" Here are some thoughts from researchers in the field:

> "People in organizations are already using storytelling. The questions are: Are they using it wisely? Are they using it strategically?" (David Boje)

> "[While] it's not easy, you just need to start. You need to try it out in a safe environment and see how it works." (Robert Dennehy)

> "Start by finding an intractable problem. Focus on the narrative of the problem, and forget about storytelling. With storytelling, you end up with entertainment but not learning." (David Snowden)

> "Learn to create experiences that make people want to tell stories of that experience—their own experience. . . . And go to the CEO. Go to him first, and ask for a couple of hours and ask him to tell stories." (Roger Schank)

Boje also offers a caution: "[Don't] buy the hype and illusion of the storytelling consulting books. Stop seeing story just as 'text' as in academic narratology work. My advice is to dig into all the many modes of storytelling that are simultaneous, distributed, and part of the storytelling organization: its system, strategy, leadership and daily behavior." Simon Kelly agrees: "Organizations are already engaging in their own anthropology, in their own ethnography. They're sharing stories all the time. It's about describing what's happening, providing a rich description of the accomplishments of work."

Kelly identifies one requirement: "[Storytelling] does require trust, so one role practitioners can have is to help make the process safer." Snowden echoes these sentiments and reminds us that organizational storytelling is laden with issues around the ownership of stories by the people who tell them: "Narrative, properly used, represents a form of self-organizing anthropology. It requires considerable attention to ethical issues in its use, and to the dangers of expert or managerial prejudices creeping in."

Ultimately, Barbara Czarniawska advises, "Don't make such a big fuss about storytelling. I am reminded of the character from Molière who has been speaking prose his whole life, but he never realizes it. Of course workers are already telling stories, but they don't talk about it that way. Practitioners need to realize that because it's already happening naturally, they will kill it if they make it too systematic."

For organizational leaders who remain unconvinced by an employee's call to focus on storytelling, Czarniawska has a clear and simple message: "Storytelling is a valid human way of communicating. If someone doesn't want to believe it, they do so at their own peril."

Note: Simon Kelly is an independent researcher whose research project on storytelling and leadership in further education has been funded by but does not necessarily reflect the views of the Centre for Excellence in Leadership.

CHAPTER FIFTEEN

There Are Five Sides to Every Story

Which Are You Missing?

Lori L. Silverman

"Are you getting what you want in your organization? Are you fulfilling your mission?" asks Sylvia L. Lovely, executive director and CEO of the Kentucky League of Cities and president of NewCities Institute. "To get results, leaders need to shift paradigms and start seeing stories." According to Michael Margolis, founder and CEO, THIRSTY-FISH Story Marketing, "Story is hiding in plain sight. Leaders must recognize the strategic importance of stories and invest in practices to make them a part of the culture for doing business."

What the organizations in this book have collectively demonstrated are five practices for strategically integrating stories into how they function. They know they get results when they find, dig into, select, craft, and embody stories, as illustrated in Figure 15.1.

Lovely and Margolis have recognized these practices in their work. So have Cathryn Wellner of Interior Health; Karen Dietz, Ph.D., of the National Storytelling Network; Jo Tyler, Ed.D., of Pennsylvania State University; Alicia Korten of Renual; Joan Lipkin of That Uppity Theatre Company; Major Patrick Michaelis and Major Mark Tribus of the U.S. Army; and Gayle Shaw-Hones, BSN, MSIT, and Ashesh Gandhi, PharmD, of Wyeth Pharmaceuticals.

Figure 15.1. The Five Sides of Story.

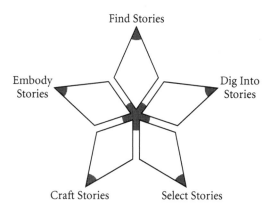

FINDING STORIES

To find stories, one must know what they are. According to Karen Dietz, executive director of the National Storytelling Network, "A story is an act of communication that provides people with packets of sensory material that allow the listener to quickly and easily internalize the material, understand it, and create meaning from it." Michael Margolis says, "You can't have a story without a listener. It's what defines story as two-way communication. What makes or breaks a story is how people choose to receive it."

"We need to listen with an appreciative ear, not interrupting to get facts straight, judging what's being said, or responding with our thoughts," Dietz says. Cathryn Wellner, food and health project manager for Interior Health, suggests, "Listen intently. Give people your undivided attention. They'll feel heard and validated." Dietz adds, "Listening in these ways encourages the person telling the story to keep going. They'll tell you a story instead of telling you *about* a story. You'll receive more sensory details, emotions, and emotional accuracy."

Alicia Korten, founder and executive director of Renual, uses this exercise to help people listen more effectively to stories. "In a group of twenty-five people, select a leader and assign roles such as daydreamer, criticizer, and 'the star' to six more individuals. These roles represent activities we all sometimes do instead of listen. In a fishbowl setting, give these seven people a task—like organizing a company holiday party—and have them act out the characters. Debrief what happens. I'll usually follow this with a deep listening exercise where people try to listen to one another's stories without interruptions or judgment."

Jo Tyler, assistant professor of Training & Development at Penn State, suggests, "Listen for all types of stories by 'tuning your ear.' Familiarize yourself with the overall discourse of the organization. Connect different pieces of the story from various people. Realize that if you have a goal [for listening], you may overlook stories equally important to those you acknowledged." As Wellner points out, "It's beneficial to have a framework for listening to capture the correct stories. You can get this by knowing the meta-narrative. For example, in public health it's the larger story about health and why we need to work upstream. With this framework you can ask, 'How does this story fit? What does it mean? How can I use it?' We all live within our own meta-narrative and that of our organization and society. We can't listen for stories tabula rasa. We all have filters."

"I focus on the absence of stories as well as their presence," comments Joan Lipkin, founder and artistic director of That Uppity Theatre Company. "I notice what or who is not in the room. Then I ask questions about what's missing. This is how the DisAbility Project started in 1995. The absence of people with disabilities from cultural life is glaring. Now this project empowers individuals, honors their stories, sparks imagination, fosters community, encourages civic dialogue, and enhances public awareness about disability through innovative theater of the highest quality."

Dietz notes, "Evoking stories is a core leadership activity. Get out of your office and chat with employees. Have people relate experiences instead of data, thoughts, and opinions. Use, 'Tell me about a time . . .' followed by 'What happened then?' Or try, 'Tell me what happened with . . . ' These prompts ask people to use story language. They differ from 'Did you have any problems today?' which is an information-gathering technique where someone *reports* on a situation."

"Depending on the prompt, you can co-create stories to address situations rather than impose solutions. Because I'm more interested in what's right than examining what's wrong, I use prompts that elicit positive stories," Wellner says. Some of her favorites are on page 217.

Gayle Shaw-Hones, associate director of learning and performance for Global Medical Affairs at Wyeth, used this approach as manager of instructional design for sales training. "I wanted to learn how sales reps were using detail aids on a specific drug in their talks with physicians. These detail aids are approved promotional materials that pro-

STORY PROMPTS

Contributed by Cathryn Wellner

- Tell a story about a time when you felt passionate and alive in your work.
- What stories do you find yourself telling repeatedly about your work?
- Tell a story that demonstrates your [values, a program's objectives, or a mandate] in action.
- If you could tell one story to explain what you do, what would it be?
- What stories do you tell to make what's at stake [your research, program, or organization] clear to someone who knows nothing about it?
- Tell the story of one of your professional successes.
- Tell the story of a time when something you believed was true turned out to be false.

vide key points about a drug; [they are] used in detailing physicians on our products. Via mass distribution by e-mail and voicemail I said, 'Tell me how you use these detail aids. Then I'll collect these accounts and use them to create learning aids for [you].' More than 130 reps shared actual stories through voicemail—you could hear their excitement. The six most relevant stories were approved by our promotional review process and put onto audio CDs accompanied by content on best practices. [The CD] was also an interactive CD-ROM with visual supports depicting the detail aid along with an explanation about how the conversation progresses at various points."

Even with successes like these, there are some pointers to note. "Give people at least two different story prompts in case one doesn't trigger a story. I prep people one-on-one prior to a facilitated session if the environment is difficult or trust hasn't been established," Korten says. Tyler suggests, "Pay attention to the organization's power dynamics. If a vice president isn't trusted he'll get one type of story. If he sends out people, they'll get different stories. We only hear stories within our own social networks. How do you talk about your purpose for evoking a story? Who do you send to listen for them? Why and how are they asking? What is the climate in the organization? You need to consider these issues." Dietz adds, "Use this approach judiciously. It's not a catch-all for every single conversation."

Evoking stories from the distant past is as valuable as listening to those happening right now. According to Margolis, "We need to give ourselves permission to harvest the gemstones from history that represent 'who we are' and inform how we do things. These core stories are the source of motivation to propel organizations forward. You have to know where you come from to know where you're going."

He provides an example: "Use anniversaries as the centerpiece for a strategic communication campaign that educates staff around the organization's core identity. Invite people into the process by explaining why you want to uncover certain types of stories. These rich legacies can legitimize credibility, reinforce what's good and unique about the organization, instill a sense of pride, and give people a filter to look at their daily work experiences. If you translate them to the external world, you can reinforce and boost market presence and contribute to your industry's larger body of knowledge."

To find stories requires listening appreciatively to communications and tuning in to all types of conversations within the organization—as well as paying attention to what is not said. Thoughtful, well-structured story prompts can elicit stories about the past, present, and future and help uncover those that are hidden from view.

DIGGING INTO STORIES

Having people share stories is one thing. Identifying the stories' deeper meaning holds even more value. "I hold sharing circles with the Dis-Ability Project ensemble to identify what's important to people with disabilities," Joan Lipkin explains. "Without interruption, people tell a story about what's on their mind or what's going on with them. Afterwards, I might ask questions to get more details. Then after each story I usually ask, 'Does this happen to any of the rest of you?' Their responses lead me to figuring out the next step. For example, if people are talking about the idea of being cured, I'll divide them into working groups using the themes I heard such as, 'it's your fault', 'tel-evangelism', and 'religion and disability' and have them create theatrical pieces around them. We push the envelope on metaphors to reframe experience. For example, one ensemble member who has advanced multiple sclerosis had another hospitalization. When asked, 'How are you doing? How was it?' he said, 'It was like Club Med.' So I had him develop a comic monologue as though going to the hospital were a vacation."

In addition to reframing situations, digging into stories can help people explore a topic in greater depth. "To create a values statement, I'll have people tell stories about moments of great pride, a person who's greatly impacted the organization's culture, or an organizational leader who's greatly impacted the world—and I'll have people title their stories," Alicia Korten says. "After a half hour, I'll ask the entire group, 'What values are you hearing?' We blend various stories, comparing and contrasting them. Let's say credibility gets identified as a value. I'll ask, 'In what stories did you hear this value?' I'll list the titles of these stories next to the word, credibility." She adds, "People love this exercise. It really brings values to life and helps to show the multidimensional ways in which a value might manifest within an organization."

Michael Margolis points out, "When working beneath the surface of stories, you'll confront mental models, assumptions, feelings, and beliefs—the dominant existing narrative. If you're doing something new or different, you must also understand the counter-narrative. The dominant surface narrative controls perceptions of what's right or wrong. Many counter-narratives provide a new claim or definition of truth and what's right. For example, the dominant narrative story in the United States around the juvenile justice system is that it's legal and punitive. Because of its businessification, the prison system needs to grow. The new counter-narrative is about humanizing the prison system. The challenge is bringing this new story into popular culture. One way is to look for 'untold stories'—aspects of the universal story that aren't being told around the issue."

In her current role in medical affairs, Gayle Shaw-Hones took the initiative to search for and understand 'untold stories' as a member of a multidisciplinary team tasked to create training on the promotional review process, which, for example, ensures detail aids are properly reviewed before release to sales representatives. "The team talked with people about specific process steps, but I was interested in the white spaces between them as well as the whole process. I volunteered to review current training [because] I wanted to identify root causes of what wasn't going well," she says.

"In the process, editorial, medical, legal, and regulatory employees conduct individual reviews. Then they come together for a review meeting where everyone's comments are shared," she continues. "So,

I suggested [we] interview people in medical affairs who do this work. The interviewers asked the reviewers, 'Tell about [medical affairs'] role in the promotional review process. Tell about problems [medical affairs] is facing. What things are going well? When you're interacting with people, what's not explicit in the process?' We were looking for know-how—tacit knowledge. To get a fuller picture, [interviewers] also interviewed legal and marketing staff. In all, the interviewers did thirty-nine interviews and captured three stories from each person." Below is an excerpt from one of these stories, from Ashesh Gandhi, director of medical communications, cardiovascular & gastrointestinal, in Global Medical Affairs.

"Through these stories I learned their work is very subjective and difficult to learn to do well. I realized relationship building and subjective aspects of the process weren't being captured or shared by anyone," Shaw-Hones notes. "Physician and scientist reviewers have different sets of problems so I identified the top three facing each group. Then I went back to the stories to figure out who had a story that explained how they solved these problems. The interviewers talked to these people and got the details."

"To address these problems, I created an e-learning piece. With help from others, I built a character and story line to create 'a day in the life of a new promotional reviewer.' It covers problems, tools used

REVIEWING PROMOTIONAL MATERIALS
Contributed by Ashesh Gandhi, PharmD

One time I received this piece from the managed care side of our marketing team. I began to review the piece and had a difficult time because I had no background on the piece at all. What I knew to do before passing it along, or rejecting the piece altogether, was to give the marketing contact a call. I asked him to provide me with the background as to why this piece was created and what the intent was [for it]. With that context, shared through a story of the product, I could review the piece with the correct perspective, which was to meet the goals of the brand and at the same time to confirm the medical and scientific accuracy of the content.

to overcome them, and how to collaborate with others in the process," she explains. What is she doing with the remaining stories? "I'm keeping them to populate new learning—to uncover new and different problem-solving techniques. In the future I'd like to build a database where someone can search based on a problem and find a story that solved it."

Shaw-Hones also had a surprise when soliciting stories: "In early interviews, the interviewer got executive bullet point summaries. So she added the word *story* to her conversation: 'Continue your story.' 'Tell me another story.' 'Tell me a story about. . . .' To get the story's premise and the outcome, she had to let them explain all points, connections, and characters. It's not enough just to get the facts straight."

Going below the surface of stories can help people reframe situations in a new light, help them explore a critical topic in greater detail, and call forth the structure of the dominant story narrative. At this depth, untold stories and relationships may emerge, making possible the creation of innovative approaches.

SELECTING STORIES

"To select stories you need to understand the goals of your organization. Strategic storytelling is about directly connecting stories to highly relevant goals in the organization," Jo Tyler comments. Cathryn Wellner adds, "Look for cogent defining stories—stories that convey something about what's valued in the organization and what's done through people's work."

Karen Dietz defines this further: "The stories you select depend on the issue and what you're trying to reinforce or accomplish. Are you rethinking your marketing or branding or are you going through a culture change? Because stories are multi-faceted, the same story can be assessed from different viewpoints and mean different things. For example, a customer service story seen through a different lens might be about an internal process or company value."

Do all stories contain value? According to Tyler, "Don't ignore or silence stories that live in the shadows of the organization. If you do, people might not find themselves within the stories you tell. If you don't acknowledge these stories, sanctioned stories may not be taken as seriously. How do you honor difficult stories within the organization? By saying, 'This happens here.' [For example], acknowledge a disconnect between a story and the stated corporate values. If you don't, you risk making decisions that only cater to the happy, upbeat side of the organization." Dietz adds, "You need dark stories as much as wonderful stories. Life is about balancing dark and light stories. If the organization's dominant stories are dark, leaders need to tell light stories so it can move closer to a state of equilibrium."

These challenges around story selection faced Major Patrick Michaelis—executive officer, 1st Squadron, 7th U.S. Cavalry, 1st Cavalry Division—who served as the division's chief knowledge officer during Operation Iraqi Freedom II. "In 2004, the Army's 1st Cavalry Division of thirty thousand troops found itself stationed in Baghdad. Army junior leaders were dealing with an adaptable and agile enemy that, in some cases, evolved their tactics every three to five days. Patrol leaders needed to prepare for combat patrols that went out every six to twelve hours. Because these leaders were separated by space and a hierarchical culture, it became apparent that although the enemy was tactically evolving rapidly, our counter-learning process was not fast enough to keep pace with our insurgent opponent. Not all tactics, techniques, and procedures (TTPs) are common knowledge," Michaelis notes. "Our challenge was figuring out how to rapidly share actionable knowledge through linking leaders together in a discussion or forum about emerging enemy and friendly tactics and procedures. After-action reviews (AARs), which we're good at doing, take a long time to diffuse across the division, and were filtering out situational context."

With approval from Major General Peter Chiarelli, Michaelis and his team developed a Web site called CAVNET, which was tailored to the approximately 220 company-level commanders and their environment. "It cost us $2,500 for messaging board software that was simple and intuitive to use. Our first challenge was establishing credibility with leaders we wanted to interview who work sixteen- to eighteen-hour days. How could we be both humble and inquisitive in our inquiry? We established an 'embed' program where we placed an officer dedicated to building rapport with the junior leaders in order to harness what was being learned, and educate leaders about the CAVNET in each Brigade. We decided to look at what they were doing right and not wear rank when accompanying troops on patrol," he describes. "Because we only had twenty-four to forty-eight hours with each unit, we hung out with platoon leaders, first sergeants, and company commanders. We'd ask, 'What do you know now that you wished you had known forty-five days ago?' With a digital tape recorder, we'd capture responses. We also got stories on patrol, after dinner, or when they debriefed the patrol and did an AAR."

How did Michaelis select stories for the Web site? "I looked for patterns—things I could corroborate—rather than single instances. I looked for indicators around what was working for the United States and what was identified from the enemy. These were based on experience and their defined impact. I also looked for patterns relevant to the Commanding General and Brigade Commanders," he explains.

"We'd populate CAVNET with an overarching story: 'Here's what particular units have seen,' and then ask, 'What are you seeing?' to promote conversation and evoke more stories to harness what others were learning. We wanted CAVNET to be just like breathing. Any one of 220 company commanders could put something on it; 85 percent had access to it. They each got one to five postings a day. Intell guys used it and we talked with embeds every day or two to get information into classified public forums so it could be used by our forces in their decision cycle against an evolving enemy," Michaelis says. Did it work? "The site had 50,000 hits in its last month."

Some stories traveled further. "Every month we put together a collection of the ten to fifteen most important posts. They were selected based on their relevance across the division's entire battle space and their immediate impact and universality," Michaelis reports. "I've taken what I've learned to new officers attending the Army's Infantry and Artillery School, and the current unit that replaced us, so they can learn what's being done on the ground. I'm currently working on an advanced version that combines information, data, and knowledge together into one system."

Before you can select stories, you have to capture them. Wellner recommends, "Capture stories that spark your imagination even without knowing how you'll use them." She has a simple approach. "I give people a pocket-sized notebook and tell them to record an outline of the story, how it could be used, what it means in the context of their work as well as a title and potential audiences for its use."

The Kentucky League of Cities (KLC) goes a step further. "All staff and interns systematically collect stories from members in phone calls, roundtable discussions, board meetings, and informal conversations. We also ask for them on the home page of KLC's Web site. Over the years, we've captured hundreds of stories from communities throughout Kentucky. They're stored in an intranet story pool that's organized by city and topic and is searchable by key word," Sylvia L. Lovely says.

Be strategic and deliberate in the selection of stories for ongoing use in the organization, recognizing the stories waiting in the shadows also need to be fully acknowledged. For this to happen, you need a system in place to capture them.

CRAFTING STORIES

How can organizations set the stage for using story structure as a communication vehicle? "We talk about the approach in our staff policy manual," explains Sylvia L. Lovely. The text is presented in the box below.

"Stories have a pattern: a beginning that hooks the listener, a middle that unrolls the conflict, and an ending that ties it all together with a satisfying sigh," Cathryn Wellner explains. Jo Tyler adds, "Be clear right away on the relevance of the story." Wellner says, "The elements of a story include a main character who's worth knowing about, a hook that makes the audience want to hear more, details that are both familiar and intriguing, and a mood conveyed through language and storytelling techniques." Character dialogue—both spoken words and inner thoughts—also help differentiate stories from other forms of communication.

"Watch that the end of the story isn't fluff. In learning organizations the *end* is what provides value. You need to include the lesson—

TELLING THE STORY
Contributed by the Kentucky League of Cities

To ensure consistent and quality branding throughout all communication mediums, we shall use the storytelling format. Lessons and insights are always best absorbed—and retained—if there is an interesting story that demonstrates them, whether the message is sad, humorous, dramatic, angry, or simply entertaining. Any story that reflects human struggle and human triumph offers a far more compelling way to engage people at every level—from commitment to a cause to understanding of an issue at a deeper and more personal level.

From *Kentucky League of Cities Department User's Guide*, February 2006. All rights reserved. Used with permission.

the ultimate meaning of the story. This is where real learning happens. You can't superimpose this meaning. You must go back to the teller of the story to build it. Otherwise learning will be disconnected from the story," Karen Dietz points out. "Much of what happens in organizations is story interruptive—telling of a story with no ending. An example is 'ain't it awful' stories. To end them you'd have to add, 'Here's the difference it made for me . . .' or 'Here's how I decided to operate or make a decision . . .'"

Wellner says, "I have people draw the story. It goes beyond language, to language of the inner eye. Words somehow skew the way we look at stories. Drawings move people to concepts and abstractions. Then they can add words."

According to Lovely, "At KLC and the NewCities Institute, we craft stories about people who touch our organization. We often take one story and craft it in different lengths for different uses." Is there an optimal story length? "My research shows business listeners don't like stories longer than twelve minutes," Tyler says. Here is the short version of one story KLC staff members tell that models the story structure outlined earlier.

HOW MAKING A DIFFERENCE CAN SAVE A LIFE

Written by John McGill, senior writer

Being mayor of a small town is never easy.

Glenn Caldwell became mayor of Williamstown, Kentucky, in 1997. It was a natural choice. His uncle, Herbert Caldwell, had been mayor of the same town for twenty-five years. Glenn believed that serving in local government was a way to make a difference. He had learned that by the example his uncle had set.

Glenn's son Brent was also serving the public. He was a police officer in Warsaw, Kentucky. On August 2, 2002, Glenn received the phone call every relative of a police officer fears.

Glenn had been asleep for about an hour when the phone rang. It was nearly 1:30 in the morning. *Something's wrong. I shouldn't be getting a call now.*

"Hello."

(Continued)

"Dad, I needed to call you. I've had an incident. I was shot, but I'm OK."

An incident? Brent? Shot? Is this really happening?

"Everything's all right. But there's news media all over the hospital and I didn't want you to wake up and hear about it on TV."

My God, Glenn thought. He's only been wearing that vest for a couple of weeks! I told him he ought to tell his mayor to buy those things for his officers.

Later that day when Glenn went to visit his son, Brent raised his shirt to show what had happened. On the right side of his abdomen was a deep purple splotch of ugliness, about five inches in diameter. In the center of it, right where the bullet had hit the vest, there was a splotch of blood that had risen up under the skin, not breaking it, but visible to the eye.

Five months later, you could still see the bruised area.

What made all the difference had been the ballistic vests that Glenn had gotten for his own police force eight months prior to the shooting. He'd bought them because a safety grant program provided by the Kentucky League of Cities had underwritten much of the cost.

Glenn recalls telling Brent about the vests and encouraging him to press the mayor in Warsaw to do the same. Glenn never asked if his son had actually talked to his superiors. What mattered, after all, was that they had applied for the grant and gotten them.

Today, Brent is still a police officer in Warsaw and Glenn is still the mayor of Williamstown. They do their jobs. They do them because they believe they can make a difference.

Glenn now serves on the KLC board of directors. As he puts it, "Serving on the board is a way to help make a difference in other communities. Sometimes it's the small things we do that matter most. In my case, a $200 item helped my son stay alive."

Glenn and Brent make a difference in people's lives. So does the Kentucky League of Cities. You can make a difference, too. Join KLC by getting involved in your own city. Get involved in a committee. Run for the board. Lobby congresspeople. You never know whose life you may save.

"In my organization, situations like these, when crafted using a storytelling format, spark bigger and more humanitarian thoughts about how we can care for one another. It helps other people realize they also have stories to tell. Together, these stories build better communities," Lovely emphasizes.

Stories have structure and identifiable elements. And stories are an art form. The ultimate meaning of a story in the eyes of its rightful owner needs to be linked to it in order for learning to occur. Attend also to length when using stories in a business context.

EMBODYING STORIES

"Too often organizations treat storytelling as another project that sits in a binder on the shelf. It's the lifeblood of the organization. It's always present," Karen Dietz observes. "Take stories and repeat them. Bring them into everyone's consciousness on a daily basis."

Major Mark Tribus, an officer in the Personnel Management System Task Force, U.S. Army Human Resources Command, follows this philosophy. "In August 2003, I was stationed in Hawaii as the brigade personnel officer for four thousand soldiers to be deployed to Afghanistan. To help them better prepare for the situation they were about to enter, colleagues from the companycommand.com team and I designed a multi-pronged leader development program built on stories for seventy of the brigade's key leaders," he says. For more information on companycommand.com, see the book *Company Command*, in the References.

"Five months before deployment, we provided the key leaders the book *Taliban: Militant Islam, Oil and Fundamentalism in Central Asia*, to help build context and cultural awareness," he notes. "We then surveyed one hundred company commanders who'd served in Afghanistan using questions garnered from the seventy key leaders. About 50 percent responded with short stories and examples to the questions. We mined them for themes and put them into a book along with their contact information. The final book contained the responses from forty-two company commanders. We gave them to the same seventy leaders."

Tribus continues, "Six weeks before departure, we flew in six company commanders and two of their spouses so these leaders could go face-to-face with those who gave stories. The first day the six commanders rehearsed their stories. We had them tie in the effects on soldiers, superiors, and subordinates and build their stories so people were drawn into them. On day two, we had a lunchtime opening session—

all six told three short stories with no props. The next day these six went to separate units to speak or answer questions. On day four they taught classes on topics within their expertise."

How did these various embodiments of story help the seventy commanders? "We were able to connect what's explicit and known with emergent knowledge and to do so in meaningful ways. The stories also helped shape conversations," Tribus notes.

Tribus's initiative included oral storytelling. For Dietz, "I recommend oral storytelling over videotaping someone telling the story. It's a whole body, whole brain experience that captures the senses. Because the teller and audience participate together, it builds bonds, trust, and credibility and makes stories real. Video and audio are passive. They are support devices for sharing stories but not a replacement for oral tradition. Live webcasting is closer to oral tradition, but still isn't quite the same."

Jo Tyler reminds us, "Telling a story is different from being an actor on a stage. You need to subtly shift the story as you're telling it to engage people and meet their needs in the moment." Michael Margolis notes, "Storytellers are ultimately at the mercy of the audience even if reading a story in print. The audience has the power to decide what has meaning and makes sense to them. The ultimate litmus test is believability." Tyler adds, "People get cynical when they experience a disconnect between the person and the nature of story. It can be as simple as what someone wears—'he wore a sweater when he normally wears a suit.' It's a question of authenticity. This is also an issue when a person tells someone else's story. Get permission to retell it—and practice it until you get the story sanctioned as accurate by the story's owner."

The DisAbility ensemble embodies personal stories in the skits that it performs. It holds a debriefing session after each show that also personifies stories in several ways. "We have audience members partner and share reactions to what they saw. The ensemble then comes back on stage to introduce themselves and their disability. Then we dialogue with the audience. People ask informational questions. I also ask, 'What pieces spoke to you? What part of your own personal experience got triggered?' We hear their stories," Joan Lipkin explains. "I'll also say, 'There are empty chairs on stage—we are always looking for people to join us. You can do so for the rest of the conversation if you'd like." The empty chairs symbolize a story waiting to be told.

Margolis says, "Artifacts and icons create containers for stories to travel." Alicia Korten acknowledges this in her work, as well: "Let's say a foundation wants to highlight a particular impact it would like to have in the world—such as to support the growth of community-based enterprises. In retreat settings, I'll ask people to identify their best example of when the organization has supported this outcome in the past and encourage them to bring a photo, letter, or object—such as a woven basket—that can help tell their stories. A picture tells a thousand words. Imagine a photograph of a community sorting and selling garbage—the picture provides a richer understanding of an impact. With indigenous people, bringing crafts of great beauty helps people to see the value of the product and tells something about the people who created it."

There are myriad ways to embody stories: oral storytelling, print materials, audio- and videotape recordings, performance pieces, symbolic objects, and artifacts and icons. While each has its own benefits and drawbacks, face-to-face live storytelling has attributes that go beyond those found in other media.

MOVING FORWARD

Finding stories. Digging into them. Selecting stories. Crafting them. Embodying stories. As the organizations in this book have shown, embracing the five sides of story brings significant benefits to an organization, both short and long term. However, we cannot forget that stories and story work already exist. As Cathryn Wellner aptly puts it, "Celebrate and honor the story knowledge that already exists within your organization. None of us are experts when it comes to the stories embedded in an [enterprise]. We are just at their service. We should feel honored when we are able to connect people with the stories and skills that are already there and perhaps just need to be teased out."

⎯ᴧᴧ⎯ Tell Me Your Story

You have had the opportunity to read about story work from myriad organizations around the world. Now it is your turn. How is your organization consciously and purposefully engaging in story work? How is it finding stories and digging into them? How is it selecting stories? And crafting them? In what ways is the organization embodying stories? What kinds of outcomes is the organization achieving as a result?

Join me in adding to the examples in this book—and knowledge and practices in the field of story and storytelling—by sharing your experiences. Here are several ways for you to provide them:

- By Web site:

  www.wakeupmycompany.com

  www.sayitwithastory.com
- By e-mail: lori@partnersforprogress.com
- By phone: (800) 253-6398

Appendix 1:
About the Interviewees

- AARP Services, Inc., Washington, D.C.

  Liz Kelleher, manager of client services, Web Strategy and Operations

  Mike Lee, director of client services, Web Strategy and Operations

- Alternatives Federal Credit Union, Ithaca, New York

  Joe Cummins, community development educator

  Dierdre Silverman, director of development and community ventures

- BMC Software, Inc., Houston, Texas

  Ashley Fields, director, Organization Development & Diversity

  Armida Mendez Russell, head of global diversity and inclusion

- BP, Houston, Texas

  Laura Folse, vice president, Exploration & Production Technology

  Stephanie Moore, vice president, Human Resources, Exploration & Production Technology

- Bristol-Myers Squibb, New York, New York

  Melinda J. Bickerstaff, vice president, Knowledge Management and chief knowledge officer (CKO)

  Stephan Taylor, Ph.D., director, Learning and Informatics Solutions, Process R&D

- California Department of Social Services, Sacramento, California

  Dennis Boyle, director

  Michelle Schmitt, program manager, Office of Professional Management Development

- Cele Peterson's Fashions, Tucson, Arizona

  Susanna Moon, sales associate

  Cele Peterson, founder and president

- Cerium Laboratories, LLC, Austin, Texas

  Lynette Ballast, section manager

  Clayton Fullwood, managing director

- Cheskin, Redwood Shores, California

  Terri Ducay, vice president, Design Strategy

  Lee Shupp, vice president, Business Strategy

- Chivas Brothers Ltd., a business unit of Pernod Ricard, London, United Kingdom

  Han Zantingh, international marketing manager

- City Year, Inc., Boston, Massachusetts

  Michael Brown, co-founder and president

  AnnMaura Connolly, senior vice president, Public Policy and Special Initiatives

  Alan Khazei, co-founder and CEO

  Stephanie Wu, senior vice president, People and Programs

- Development Dimensions International, Inc., Bridgeville, Pennsylvania

  Jim Concelman, manager, Leadership Development

Pam Gardner, manager, Sales Productivity

Sheryl Riddle, senior vice president, Consulting Services

Bob Rogers, president

- Endevco Corporation, a Meggitt group company, San Juan Capistrano, California

  Eric Ovlen, group vice president, Human Resources & Organization Development, Meggitt Aerospace & Equipment; formerly vice president, Organizational Effectiveness, Meggitt Electronics

  David Savage, president, Meggitt Electronics

- Erbert & Gerbert's Subs & Clubs (E & G Franchise Systems), Eau Claire, Wisconsin

  Tammy Berend, director, Training

  Michelle Ranum, director, Marketing and Brand Development

- Fisher & Paykel, Auckland, New Zealand

  Craig Douglas, vice president, Sales and Marketing, Fisher & Paykel Appliances, Ltd.

  Malcolm Harris, chief operating officer, New Zealand

- FivePoint Federal Credit Union, Port Arthur, Texas

  Kristen Bellanger, senior vice president, Operations

  Erik Shaw, president and CEO

- Gaylord Hospital, Wallingford, Connecticut

  Dorothea Brennan, board member

  Jim Cullen, president and CEO

  Janine Ross, chief financial officer

  Rick Serafino, administrator, Sleep Medicine Program

- Gen-i, a subsidiary of Telecom New Zealand, Auckland, New Zealand

  Chris Quin, general manager

  Brian Smith, operations manager of field force

- Ginger Group Cooperative, Ottawa, Canada

  Marilyn Hamilton, Ph.D., CGA, meshworker

  Kate McLaren, organization development consultant

- Goizueta Business School, Emory University, Atlanta, Georgia

  Molly Epstein, Ph.D., assistant professor, Practice of Management Communication

  Kembrel Jones, Ed.D., associate dean for the full-time MBA program; assistant professor, Practice of Marketing

- Göteborg University, Göteborg, Sweden

  Barbara Czarniawska, M.A., E.D., The Swedish Research Council & Malmsten Foundation chair of management studies, Gothenburg Research Institute

- Groh Productions and Groh Records, Chicago, Illinois

  Katalina Groh, founder and president

  Stefani Piermattei, production coordinator

  Cynthia Stewart, director, Global Customer Community Development

  Lynne Wiklander, live learning and interactive media instructional designer

- HEALTHSERV, Saskatoon, Saskatchewan, Canada

  Arlene Jorgenson, BScN, RN, COHN-C, president and CEO

- Hewlett-Packard, Palo Alto, California

  Jim Arena, director of strategic change, Merger Integration Office

Leslie J. Berkes, Ph.D., director, Organizational Effectiveness Center of Expertise, Workforce Development and Organizational Effectiveness

Pat Duran, senior business consultant, Global Operations Strategy and Planning

Sandy Lieske, director of engineering, IPG Embedded System Lab, Hewlett-Packard IPG Business Unit

- i.d.e.a.s. (innovation, design, entertainment, art and storytelling), Lake Buena Vista, Florida

   Robert Allen, founder and CEO

   Duncan Kennedy, vice president, Innovation

- Incredible Pets, Rocklin, California

   Sharon Love, owner

   Tracy Storck, assistant store manager

- Information Resources, Inc., Chicago, Illinois

   Gordon Peterson, vice president, Organizational Effectiveness

   Kevin Yates, director, Learning Solutions

- Interface, Inc., Atlanta, Georgia

   Dan Hendrix, president and CEO

John Wells, president and CEO, Interface Americas

- Interior Health, Kelowna, British Columbia, Canada

   Cathryn Wellner, food and health project manager

- Kaiser Permanente, Oakland, California

   Tom Debley, director, Heritage Resources

   Mike Lassiter, vice president, Media & External Relations

- Kentucky League of Cities and NewCities Institute, Lexington, Kentucky

   Sylvia L. Lovely, executive director and CEO, Kentucky League of Cities; president, NewCities Institute

   John McGill, senior writer

- Kimberly-Clark Corporation, Neenah, Wisconsin

   Jeff Drake, director of marketing research

   Hedy Lukas, senior director, Marketing Services

- Kimpton Hotel and Restaurant Group, LLC, San Francisco, California

   Jimmy Hord, general manager, Hotel Monaco San Francisco

   Tom LaTour, chairman and CEO

   Niki Leondakis, chief operating officer

Steve Pinetti, senior vice president, Sales and Marketing

Angela Prager, chief concierge, Hotel Monaco San Francisco

• KYGO FM, Denver, Colorado

Craig Hunt ("Catfish Hunter"), on-air personality

Sondra Singer, certified radio marketing consultant

• Lancaster University, Lancaster, United Kingdom

Simon Kelly, Ph.D., research associate, Centre for Excellence in Leadership, Lancaster University Management School

• Lands' End, Dodgeville, Wisconsin

Nora Halverson, Internet customer service specialist

Anne Hore, director, Employee and Customer Communications

Diane Huza, call center manager

Sandy Johns, learning and development manager

Jackie Johnson-Caygill, director, Lands' End Business Outfitters Contact Center

Kelly Ritchie, senior vice president of employee and customer services

• Levi Strauss & Company, San Francisco, California

Scott LaPorta, president, Levi Strauss Signature®

Thom Masat, vice president of design, Levi Strauss Signature®

Michael Perman, senior director of consumer insight

• Lockheed Martin Space Systems Company, Sunnyvale, California

Arthur L. Major, director, System Safety, Product Assurance & System Safety

Anastasia Walsh, two-way communication program manager

• Microsoft Corporation, Redmond, Washington

Christopher J. Frank, director, Corporate Research

R. Jeff Hansen, general manager

• Molson Coors Brewing Company, Golden, Colorado

Cathy Krause, program manager, Global People Development

Bob Merchant, vice president, Manufacturing & Planning, Coors Brewing Company

Vonda Mills, vice president, Global People Development

Flo Mostaccero, vice president, Technical Services and Business Process Development, Coors Brewing Company

- Motorola, Schaumburg, Illinois

  Orlando Ashford, vice president, Human Resources Strategy & Organization Development

- NASA, Goddard Space Flight Center, Greenbelt, Maryland

  Sandra Cauffman, assistant director, Flight Programs & Projects Directorate

  Marty Davis, program manager

  Kanu Kogod, program designer and facilitator, Leadership Alchemy Program

  Rich Rogers, program graduate and mentor, Leadership Alchemy Program; pilot and aviation safety officer, Wallops Flight Facility

  Kim Toufectis, program supervisor and mentor, Leadership Alchemy Program; supervisor, Facilities Planning Office

  Gail Williams, program manager, Leadership Alchemy Program

- National Speakers Association, Tempe, Arizona

  Marsha Mardock, APR, CAE, director of communications

  Lee Robert, president, Cavett Robert Communications

  Stacy Tetschner, CAE, executive vice president

- National Storytelling Network, Jonesborough, Tennessee

  Karen Dietz, Ph.D., executive director

- Newark Beth Israel Medical Center, Newark, New Jersey

  Marcia McGregor, RN, BSN, nursing director, Telemetry Unit

  Nancy Shendall-Falik, RN, MA, vice president, Patient Care Services

- New Mexico State University, Las Cruces, New Mexico

  David Boje, Ph.D., professor of management, Department of Management and Arthur Owens Chair in Business Administration

- oneVillage Foundation, San Jose, California

  Jeff Buderer, program development manager

  Joy Tang, founder

- Orlando Regional Health-care, Orlando, Florida

  Tracey Briggs, communications representative

  Martha Johnson, manager, 55PLUS Program
- Pace University, Pleasantville, New York

  Robert Dennehy, Ph.D., professor of management
- Pennsylvania State University, Middletown, Pennsylvania

  Jo Tyler, Ed.D., assistant professor, Training & Development
- Procter & Gamble Company, West Chester, Ohio

  W. Scott Cameron, global process owner-project management, Corporate Engineering

  Andrew R. Poole, manager, Global Engineering Learning Solutions
- Renual, Washington, D.C.

  Alicia Korten, founder and executive director
- RS Information Systems, Inc., McLean, Virginia

  Robert S. Frey, senior vice president, Knowledge Management & Proposal Development

  Rick Stalnaker, director of NASA Programs
- Rush-Copley Medical Center, Aurora, Illinois

  Jodie Beverage, RN, Operating Room

  Shawn Tyrrell, MSN, CNAA, CHE, vice president, Nursing Services
- Saatchi & Saatchi, New York, New York

  Bob Isherwood, worldwide creative director

  Kevin Roberts, CEO worldwide
- St. Andrew's United Church, Edmonton, Alberta, Canada

  Alan Shugg, congregation member

  The Reverend Dr. Geoffrey Wilfong-Pritchard, minister
- Shell Exploration & Production Company, Houston, Texas

  Larry Forster, staff engineer, Technology Planning & Implementation
- Society for the Protection and Care of Children (SPCC), Rochester, New York

  Trina Laughlin, LCSW-R, clinical supervisor, Family Violence Program

  Kelly Reed, president and CEO
- SocraticArts, Stuart, Florida

  Roger Schank, Ph.D., CEO

- Spare Key, St. Paul, Minnesota

  Patsy Keech, co-founder

  Kim Lovrich, executive director

- State of Wisconsin Department of Natural Resources

  John DeLaMater, retired

  Bruce Neeb, government outreach supervisor, West Central Region

  Ralph Schwartz, director, Leadership and Staff Development

  Scott Watson, watershed supervisor, West Central Region

- That Uppity Theatre Company, St. Louis, Missouri

  Joan Lipkin, founder and artistic director

- The Asset-Based Community Development Institute, Evanston, Illinois

  Tom Mosgaller, adjunct faculty

- The Cynefin Centre, Marlborough, United Kingdom

  David Snowden, founder

- The United Illuminating Company, New Haven, Connecticut

  Dorothea Brennan, director, Process Improvement

- THIRSTY-FISH Story Marketing, Washington, D.C.

  Michael Margolis, founder and CEO

- Tutta Bella Neapolitan Pizzeria, Seattle, Washington

  Joe Fugere, owner

  Brian Goidjics, chef

  Greg Nickels, mayor, City of Seattle, Washington

- University of North Carolina at Greensboro, Greensboro, North Carolina

  Kimberly Cuny, director, The University Speaking Center

  April Reece, manager, The University Speaking Center

- U.S. Air Force Research Laboratory, Rome, New York

  Captain Gabe Mounce, lead engineer, Information Directorate

  Major Dan Ward, project manager, Information Directorate

- U.S. Army (worldwide)

  Major Patrick Michaelis, executive officer, 1st Squadron, 7th U.S. Cavalry, 1st Cavalry Division

  Major Mark Tribus, officer, Personnel Management System Task Force, U.S. Army Human Resources Command

- U.S. Department of the Treasury, Washington, D.C.

  Lynne Feingold, program analyst and one founder of Golden Fleece

- U.S. Environmental Protection Agency, Washington, D.C.

  Jamie Langlie, program analyst, Office of Human Resources/Office of Administration & Resources Management

  Susan Smith, senior program analyst, Executive Resources, Office of Human Resources

- U.S. Geological Survey, Denver, Colorado

  Nancy Driver, leadership program manager, Office of Employee Development

- United Way of York County, York, Pennsylvania

  Deb Gogniat, director, Major Gifts

  Robert Woods, executive director

- UTSA's Institute of Texan Cultures, San Antonio, Texas

  Mary Grace Ketner, education specialist, Programs Management Department

- Verizon, New York, New York

  Lee Brathwaite, vice president, Verizon Real Estate

  Karin B. Hurt, director, Verizon Partner Solutions

  Dennis Metzger, manager, Workforce Development and Performance Management, Network Services Group

  Raymond Wierzbicki, senior vice president, Enterprise Customer Service, Enterprise Solutions Group

- VSM Geneesmiddelen bv (VSM Pharmaceuticals), Alkmaar, The Netherlands

  Johan van der Molen, senior product manager

  Maarten van Walsem, program manager

  Jan Zwoferink, CEO

- *Washington Business Journal,* Arlington, Virginia

  Terry Nicholetti, sales trainer and account executive

- Washington Mutual, Irvine, California

  Mark Steiman, first vice president and senior human resources manager, Home Loans Division

- Winning Ways, Inc., Oakton, Virginia

  Joan Fletcher, owner

- World Vision U.S., Federal Way, Washington

    Kari Costanza, communications, manager, Information Resources

    Tom Costanza, photojournalist and senior video producer, Creative Solutions

    Marilee Pierce Dunker, child sponsorship advocate

    Karen Kartes, communications manager

    Richard E. Stearns, World Vision president

- Wyeth Pharmaceuticals, Philadelphia, Pennsylvania

    Ashesh Gandhi, PharmD, director of medical communications, cardiovascular & gastrointestinal, Global Medical Affairs

    Gayle Shaw-Hones, BSN, MSIT, associate director, Learning and Performance, Global Medical Affairs

—⁓— Appendix 2: About the Contributors

Madelyn Blair, Ph.D., president, Pelerei, Inc.
2379 Broad Run Court
Jefferson, MD 21755
Phone: (301) 371-7100
E-mail: mblair@Pelerei.com
Web site: www.Pelerei.com
Madelyn is the founder of Pelerei, Inc., a firm dedicated to helping clients turn vision into reality. She provides innovative management solutions to help organizations transform themselves through an environment of learning and encouragement, building on their own strengths. "She seems to bring everyone up to her level of thinking effortlessly, because she listens so well," says one of her clients. Madelyn delivers on time, within budget, often doing what her clients call "the impossible." Her current projects include one dedicated to changing the world through story. Madelyn is an associate of the Taos Institute. She received her doctorate in organizational psychology from the University of Tilburg, The Netherlands. She writes extensively and is a regular conference speaker.

Evelyn Clark, the corporate storyteller
501 Kirkland Avenue, Suite 305
Kirkland, WA 98033
Phone: (425) 827-3998
E-mail: evelyn@corpstory.com
Web site: www.corpstory.com
Author of *Around the Corporate Campfire: How Great Leaders Use Stories to Inspire Success,* Evelyn works with leaders who want to maximize results. She helps them achieve their goals by developing powerful communication strategies and compiling values-based stories that inspire

and sustain success. Evelyn also delivers keynote addresses and facilitates customized workshops and retreats. Her client list includes premier organizations such as National Reconnaissance Office, Microsoft, VeriSign, World Vision, and Costco Wholesale.

Karen Dietz, Ph.D., executive director, National Storytelling Network
132 Boone Street
Jonesborough, TN 37659
Phone: (800) 525-4514, x205 or (423) 913-8201, x205
Cell: (423) 426-1637
Fax: (423) 753-9331
E-mail: Karen@storynet.org
Web site: www.storynet.org
Karen is executive director of the National Storytelling Network, a membership association based in Jonesborough, Tennessee. She has applied her rich cross-training as a folklorist, communication specialist and storyteller, leadership and organizational consultant, and coach and professional speaker to help people and organizations improve their leadership, culture, products, and services for more than twenty-two years. With clients she has worked on projects that include large-scale organizational change, leadership development, strategic planning, visioning, and the application of storytelling in core business issues. She has worked with businesses including Walt Disney Imagineering, Chase Manhattan Bank, Securities Industry Automation Corporation, Idec Pharmaceuticals, Avery Dennison, and Toyota. Karen attended the University of Pennsylvania, receiving her M.A. and Ph.D. degrees in folklore from the University of Pennsylvania.

Marcy Fisher, organization development and human resources
    professional
1306 Pine Bluff Drive
Saint Charles, MO 63304
Phone: (636) 922-0905
E-mail: marcylfisher@yahoo.com
Marcy has more than thirty years of industry experience with leading firms: Procter & Gamble, Royal Dutch Shell, Eli Lilly, and Ingersoll-Rand. Her recent experience has centered on the redesign and development of corporate culture. She is currently affiliated with Resources Global Professionals, where she contributes to client organizations in the area of organization design and development. Marcy possesses

strong functional and technical knowledge in organization design and
development, management, alliances, globalization, leadership development, coaching, and manufacturing management. She holds a B.S.
degree in industrial management and computer science from Purdue
and an M.S. degree in human resource and organization development
from the University of San Francisco.

Alicia Korten, founder and executive director, Renual
4801 Connecticut Avenue, NW
Washington, DC 20008
Phone: (202) 364-5369
E-mail: akorten@renual.com
Web site: www.renual.com
Alicia is the director of Renual, a firm that offers strategic planning,
evaluation, and writing services to foundations, nonprofits, and socially
responsible businesses. An author, facilitator, and speaker, Alicia most
recently published *Staying Power: Using Technical Assistance and Peer
Learning to Enhance Donor Investments.* She is fluent in Spanish, and
wrote her first book as a Fulbright Scholar to Costa Rica. Her clients and
workshop sponsors include the Ford Foundation, the Inter-American
Foundation, the Share Foundation, the Smithsonian Associates Program, Johns Hopkins School of Medicine, CARE-USA, and the International Monetary Fund. The narrative methodologies that Alicia
infuses throughout her work with organizations are informed by seven
years of working with native peoples in Central America. She has a B.A.
degree in Latin American studies from Brown University.

Denise Lee, senior consultant, OmniSolve
103873 Park Center Road, Suite 350A
Herndon, VA 20171
Phone: (703) 850-7450
E-mail: dlee@cox.net
Denise has more than twenty years' experience in the areas of human
capital, organizational learning, leadership development, and project
and knowledge management. She has expertise in projects that help
organizations create a knowledge-centric culture based on leveraging
knowledge and human capital resources through storytelling and
communities of practice. Denise is an adjunct professor at Johns Hopkins University in strategic human capital and has presented at conferences, universities, and associations across the United States. She

contributes to knowledge management and organizational learning books and articles and is a board member for the *International Journal of Knowledge and Learning*. She earned an M.S. degree in social and organizational learning from George Mason University, a B.A. degree in business administration from Averett University, and a certificate in measurement and evaluation from Georgetown University.

Sylvia L. Lovely, executive director and CEO, Kentucky League of
    Cities; president, NewCities Institute
100 E. Vine Street, Suite 800
Lexington, KY 40507
Phone: (859) 977-3700
Fax: (859) 977-3703
E-mail: slovely@klc.org
Web site: www.klc.org
Sylvia jokes about being born in city hall—but she's only half kidding. The hospital in the Appalachian hills of Kentucky where she was born was later transformed into the city hall of Frenchburg, her hometown. The symbolism fits. Sylvia is executive director and CEO of the Kentucky League of Cities and president of the NewCities Institute. She has long understood the importance of storytelling. Her book, *New Cities in America: The Little Blue Book of Big Ideas,* includes a number of success stories. Recognized as a champion of cities and the power of people to create positive change, Sylvia has appeared on CNN's *Lou Dobbs Tonight,* CNBC's *Power Lunch,* and ABC radio. Her opinion columns have appeared in the *Miami Herald, Indianapolis Star,* and *Cincinnati Enquirer.*

Michael J. Margolis, founder and CEO
THIRSTY-FISH Story Marketing
3233 M Street NW, 4th Floor
Washington, DC 20007
Phone: (202) 319-2814
Fax: (202) 965-1298
E-mail: michael@thirsty-fish.com
Web site: www.thirsty-fish.com
Michael is CEO and founder of THIRSTY-FISH Story Marketing. Specializing in the marketing of both social and business innovation, Michael translates new, different, and complex ideas into stories that can travel across culture. In practical terms, these stories help organi-

zations raise more money, boost recognition, build brand presence, improve stakeholder relations, and shepherd new ideas into cultural acceptance. Michael has consulted to more than thirty organizations including AARP, Ernst & Young, LLP, NASA, The Nature Conservancy, and countless emerging enterprises. His unique story perspective draws upon varied adventures as a pop anthropologist, social marketer, and successful entrepreneur. A frequent conference speaker and workshop leader, Michael presents a fresh approach to meaningful marketing and cultural renewal.

North McKinnon, co-founder, Parnassus Consulting, LLC
257 Avenida Madrid #A
San Clemente, CA 92672
Phone: (949) 248-7784
Fax: (949) 248-7742
E-mail: mckinnon@cox.net
Web site: www.ParnassusConsulting.com
North is a co-founder of Parnassus Consulting, LLC, a firm dedicated to creating a better world by facilitating strategic visioning and transformational experiences for organizations, groups, leaders, and individuals. He has twenty years' experience as a corporate marketing executive and as an organization development consultant and facilitator. He is certified in a variety of assessments and uses storytelling, positive psychology, and visual language in the course of his work. He has a contagious passion for creativity and authenticity that enables individuals and teams to make positive change. Besides Parnassus Consulting, North has worked with Big Four consulting firms providing organizational change facilitation and communication. He holds an M.B.A. in marketing and strategy from Pepperdine University and a B.S. in education from the University of Tennessee, Knoxville.

Susan J. Moore, marketing consultant
4008 42nd Avenue South
Seattle, WA 98118
Phone: (206) 393-0934
E-mail: sjmooremarketing@yahoo.com
Susan was recently senior research manager with Microsoft in corporate marketing. She works with global companies to bring customer satisfaction data and insights to senior leadership with discipline, passion, and focused understanding. She has also led qualitative research

techniques at Eastman. For her clients in the retail, building products, banking, and energy sectors, she co-developed a methodology for driving customer-centric initiatives. Her work with global companies was cited in *Mastering Customer Value Management,* and her former clients have presented on customer satisfaction at American Marketing Association conferences. Susan earned her M.B.A. in marketing at the University of Chicago Graduate School of Business and has guest lectured at Auckland Graduate School of Business, Auckland, New Zealand.

Susan M. Osborn, Ph.D., M.S.W.
7541 Wooddale Way
Citrus Heights, CA 95610
Phone: (916) 722-3452
Fax: (916) 722-3452
E-mail: sosborn@ix.netcom.com
Web site: http://susan.osborn.bz
Susan is a storyteller, coach, and consultant. She gives presentations and facilitates workshops titled "Leader as Storyteller," "Creating a Shared Story," "Presenting with Pizzazz," "Old Stories, New Stories—Changing Your Personal Mythology," and "A Narrative Approach to Knowledge Management." For six years she has taught "Storytelling as a Leadership Tool" at Chapman University. Her background includes twenty-five years as a management and organization consultant, and experience as a human resources manager, corporate trainer, adult educator, therapist, career coach, director of a prisoner rehabilitation program, parole agent, and talk show guest. Her book, *The System Made Me Do It! A Life Changing Approach to Office Politics,* shows how to transform organizations by becoming the authors of our own stories.

Ashraf Ramzy, M.A., CEO, Narrativity Strategy & Story B.V.
P.O. Box 271
1180 AG Amstelveen, The Netherlands
E-mail: aramzy@narrativity.net
Web site: www.narrativity.net
Ashraf heads Narrativity, a strategy consultancy based in Amsterdam, The Netherlands, with affiliations in the United States. Prior to launching Narrativity in 2002, he worked at a.o. BBDO, TBWA, and Publicis for fifteen years as a brand strategy director. Ashraf views corporate and brand identity as a story that an organization writes with its character and tells with its actions. With a proprietary narrative method, he helps companies discover, develop, and deliver their story, grow

their business, and build their brands. Ashraf has worked with numerous organizations, including Nissan Automobiles Europe, Canon Europe, Frito Lay, ABN AMRO, Expatica Media, KLM Cargo, RTL Netherlands, and VSM Pharmaceuticals. He has a master's degree in film with a specialization in narratology from the Catholic (now Radboud) University of Nijmegen.

Steven N. Silverman, Ph.D., senior research manager,
    Central Marketing Research and Insights, Microsoft
One Microsoft Way
Redmond, WA 98065
Phone: (425) 705-4104
Fax: (425) 936-7329
E-mail: steven.silverman@microsoft.com
Steven is a senior research manager and strategist for Microsoft Office research in Microsoft's Central Marketing Group in Redmond, Washington. He has been with Microsoft since March 2004. Prior to joining Microsoft, Steven led the research organization for the fibers group at DuPont and was a consultant with Monitor Group. He served on the faculty of the School of Business at Washington State University in Pullman, Washington, from 1996 through 2000. He received a Ph.D. in marketing and strategy from the University of Pittsburgh in 1996 and holds an M.B.A. in marketing and a B.A. in psychology and communications from the University of Wisconsin-Madison.

Susan Stites, head alligator, Management Allegories
3788 Highridge Road
Madison, WI 53718
Phone: (608) 837-7978
Fax: (608) 825-8418
E-mail: alligat@aol.com
Susan owns Management Allegories, a writing and training firm specializing in leadership development and customer service. She has helped dozens of organizations build and maintain strong customer relations. She speaks throughout the United States on a variety of business topics. Susan is the author of ten books, dozens of articles, three business simulations, and numerous training programs. Prior to starting her business, Susan was director of human resources for Central Life Assurance and manager of training for Lands' End. Her master's degree is from Northwestern University in industrial education. She is currently working on a collection of satirical business stories.

Joanna Truitt, Washington, D.C., director, American Legion Auxiliary
1608 K Street NW
Washington, DC 20006
Phone: (202) 861-1365
Fax: (202) 861-1352
E-mail: jtruitt@legion-aux.org
Joanna believes in the power of stories. Growing up, she watched stories about "the old country" told at family gatherings keep a culture alive. Images of "dancing fireflies" remind her of good times around campfires at Girl Scout camp. Stories of courage, fear, and camaraderie from her dad's experiences in WWII and the Korean War instilled respect and pride for fighting soldiers. Joanna has twenty-two years' experience as a university administrator. Stories of institutional traditions, building a campus from scratch, and turning around a department or service make for strong connections and ties to challenges she has faced and people she has worked with over the years. She has a B.S. in recreation administration and an M.S. in college student personnel, both from the University of Wisconsin-LaCrosse.

Jo Tyler, Ed.D., assistant professor, training and development,
     Pennsylvania State University
W331-A Olmsted Building
777 West Harrisburg Pike
Middletown, PA 17057-4898
Phone: (717) 948-6387
Fax: (717) 948-6064
E-mail: jat235@psu.edu
Jo is an assistant professor at Pennsylvania State University, in the master's program in training and development. Prior to joining Penn State, Jo was vice president of organization and management development at Armstrong World Industries in Lancaster, Pennsylvania. Her earlier career included progressive roles in training, management, and organizational development at Hewlett-Packard, Otis Elevator, and Pratt & Whitney. Jo's doctorate in education is from Columbia University (2004), where her dissertation focused on the strategic use of storytelling in for-profit settings. Her research interests include storytelling in a range of applications, organizational development, and adult literacy. Her storytelling draws on the details that make the personal universal and her belief in the possibilities associated with risk taking.

━⁓━ References

Introduction

Deutschman, A. (2005, May). Change or die. *Fast Company*, p. 53.

Echols, M. E. (2005, February). Engaging employees to impact performance. *Chief Learning Officer*, p. 44.

Groff, L. (1996). Social and political evolution. In G. Kurian & G. Molitor (eds.), *Encyclopedia of the Future*, Vol. 2, p. 855. New York: Simon & Schuster.

Jensen, R. (2001). *The dream society: How the coming shift from information to imagination will transform your business.* New York: McGraw-Hill.

Halal, W. E. (1996, November–December). The rise of the knowledge entrepreneur. *The Futurist*, p. 14.

Meister, J. C. (2005, November). What's on the mind of your senior executives? *Chief Learning Officer*, p. 66.

Pink, D. H. (2005). *A whole new mind: Moving from the information age to the conceptual age.* New York: Riverhead Books.

Terzo, G. (2005, February). Report links engagement to profitability. *Workforce Management*, p. 19.

Thurm, S. (2006, January 23). Companies struggle to pass on knowledge that workers acquire. *Wall Street Journal*, p. B1.

Zukav G. (2001). *The dancing Wu Li masters: An overview of the new physics.* New York: HarperCollins, p. 18.

Chapter One

All honor to you who put the customer 1st. (1991). Dodgeville, WI: Lands' End, Inc.

Careholders' report 2004. (2004). Orlando, FL: Orlando Regional Healthcare.

Lands' End at your service: The people, the stories, the traditions. (2000). Dodgeville, WI: Lands' End, Inc.

Chapter Two

Extraordinary care: A collection of stories from the nurses at Rush-Copley Medical Center. (2004, May). Aurora, IL: Rush-Copley Medical Center.

Hayles, V. R., & Russell, A. M. (1997). *The diversity directive: Why some initiatives fail and what to do about it.* New York: McGraw-Hill, p. 7.

Hesse, H., & Rosner, H. (1956). *The journey to the East.* New York: Picador.

Chapter Three

None

Chapter Four

Cuny, K. (2003, Fall). Don't be a Bob. E-mail correspondence to staff.

DeLaMater, J. (2002, November 19). Changing jobs. Oral history interview.

Hurt, K. B., & Metzger, D. (2000, 2003). *Info-line: Storytelling.* Alexandria, VA: American Society for Training & Development.

Riddle, S. (2005, August 6). Honest is as honest does. E-mail correspondence.

Chapter Five

Davis, M. (2003, December). A good man is hard to find. *ASK Magazine,* 15, 12–15.

Frey, R. (2005, Spring/Summer). Winning federal government contracts through fact-based storytelling. *Proposal Management,* pp. 50–59.

Ward, D. (2005). *The radical elements of radical success.* New Hartford, NY: Rogue Press.

Chapter Six

Alternatives Federal Credit Union. Available online: www.alternatives.org. Last visited: April 2006.

Anderson, R. (2005, June 20). Speech at the Shared Air Summit, Toronto, Canada.

Celebrating: Annual report 2003. (2003). Ithaca, NY: Alternatives Federal Credit Union.

Gaylord Hospital. Available online: www.gaylord.org. Last visited: April 2006.

Interface, Inc. Available online: www.interfaceinc.com. Last visited: April 2006.

Interface sustainability. Available online: www.interfacesustainability.com. Last visited: April 2006.

Press release: Interface celebrates ten years of sustainability in action. (2004, August 31). Atlanta: Interface, Inc.

Press release: Interface posts global environmental progress with 2004 eco-metrics report—progress seen on reducing emissions and reclaiming carpet for recycling. (2005, July 28). Atlanta: Interface, Inc.

Press release: Interface puts more distance between manufacturing and the well head—innovative new backing technology decreases dependence on petroleum and offers flexible system for experimentation with emerging polymers. (2005, November 8). Lagrange, GA: Interface, Inc.

Storylines: Interface, Inc. 2003 annual report. (2003). Atlanta: Interface, Inc.

Chapter Seven

Brand launch employee information kit. (2004, August 25). Port Arthur, TX: FivePoint Federal Credit Union.

Chapter Eight

Arthur, M. A. (1994). Fusion Forum interview guide. Internal memo, pp. 1–3.

Brown, M., & Khazei, A. (2004, July). The traveler. *Founding Stories.* Boston: City Year, Inc.

Chapter Nine

Debley, T. (2005, August–September). Diversity as a Kaiser Permanente value born on the home front of World War II. Based on articles posted on Kaiser Permanente's employee intranet.

Dunker, M. P. (2005). *Man of vision.* Waynesboro, GA: Authentic Publishers.

National Speakers Association. Available online: www.nsaspeaker.org. Last visited: April 2006.

National Speakers Association. (2006). *The magic of community: 2006 annual member handbook.* Tempe, AZ: National Speakers Association.

Reed, K. (2001, November). *SPCC: A long proud history.* Rochester, NY: Society for Prevention of Cruelty to Children.

Robert, C., & Robert, L. E. (1998). *Cavett Robert: Leaving a lasting legacy.* Minneapolis: Creative Training Techniques International.

Society for Prevention of Cruelty to Children. Available online: www.
spcc-roch.org/FLASHPAGE.html. Last visited: April 2006.

World Vision. Available online: www.worldvision.org. Last visited: April 2006.

Chapter Ten

Allen, R. (2001). i.d.e.a.s.: The story. Story used internally.

Bristol-Myers Squibb process R&D embraces the new world of electronic
scientific knowledge management. (2005, January). Future story
used internally.

Bristol-Myers Squibb named top-ranked global pharmaceutical company:
Managing intellectual assets attracts top BMS alliances—blockbuster
drugs follow. (2001). Future story used internally.

Chapter Eleven

Fisher & Paykel: About us. Available online: http://usa.fisherpaykel.com/
about-us/about-us.cfm. Last visited: January 2006.

Tutta Bella story. Available online: www.tuttabellapizza.com/story.html.
Last visited: January 2006.

Chapter Twelve

Berta, D. (2005, May 9). Erbert & Gerbert's builds brand by recruiting
"storytellers." *Nation's Restaurant News.* Available online: www.nrn.
com. Last visited: April 2006.

E & G Franchise Systems, Inc. (2002). Boney Billy poster. Used in all Erbert
& Gerbert Subs & Clubs locations since 1988.

Erbert & Gerbert's Subs & Clubs. Available online: www.erbertandgerberts.
com/aboutus.html. Last visited: April 2006.

Hendrie, R. (2004, November 18). Your experience is the brand. Available
online: www.hotelnewsresource.com/article13842.html. Last visited:
April 2006.

Hodgson, L. (2002, April 4). Levi's get leg up with new and polished look.
International Market News. Available online: www.tdctrade.com/
imn/o2040401/clothing37.htm. Last visited: April 2006.

Hotel Monaco San Francisco. Available online: www.monaco-sf.com. Last
visited: April 2006.

Kimpton Hotels and Restaurants. Available online: www.kimptonhotels.com.
Last visited: April 2006.

Levi Strauss Signature®. Available online: http://levistrausssignature.com.
Last visited: April 2006.

Ramzy, A., Valkema, G., & Zwoferink, J. (2005). *The Adonis*. Alkmaar, The Netherlands: VSM Geneesmiddelen bv.

Tate, R. (2005, January 28–February 3). Kimpton Hotels remakes its beds. *San Francisco Business Times.*

The Chivas legend. (2003). Chivas Brothers Ltd., Pernod Ricard SA.

Chapter Thirteen

Brennan, D. (2004). When the lights go out, it's our time to shine! *Process Overview Training.*

Feingold, L. (2002, February). Swept off your feet. Unpublished story.

Gohn, K. (2004). *Celebrating 125 years of the U.S. Geological Survey.* U.S. Geological Survey Circular 1274.

Ketner, M. G. (2001). *LIFETIMES: The Texas experience.* San Antonio: The UTSA's Institute of Texan Cultures.

The Asset-Based Community Development Institute. Available online: www.northwestern.edu/ipr/abcd.html. Last visited: April 2006.

Chapter Fourteen

Boje, D. M. (1991, March). The storytelling organization: A study of story-telling performance in an office supply firm. *Administrative Science Quarterly,* pp. 106–126.

Boje, D. M., Rosile, G. A., Dennehy, R. F., & Summers, D. J. (1997). Restorying reengineering. *Communication Research, 24*(6), 631–668.

Boje, D. M., Rosile, G. A., & Garner, C. (2004, August). Antenarratives, narratives and anaemic stories. Paper presented in Showcase Symposium, Academy of Management, New Orleans. Available online: http://peaceaware.com/McD/. Last visited: April 2006.

Czarniawska, B. (1998). Metaphor and organizations. *Management Learning, 29*(3), 389–391.

Czarniawska, B. (2001). Is it possible to be a constructionist consultant? *Management Learning, 32*(2), 253–266.

Czarniawska, B. (2003). Forbidden knowledge: Organization theory in times of transition. *Management Learning, 34*(3), 355–365.

Dennehy, R. F. (1999). The executive as storyteller. *Management Review, 88*(3), 40–43.

Kelly, S., White, M. I., Rooksby, J., & Rouncefield, M. (2005). *Storytelling and design: The problem of leadership.* Unpublished manuscript, Centre for Excellence in Leadership, Computing Department, Lancaster University, U.K.

Morgan, S., & Dennehy, R. F. (2004). Using stories to reframe the social construction of reality: A trio of activities. *Journal of Management Education, 28*(3), 372–389.

Schank, R. C. (2000). A vision of education for the 21st century. *T.H.E. Journal, 27*(6), 42–49.

Schank, R. C. (2002). Every curriculum tells a story. *Tech Directions, 62*(2), 25–29.

Snowden, D. (2002). Complex acts of knowing: Paradox and descriptive self-awareness. *Journal of Knowledge Management, 6*(2), 100–111.

Snowden, D., & Kurtz, C. F. (2003). The new dynamics of strategy: Sense-making in a complex and complicated world. *IBM Systems Journal, 42*(3), 462–482.

Chapter Fifteen

Dixon, N., et al. (2005). *Company command: Unleashing the power of the Army profession.* West Point, NY: Center for the Advancement of Leader Development & Organizational Learning.

Michaelis, P. R., & Spain, E.S.P. (2005, May–June). Knowledge shared is power. *Leader to Leader Special Supplement,* pp. 60–66.

That Uppity Theatre Company, (2005, Fall). *Fall 2005 newsletter.*

That Uppity Theatre Company. (2005, Fall). *The DisAbility Project Fall 2005 newsletter.*

—✺— Suggested Resources

Joanna Truitt

BOOKS AND PAMPHLETS

Allan, J., et al. (2002). *The power of the tale: Using narratives for organizational success.* Hoboken, NJ: Wiley.

Armstrong, D. (1992). *Managing by storying around: A new method of leadership.* New York: Currency/Doubleday.

Armstrong, D. (1998). *Once told they're gold.* Three Rivers, MI: Armstrong International.

Atkinson, C. (2005). *Beyond bullet points: Using Microsoft PowerPoint® to create presentations that inform, motivate and inspire.* Redmond, WA: Microsoft Press.

Berry, T. (1988). *The dream of the earth.* San Francisco: Sierra Club.

Bocchi, G., & Ceruti, M. (2001). *The narrative universe: Advances in systems theory, complexity, and the human sciences.* Mt. Waverly, VIC, Australia: Hampton Press.

Bonnet, J. (1999). *Stealing fire from the gods: A dynamic new story model for writers and filmmakers.* Studio City, CA: Michael Wiese Productions.

Booker, C. (2005). *The seven basic plots: Why we tell stories.* New York: Continuum International.

Brown, J. S., Denning, S., Groh, K., & Prusak, L. (2004). *Storytelling in organizations: How narrative and storytelling are transforming 21st century management.* Woburn, MA: Butterworth Heinemann.

Bystedt, J., et al. (2003). *Moderating to the max.* New York: Paramount Market.

Campbell, J. (1972). *Myths to live by.* New York: Bantam.

Campbell, J. (1973). *The hero with a thousand faces.* Princeton, NJ: Princeton University.

Campbell, J. (1988). *The power of myth.* New York: Doubleday.

Cassady, M. (1990). *Storytelling step by step.* San Jose, CA: Resource Publications.

Chamberlin, J. (2004). *This is your land, where are your stories?* Berea, OH: Pilgrim Press.

Clandinin, D. J., & Connelly, F. M. (2000). *Narrative inquiry.* San Francisco: Jossey-Bass.

Clark, E. (2004). *Around the corporate campfire.* Sevierville, TN: Insight.

Clarke, C. A. (2001). *Storytelling for grantseekers: The guide to creative nonprofit fundraising.* San Francisco: Jossey-Bass.

Cornog, E. (2004). *The power and the story.* New York: Penguin Press.

Cox, A., & Albert, D., eds. (2003). *The healing heart for communities: Storytelling for strong and healthy communities.* Gabriola Island, BC, Canada: New Society.

CUNA & Affiliates. (2001). *Real stories from credit unions.* Dubuque, IA: Kendall/Hunt.

Davenport, T. (2003). *What's the big idea? Creating and capitalizing on the best management thinking.* Boston: Harvard Business School Press.

Davis, D. (1993). *Telling your own stories.* Little Rock, AR: August House.

Denning, S. (2001). *The springboard: How storytelling ignites action in knowledge-era organizations.* Woburn, MA: Butterworth Heinemann.

Denning, S. (2004). *Squirrel Inc.: A fable of leadership through storytelling.* San Francisco: Jossey-Bass.

Denning, S. (2005). *The leader's guide to storytelling: Mastering the art and discipline of business narrative.* San Francisco: Jossey-Bass.

Dixon, N., et al. (2005). *Company command: Unleashing the power of the Army profession.* West Point, NY: Center for the Advancement of Leader Development & Organizational Learning.

Donato, J. (2000). *Storytelling in emergent literacy: Fostering multiple intelligences.* Florence, KY: Thomson Delmar.

Fog, K. (2005). *Storytelling: Branding in Practice.* New York: Springer.

Fulford, R. (2001). *The triumph of narrative: Storytelling in the age of mass culture.* New York: Broadway Books.

Gabriel, Y. (2000). *Storytelling in organizations: Facts, fictions, and fantasies.* New York: Oxford University Press.

Galvanek, J., & Konczal, E. (2005). *Simple stories for leadership insights in the new economy.* New York: University Press of America.

Gargiulo, T. (2002). *Making stories: A practical guide for organizational leaders and human resource specialists.* Westport, CT: Quorum Books.

Gargiulo, T. (2005). *The strategic use of stories in organizational communication and learning.* Armonk, NY: Sharpe.

Gathering Waters Conservancy. (2003). *In their own words: Stories of protecting land in Wisconsin.* Madison, WI: Gathering Waters Conservancy.

Gibson, E. (1999). *Story sells: Winning ways to fame and fortune.* Carmichael, CA: Gibson.

Gobe, M. (2001). *Emotional branding.* New York: Allworth Press.

Gobe, M. (2002). *Citizen brand: 10 commandments for transforming brands in a consumer democracy.* New York: Watson-Guptil.

Godin, S. (2005). *All marketers are liars: The power of authentic stories in a low trust world.* New York: Penguin Press.

Heriot, J., & Polinger, E., eds. (2002). *The use of personal narratives in the helping professions.* Binghamton, NY: Haworth Press.

Herman, D. (2002). *Story logic: Problems and possibilities of narrative.* Lincoln: University of Nebraska Press.

Hughes, R. K. (1998). *1001 great stories and quotes.* Wheaton, IL: Tyndale House.

Hurt, K. B., & Metzger, D. (2000, 2003). *Info-line: Storytelling.* Alexandria, VA: American Society for Training & Development.

Hutchens, D. (1999). *Shadows of the Neanderthal: Illuminating the beliefs that limit our organizations.* Waltham, MA: Pegasus Communications.

Hutchens, D. (2000a). *Outlearning the wolves: Surviving and thriving in a learning organization.* Waltham, MA: Pegasus Communications.

Hutchens, D. (2000b). *The lemming dilemma: Living with purpose, leading with vision.* Waltham, MA: Pegasus Communications.

Jensen, R. (2001). *The dream society: How the coming shift from information to imagination will transform your business.* New York: McGraw-Hill.

Koppett, K. (2001). *Training to imagine: Practical improvisational theater techniques to enhance creativity, teamwork, leadership and learning.* Sterling, VA: Stylus.

Lambert, J. (2002). *Digital storytelling: Capturing lives, creating community.* Berkeley, CA: Digital Diner Press.

Lindstrom, M. (2005). *Brandsense: How to build powerful brands through touch, taste, smell, sight and sound.* Sussex, UK: Gardners Books.

Lipman, D. (1995). *The storytelling coach: How to listen, praise and bring out people's best.* Little Rock, AR: August House.

Lipman, D. (1999). *Improving your storytelling: Beyond the basics for all who tell stories in work or play.* Little Rock, AR: August House.

Livo, N. J., & Rietz, S. A. (1986). *Storytelling process and practice.* Littleton, CO: Libraries Unlimited.

Lovely, S. L. (2004). *The little blue book of big ideas.* Louisville, KY: Minerva.

Maguire, J. (1998). *The power of personal storytelling: Spinning tales to connect with others.* New York: Tarcher/Putnam.

Mark, M., & Pearson, C. S. (2001). *The hero and the outlaw: Building extraordinary brands through the power of archetypes.* New York: McGraw-Hill.

May, R. (1991). *The cry for myth.* New York: Norton.

Mayer, G. G., & Mayer, T. (1999). *Goldilocks on management: 27 revisionist fairy tales for serious managers.* New York: AMACOM.

McAdams, D. (2005). *The redemptive self: Stories Americans live by.* New York: Oxford University Press.

McKee, R. (1997). *Story: Substance, structure, style, and the principles of screenwriting.* New York: HarperCollins.

Meade, E. H. (2001). *The moon in the well: Wisdom tales to transform your life, family, and community.* Chicago: Open Court.

Moore, R. (1991). *Awakening the hidden storyteller.* Boston: Shambhala.

Neuhauser, P. C. (1993). *Corporate legends and lore: The power of storytelling as a management tool.* Austin, TX: PCN Associates.

Parkin, M. (1998). *Tales for trainers: Using stories and metaphors to facilitate learning.* London: Kogan Page.

Paulos, J. A. (1998). *Once upon a number: The hidden mathematical logic of stories.* New York: Perseus Books.

Pine, J. (1999). *The experience economy: Work is theater and every business is a stage.* Boston: Harvard Business School Press.

Pink, D. (2005). *Whole new mind: Moving from the information age to the conceptual age.* New York: Penguin Group.

Polkinghorne, D. E. (1988). *Narrative knowing and the human sciences.* Albany: State University of New York Press.

Rashid, M. (1993). *Considering the horse: Tales of problems solved and lessons learned.* Boulder, CO: Johnson Books.

Riessman, C. K. (1993). *Narrative analysis.* Thousand Oaks, CA: Sage.

Roberts, K. (2004). *LoveMarks: The future beyond brands.* Sydney, NSW, Australia: Powerhouse.

Robinson, G. J. (2000). *Did I ever tell you about the time. . . . How to develop and deliver a speech using stories that get your message across.* New York: McGraw-Hill.

Rydell, K., ed. (2003). *A beginner's guide to storytelling.* Jonesboro, TN: National Storytelling Press.

Sawyer, R. (1968). *The way of the storyteller.* New York: Viking.

Sewall, H. (1942). *A book of myths.* New York: Macmillan.

Shank, R. C. (1990). *Tell me a story: A new look at real and artificial memory.* New York: Scribners.

Shank, R. C. (1998). *Tell me a story: Narrative and intelligence.* Evanston, IL: Northwestern University Press.

Simmons, A. (2001). *The story factor: Inspiration, influence, and persuasion through the art of storytelling.* New York: Perseus Books.

Spaulding, A. E. (2004). *The wisdom of storytelling in an information age.* Lanham, MD: Scarecrow Press.

Stevenson, D. (2003). *Never be boring again.* Colorado Springs: Cornelia Press.

Stotter, R. (2002). *More about story: Writings on stories and storytelling, 1995–2001.* Stinson Beach, CA: Speaking Out Press.

Taylor, D. (1996). *The healing power of stories.* New York: Doubleday.

The NASA Academy of Program and Project Leadership. (2003). *Knowledge sharing initiative.* Washington, DC: NASA.

Tyler, J. A. (2004). *Strategic storytelling: The development of a guidebook for HRD practitioners using storytelling as a business strategy for learning and knowledge transfer.* Doctoral dissertation, Columbia University, UMI Dissertation Abstracts International, 65/06, AAT3135386.

VanGundy, A. B., & Naiman, L. (2003). *Orchestrating collaboration at work: Using music, improv, storytelling, and other arts to improve teamwork.* San Francisco: Jossey-Bass/Pfeiffer.

Vincent, L. (2002). *Legendary brands: Unleashing the power of storytelling to create a winning market strategy.* Chicago: Dearborn Financial.

Vogler, C. (1992). *The writer's journey: Mythic structures for storytellers and screenwriters.* Studio City, CA: Michael Wiese Productions.

Von Franz, M. L. (1997). *Archetypal patterns in fairy tales.* Toronto: University of Toronto Press.

Wacker, M. B., & Silverman, L. L. (2003). *Stories trainers tell: 55 ready-to-use stories to make training stick.* San Francisco: Jossey-Bass.

West, S., & Anthony, M. (2000). *Storyselling for financial advisors: How top producers sell.* Chicago: Dearborn Financial.

Whitney, D., & Trosten-Bloom, A. (2003). *The power of appreciative inquiry: A practical guide to positive change.* San Francisco: Berrett-Koehler.

Whybrow, H., ed. (2002). *The story handbook: Language and storytelling for land conservationists.* San Francisco: Trust for Public Land.

Winslade, J. M., & Monk, G. D. (2000). *Narrative mediation: A new approach to conflict resolution.* San Francisco: Jossey-Bass.

Yashinsky, D. (2004). *Suddenly they heard footsteps: Storytelling for the 21st century.* Toronto: Vintage Canada.

Zaltman, G. (2003). *How customers think.* Boston: Harvard Business School Press.

Zipes, J. D. (1995). *Creative storytelling: Building community, changing lives.* New York: Routledge.

ARTICLES

Accenture discovers that it really is good talk: Conversation and storytelling in management development. (2003). *Development and Learning in Organizations, (17)*2, 24–28.

Alexander, A. (2004, January 20). Once upon a time in our company . . . *Greater Baton Rouge Business Report.* Available online: www.businessreport.com/newsDetail.cfm?aid=1814. Last visited: April 2006.

A story to tell. (2005, October). *T + D,* pp. 54–56.

Bales, S. (2005, Fall). Wanted: Master storytellers. *Nonprofit Quarterly,* pp. 46–57.

Bartholome, P. (2002). Leading with stories. *Newsletter of the Council of Communication Management.* Available online: www.parallax-perspectives.com/resourceslink.htm. Last visited: April 2006.

Bartholome, P., & Clark, E. (n.d.). Story power for teams. Available online: www.parallax-perspectives.com/resourceslink.htm. Last visited: April 2006.

Bell, C. R. (1992, September). The trainer as storyteller. *T + D,* pp. 53–56.

Bennett, J. (2003). Spin straw into gold with good storytelling. Available online: www.startupjournal.com/ideas/services/20030730-bennett.html. Last visited: April 2006.

Bennis, W. (1996, February). The leader as storyteller. *Harvard Business Review,* pp. 154–160.

Berman, D. (1998, November 2). Group holds executive storytelling seminars as a communication tool. *Business Week,* p. 6.

Berta, D. (2005, May 9). Erbert & Gerbert's builds brand by recruiting "storytellers." *Nation's Restaurant News.* Available online: www.nrn.com. Last visited: April 2006.

Bianchi, A. (2005, Spring). Toolkit: I want you to meet Joe. How a riveting story can get your message across. *Stanford Social Innovation Review,* pp. 60–63.

Birchard, B. (2002). Once upon a time. *strategy + business*, Reprint 02211.

Bogdanffy-Kriegh, M. (2003, January 26). What's your story and is it big enough? Available online: www.nysec.org/new-york/sunday-addresses/. Last visited: April 2006.

Boje, D. (1999, revised 2002). Notes on the strategic stories fad: Disney and other storytellers. Available online: http://business.nmsu.edu/~dboje/. Last visited: April 2006.

Boyce, M. (1996). Organizational story and storytelling: A critical review. *Journal of Organizational Change Management, 9*(5), 5–26.

Bradfield, J. (2004, February 25). A twist in the tale: Communicating through stories. Available online: www.biz-community.com/Article/196/18/3153.html. Last visited: April 2006.

Breen, B. (2004, March). Hidden asset. *Fast Company,* pp. 93–95.

Brown, T. (2005, June). Strategy by design. *Fast Company,* pp. 52–54.

Chromatic. (2003). "Head first Java" author interview. Available online: www.onjava.com/lpt/a/3925. Last visited: February 2006.

Cloninger, C. (2005, August). A case for Web storytelling. Available online: www.alistapart.com/articles/storytelling/. Last visited: April 2006.

Collins, C. (2004). March 31). Every house tells a story. *Christian Science Monitor.* Available online: www.thechristiansciencemonitor.com/2004/0331/p11s02-lihc.html. Last visited: April 2006.

Collison, C., & Mackenzie, A. (1999). The power of story in organizations. *Journal of Workplace Learning, 11*(1), 38–40.

Cross, J. (2005, December). Storytelling: PowerPoint's new best friend. *Chief Learning Officer,* p. 15.

Cullen, E., & Fein, A. H. (2005, August). Tell me a story: Why stories are essential to effective safety training. Available online: www.cdc.gov/niosh/mining/pubs/pdfs/2005-152.pdf. Last visited: June 2006.

Deal, T. (1996, October). Telling tales. *Case Currents,* pp. 8–11.

Delin, M. (2005). The power of leadership storytelling. Available online: www.mln.org.uk/rolemodels.asp. Last visited: April 2006.

Denning, S. (2004, May). Telling tales. *Harvard Business Review,* pp. 122–129.

Drainie, B. (n.d.). Telling our story: Communicating the value of philanthropy and the voluntary sector. Available online: www.vsi-isbc.ca/eng/awareness/pdf/drainie.pdf. Last visited: April 2006.

Ellis, B. F. (1997, January). Why tell stories? *Storytelling,* pp. 21–22.

Erickson, T. (2002). Design as storytelling. Available online: www.pliant.org/personal/Tom_Erickson/Storytelling.html. Last visited: April 2006.

Fleming, D. (2001). Narrative leadership: Using the power of stories. Available online: www.leaderlinks.com/pastissues/2004/02_february/feature20040201.htm. Last visited: April 2006.

Gargiulo, T. (2003, August). 8 strategies for using stories to increase learning and facilitate trainings. Available online: www1.astd.org/News_Letter/August03/Links/Practice_gargiulo.html. Last visited: April 2006.

Garland, S. (2005, May 9). Hotels that have a story to tell. *Business Week,* pp. 104–105.

Godin, S. (2005). The storytellers. *CMO Magazine.* Available online: www.cmomagazine.com/read/060105/storytellers.html. Last visited: April 2006.

Gold, J. (1997). Learning and storytelling: The next stage in the journey for the learning organization. *Journal of Workplace Learning, 9*(4), 133–141.

Gold, J., & Holman, D. (2001). Let me tell you a story: An evaluation of the use of storytelling and argument analysis in management education. *Career Development International, 6*(7), 384–395.

Gold, M. (2005, July 6). CBS News explores storytelling. *Los Angeles Times.* Available online: http://pqasb.pqarchiver.com/latimes/advancedsearch.html. Last visited: April 2006.

Greco, J. (1996). Stories for executive development: An isotonic solution. *Journal of Organizational Change Management, 9*(5), 43–74.

Greenhalgh, T., Collard, A., & Noorjahan, B. (2005, March 19). Sharing stories: Complex intervention for diabetes education in minority ethnic groups who do not speak English. Available online: http://bmj.bmjjournals.com. Last visited: April 2006.

Hansen, C. D., & Kahnweiler, W. M. (1993). Storytelling: An instrument for understanding the dynamics of corporate relationships. *Human Relations, 46*(12), 1391–1409.

Heckler, L. (2005, November). Making the movie go: Enhancing storytelling in our presentations. *Professional Speaker,* pp. 6–8.

Hermes, W. (1997, September–October). Too many stories: Are we getting paralyzed by narrative overload? *Utne Reader,* pp. 40–41.

Hillman, J. (1979, November). A note on story. *Parabola, (4)*4, 43–45.

Hofman, M. (2002, May). Emotional branding: How much of your life story should you use to market your company? *Inc.,* pp. 70–79.

Hummel, R. P. (1991, January/February). Stories managers tell: Why they are as valid as science. *Public Administration Review, 51*(1), 31–37.

Ibarra, H., & Lineback, K. (2005, January). What's your story? *Harvard Business Review,* Reprint R0501F.

Jones, D. (2004, September 20). Indian art of storytelling seeps into board-room. *USA Weekend*, Available online: www.usaweekend.com/ 04_issues/040118/040118storytelling.html. Last visited: April 2006.

Kaufman, B. (2003, February). Stories that sell, stories that tell. *Business Strategy*, pp. 11–15.

Kaye, B., & Jacobson, B. (1999, March). True tales, tall tales: The power of organizational storytelling. *T + D*, pp. 1–6.

Keen, J. (2003, June 15). ROI's secret ingredient. *CIO Magazine*. Available online: www.cio.com/archive/061503/value.html. Last visited: April 2006.

Kellaway, L. (2004, May 10). Once upon a time we had managers—not storytellers. *Financial Times*, p. 10.

Kim, W. C., & Mauborgne, R. A. (1992, July–August). Parables of leader-ship. *Harvard Business Review*, pp. 123–128.

King, S., & Pronovost, P. (2003, Summer). Rekindling the central fire: Stories can change your life. *Journal of Innovative Management*, pp. 66–79.

Koenig, J. M., & Zorn, C. R. (2002, September). Using storytelling as an approach to teaching and learning with diverse students. *Journal of Nursing Education, 41*(9), 393–399.

Lieber, R. (1997, February 3). Storytelling: A new way to get close to your customer. *Fortune*, pp. 102–108.

Littlemore, R. (2002, December). Long long story: Step aside consultants, accountants, system administrators . . . here comes the company storyteller. *BC Business Magazine*. Available online: www.bcbusiness magazine.com/displayArticle.php?archive=ARC&artId=252. Last visited: April 2006.

McKee, R. (2003, June). Storytelling that moves people: A conversation with screenwriting coach Robert McKee. *Harvard Business Review*, Reprint R0306B.

McNamee, T. (1994, July/August). The power of story. *Case Currents*, pp. 28–32.

Messinger, L. (2001, March). Using a story-building approach to research comprehensive community initiatives. Available online: www.nova. edu/ssss/QR/QR6-1/messinger.html. Last visited: April 2006.

Morgan, S., & Dennehy, R. (1997). The power of organizational story-telling: A management development perspective. *Journal of Management Development, 16*(7), 494–501.

Murphy, R. (2005, June). Getting to know you. *Fortune Small Business*, pp. 41–46.

Neilson, R., & Stouffer, D. (2005, May–June). Narrating the vision scenarios in action. *The Futurist*, pp. 26–30.

Nussbaum, B. (2005, August 1). How to build innovative companies. *Business Week*, pp. 60–68.

Once upon a time . . . the use and abuse of storytelling and anecdote in the health sector. (2003). Canadian Health Services Research Foundation, annual conference report. Available online: www.chsrf.ca/knowledge_transfer/resources_e.php. Last visited: April 2006.

Patrick, D. (2005, February 21). Every card tells a story. *Publishers Weekly*.

Pennington, N., & Hastie, R. (1991, November). A cognitive theory of juror decision making: The story model. *Cardozo Law Review, 13*(2–3), 519–557.

Pike, L. (1992, Summer). When stories mean business. *Storytelling Magazine*, pp. 10–13.

Pink, D. (2005a, February 14). A story goes with it. *Forbes*. Available online: www.forbes.com/business/forbes/2005/0228/030.html. Last visited: April 2006.

Pink, D. (2005b, February). Revenge of the right brain. *Wired*, pp. 70–72.

Potts, D. (2004, Spring). Once upon a time . . . Storytelling as a qualitative tool. *QRCA News*, pp. 14–20.

Ransdell, E. (2000, January). The Nike story? Just tell it! *Fast Company*, pp. 44.

Ready, D. A. (2002, Summer). How storytelling builds next-generation leaders. *Sloan Management Review, 43*(4), 63–69.

Reamy, T. (2002, June). Imparting knowledge through storytelling, part 1 of a two-part article. *KMWorld*. Available online: www.kmworld.com/Articles/ReadArticle.aspx?ArticleID=9358. Last visited: April 2006.

Reamy, T. (2002, August). Imparting knowledge through storytelling, part 2 of a two-part article. *KMWorld*, Available online: www.kmworld.com/Articles/ReadArticle.aspx?ArticleID=9374. Last visited: April 2006.

Ristau, J., & Ryan, E. (1997, September–October). Exiles on Main Street: Story and the struggle for community in small-town America. *Utne Reader*, p. 48.

Sanders, S. R. (1997, September–October). The most human art: Ten reasons why we'll always need a good story. *Utne Reader*, pp. 54–56.

Shanahan, M., & Maira, A. N. (1998, Fourth Quarter). Viewpoint: Creating change through strategic storytelling. *Prism*, pp. 99–108.

Shaw, G., Brown, R., & Bromiley, P. (1998, May–June). Strategic stories: How 3M is rewriting business planning. *Harvard Business Review,* pp. 41–50.

Siegel, M. (2002, May). Accelerating insight through scenarios. Available online: www.wisdomtools.com. Last visited: April 2006.

Silverman, L. (2003). The best-kept secret in business today. Available online: www.sayitwithastory.com/Articles.htm. Last visited: April 2006.

Silverman, L. (2004, January). Story time. *Credit Union Management Magazine,* pp. 18–22.

Silverman, L. (2004, November). Strategic storytelling: A timeless tool makes its way into association management. *Association Management,* pp. 41–48.

SIO SIG lends a hand in international marketing. (2005, January/February). *Storytelling Magazine,* pp. 33–34.

Snow, D. (2005, May 12). Storytelling as a leadership tool. Available online: www.4hoteliers.com/4hots_fshw.php?mwi=691. Last visited: April 2006.

Spangler, D. (1985/86, Winter). The new storytellers. *In Context.* Available online: www.context.org/ICLIB/IC12/Spangler.htm. Last visited: April 2006.

Stepanek, M. (2000, May 15). Tell me a (digital) story. *Business Week e.biz,* pp. 90–94.

Storytelling gives business professionals a competitive edge. (2002). Available online: www.nationalbusiness.org/NBAWEB/Newsletter/171.htm. Last visited: April 2006.

Sturm, B. W. (1999). The enchanted imagination: Storytelling's power to entrance listeners. Available online: www.ala.org/ala/aasl/aaslpubsandjournals/slmrb/slmrcontents/volume21999/vol2sturm.htm. Last visited: February 2006.

Swap, W., Leonard, D., Shields, M., & Abrams, L. (2001, Summer). Using mentoring and storytelling to transfer knowledge in the workplace. *Journal of Management Information Systems, 18*(1), 95–114.

Szegedy-Maszak, M. (2005, February 28). Mysteries of the mind: Your unconscious is making your everyday decisions. *U.S. News & World Report,* pp. 53–61.

Terez, T. (2002, March). The business of storytelling. *Workforce,* pp. 22, 24.

Wang, Y. (2003, Winter). When stories mislead: Collective beliefs and corporate decision making. *Business Value Directions,* pp. 80–93.

Weil, E. (1998, June–July). Every leader tells a story. *Fast Company,* pp. 38, 40.

Welles, E. O. (1996, May 1). Why every company needs a story. *Inc.,* pp. 69–75.

Wyzga, D. (2005, January/February). Stories breathe life into law. *Storytelling Magazine,* pp. 16–17.

Zemke, R. (1990). Storytelling: Back to basics. *Training, 2*(3), 44–50.

Zipes, J. D. (1997, September–October). Tales worth telling. *Utne Reader,* pp. 39–42.

JOURNALS

Storytelling Magazine. Published bimonthly. National Storytellers Network. 132 Boone Street, Suite 5, Jonesborough, TN 37659, www.storynet.org.

Storytelling, Self, Society. Published biannually. Florida Atlantic University, Department of Communication, 777 Glades Road, Boca Raton, FL 33431-0991, www.fau.edu/storytelling/journal.html.

—ᴧᴧᴧ— Acknowledgments

Coming up with an idea for a book is easy. Bringing it to fruition, especially with a project like this one, is a monumental task. It is only through the combined efforts of hundreds of people that this book stands before you.

First and foremost are the contributors, who spent several months tracking down organizations for their specific topic; interviewing key people; ascertaining themes from their findings; and crafting practical, easy-to-read chapters. I applaud the generosity and extend my heartfelt appreciation for the gifts shared by Madelyn Blair, Evelyn Clark, Karen Dietz, Marcy Fisher, Alicia Korten, Denise Lee, Michael Margolis, North McKinnon, Susan Moore, Susan Osborn, Ashraf Ramzy, Steven Silverman, Susan Stites, and Jo Tyler. Two contributors—Marcy Fisher and Alicia Korten—went above and beyond the call to help by providing their expertise and support to several parts of this book. I could not have done this publication without these fourteen individuals.

Several people identified at the end of each chapter, along with the staff of the National Storytelling Network, assisted in identifying organizations for us to feature. I would like to thank all of them; their efforts made a significant difference. There were 171 people representing 81 organizations interviewed for this book. Their combined voices are convincing—stories work. They breathe life into organizations. My deepest thanks to each of these people for sharing practices and insights and for letting us showcase their organizations' work to the world.

I am indebted to Sylvia Lovely, who offered to write the introduction—it is truly a masterpiece. A very special thank-you to Joanna Truitt, who stepped into the project several months after its kick-off to put together a comprehensive list of suggested resources. She also worked tirelessly along with Debra Earl and Nancy Sprecher over many weeks to help me ensure the accuracy of all the quotations in this book—to each of them I offer my deepest appreciation. Chara Watson's enthusiasm and willingness to help me with whatever I needed was refreshing and invaluable.

The title of this book would not have happened without the inspiration of Steven Silverman and the phenomenal facilitation provided by Sam Horn; both continue to coach me on marketing. Laura Page captured the essence of me in the photograph she took for the book jacket. And Karen Birk took the time to read every single chapter and provide her thoughts and copyediting expertise on a moment's notice. All four of them generously gave from the heart and for this I am deeply grateful.

To my colleagues and friends who helped me solve problems, cheered me through the last fourteen months, and made certain I had fun while I worked—Liz Anderson, Maggie Brothers, Debra Earl, Marcy Fisher, Autumn Gessert, Joan Gillman, Lunell Haught, Julie Hedlund, Bruce Himelstein, Laura Page, BJ Pfeiffer, Bob McIlree, Eve Scheffenacker, Shelley Peterman Schwartz, Nancy Sprecher, and Susan Stites—you are the best. To my family, whose love and support came in numerous ways, my love to you for believing in my work and in me. For Joan Fuller, who helped me develop my inner and outer voice and kept me centered throughout the writing process, and Karen Dietz, who supported my idea from the very first day she heard it spoken in October 2003 through to its completion, may many blessings come your way.

This book would not have come about if it were not for Matt Davis at Jossey-Bass/Wiley who believed in my idea and brought it forward. My thanks to senior editor Kathe Sweeney and contracts editor Debbie Notkin for guiding me through the process of producing a trade book and ensuring all permissions were in place.

To all who read this book, thank you for recognizing the power of stories in organizations. This book confirms it. They truly can make a difference.

Lori L. Silverman

About the Editor

LORI L. SILVERMAN says, "Stories are a natural stimulant. They are the antidote to boredom and indifference." This philosophy has guided Lori's consulting work in strategy, enterprise-wide change, and performance improvement for almost twenty years. However, it was not until 1999 that she came to truly grasp the need to make story work conscious and purposeful rather than happenstance. The turning point was the night before a keynote talk to eleven hundred people in Seattle, Washington, which she planned to give without relying on visual aids. Through feedback from a friend who heard her practice she suddenly realized that something needed to replace the props—stories that brought concepts and ideas from her book *Critical Shift: The Future of Quality in Organizational Performance* to life.

Soon after, she simplified her talks and queried colleagues for tales to tell. No more brain overload for those sitting in the audience. In her consulting, varied kinds of future stories entered her strategy work, and storytelling to facilitate organizational change and performance improvement became a thoughtful occurrence. Yet something was still missing. But Lori chose to go with the flow and let life take its course. It soon brought the opportunity to coauthor *Stories Trainers Tell: 55 Ready-to-Use Stories to Make Training Stick*. While interviewing trainers, storytellers, speakers, consultants, and business leaders for the book, she stumbled onto more answers—and more questions that stimulated the current book, *Wake Me Up When the Data Is Over: How Organizations Use Stories to Drive Results*.

Lori's consulting clients in more than fifteen different industries—from financial services to petroleum, high technology, retail, paper, insurance, health care, airline, higher education, manufacturing, professional and trade associations in addition to government agencies and military units—have benefited from her deliberate work with stories. Today, she is highly sought as a keynote speaker having enhanced the lives of thousands of conference and meeting participants with her highly energized and enthusiastic approach and magical stories, inspiring her audiences to take action. Along the way, Lori also created the Web site www.sayitwithastorycom to bring a variety of story applications into workplaces around the world.

Stories are the mainstay of her teaching as an adjunct instructor for the Fluno Center for Executive Education at the University of Wisconsin-Madison and the School of Continuing Education at the University of Wisconsin-Milwaukee. And they are integral to her myriad writings. Having earned two master's degrees, in business administration and counseling, and a bachelor's degree in psychology, Lori brings a wealth of experience, knowledge, and stories to the work she engages in today.

Lori L. Silverman, owner, Partners for Progress
1218 Carpenter Street
Madison, WI 53704-4304
Phone: (800) 253-6398
Fax: (608) 241-8092
E-mail: lori@partnersforprogress.com
Web:
    www.partnersforprogress.com
    www.sayitwithastory.com
    www.wakeupmycompany.com
    www.lorisilverman.com

Index

Interior Health, 214
Internet: *Annual Member Handbook*
(NSA Web site) stories on the, 130;
CAVNET Web site stories on the,
222–223; conveying stories via the,
23–24
"Invited stories," 207, 209
"Is Our Name Telling the Right Story?"
(Shaw), 96
Isherwood, B., 116

J

Jackson, M., 125
Jacobson, D., 51
Jahnson-Caygill, J., 4
Jeff Saperstein and Associates, 184
Johns, S., 3
Johnson, M., 6, 14, 15, 16
Johnson-Caygill, J., 6, 8–9, 10, 14
Jones, K., 33, 35, 39, 40, 42, 43–44
Jorgenson, A., 188, 192, 194

K

Kahan, S., 125
Kaiser, E., 133, 134
Kaiser, H. J., 131, 133
Kaiser Permanente: "Diversity as a
Kaiser Permanente Value Born on
the Home Front of World War II"
(Debley), 133–134; legacy of found-
ing stories of, 131–132; measuring
results at, 138–139; stories capturing
history of, 132–135; stories used to
define, 126
Kartes, K., 127, 131, 136, 139
Keech, D., 86
Keech, P., 86, 90
Keech, R., 86
Kelleher, L., 36–37, 41, 44, 46
Keller, S., 140
Kelly, S., 202, 204, 206–207, 208, 211,
212
Kennedy, D., 147
Kenney, M., 92
Kentucky League of Cities (KLC), 214,
223–224, 225
Ketner, M. G., 187, 189, 198, 199

Khazei, A., 115, 120, 123
Kimberly-Clark Corporation: communicating marketing research
through stories, 162–164; learning
to use market research, 156; results
of brand name stories for, 182–183;
results of marketing stories used by,
168; stories reporting marketing
research at, 165–166; telling their
brand name story, 179
Kimpton, B., 175
Kimpton Hotel and Restaurant Group,
LLC: brand name stories used by,
170; positioning challenges
addressed by stories, 172–173;
sources for stories used by, 175
"Kitty Crates" (Love), 5
Knowledge Management Review, 150
Kogod, K., 121
Korten, A., 2, 46, 78, 110, 170, 214, 215,
219, 228–229
Krause, C., 53
Kuh, C., 134
Kull, M., 140
KYGO-FM (Denver radio station):
advertising as form of storytelling
at, 7–8; awards won by, 15; building
customer relationships using stories,
10–11; "Catfish Diaries" segment
of, 10, 11; customer service stories
used by, 3, 12; "Dewey from
Louisville" segment, 10, 11; "Take
the Plunge" event, 11

L

Lancaster University Management
School, 203, 208
Lands' End Business Outfitters Contact
Center, 4
Lands' End, Inc.: customer satisfac-
tion surveys used by, 16; customer
service philosophy of, 4, 8, 9,
14; *Legendary Customer Service
Award* of, 15; "Pre-Wedding Jitters"
story, 9
Lang, R., 9
Langlie, J., 135–136, 138